THE TRAVELERS' GUIDE TO
ASIAN CUSTOMS & MANNERS

Kevin Chambers

Meadowbrook

Distributed by Simon & Schuster

New York, New York

395
CHA

Library of Congress Cataloging-in-Publication Data

Chambers, Kevin.
  The travelers' guide to Asian customs and manners.

  1. Asia—Social life and customs.
2. Etiquette—Asia. I. Title.
DS12.C47   1988   395'.095   87-31262
ISBN 0-88166-106-6

Published by Meadowbrook, Inc.
18318 Minnetonka Boulevard
Deephaven, MN 55391.

BOOK TRADE DISTRIBUTION by Simon and Schuster, a division of Simon and Schuster, Inc., 1230 Avenue of the Americas, New York, NY 10020.

S & S Ordering: 0-671-65888-3

88 89 90 91 10 9 8 7 6 5 4 3 2 1
Printed in the United States of America

Edited by Katherine Stevenson

To my parents,
who encouraged both self-education
and travel,
and to my wife Sim,
who introduced me to Asia and
indulges me in my explorations.

ACKNOWLEDGMENTS

I wish to thank the following people for their assistance in this project: James Barnes, Elizabeth Barnet, Yatindra Bhatnagar, Jane Bock, Janet L. Bringans, Frank Brockway, Trish Brockway, Jill Carmen, Paul P. Castillejos, Bruno Cornelio, Nelda Crowell, George De Wilde, Sanjyot Dunung, Kip Farmer, Colin Goddard, John Green, Obaedul Huq, Song-Hyon Jang, Ray Klinge, Lee Lacy, Bruce Lansky, John Maysa, Kristy McCoy, Mokhtar Mohyat, John Neutze, Steve Olsen, Wesley Palmer, Mike Ransom, Camille E. Sailer, Richard B. Smith, Mike Stangeby, Katherine Stevenson, Phyllis Stevenson, Edward L. Taylor, and Sung-ro Yoon.

Contents

Introduction vi

Australia 1

Bangladesh 17

China 31

Hong Kong 57

India 84

Indonesia 119

Japan 146

Malaysia and Singapore 187

New Zealand 216

Pakistan 232

The Philippines 251

South Korea 273

Sri Lanka 302

Taiwan 326

Thailand 351

INTRODUCTION

I could feel the perspiration on my forehead as I stared across the coffee table at my Japanese contacts. Their heads were tilted back, their eyes avoided mine, and they were sucking in air between their teeth with an alarming hissing noise. Clumsily I forged ahead with my sales pitch, trying desperately to fill the void with words, but I could elicit no response.

It wasn't until months after this disastrous meeting that I realized that I'd committed a grievous mistake: I had launched into an American-style hard sell only moments after meeting my potential business clients in Tokyo.

I had failed to comprehend the importance of cultural differences. Assuming that business is business, no matter where in the world you find it, I had squandered a valuable opportunity and brought great discomfort to everyone involved.

This same cultural ignorance led me to offend my hosts and fellow guests at a Chinese banquet by sticking my chopsticks upright into a bowl of rice, and to insult my Malay host by inadvertently showing him the soles of my shoes. It was after another faux pas — congratulating a Japanese friend on a promotion by sending him an attractive Japanese card of a type used only for funerals — that I decided to write this book.

The Travelers' Guide to Asian Customs & Manners will help you avoid the most common social blunders of novice travelers in the many and varied cultures of the Asia-Pacific region. It will also help you understand the cultures, so you can enjoy your travels more fully.

I'll tell you what to do — and what not to do — in a wide variety of situations, from saying hello to bargaining in shops, giving gifts, or being a guest in someone's home. You'll learn how to do the right thing in most of the situations you'll face. And you'll feel much more comfortable in whichever countries you visit.

One caution: Although I encourage you to understand the cultures you'll be visiting and to be sensitive to the feelings of locals, don't go overboard and abandon your own culture and values. Tourists and business people who "go native" only succeed in losing the trust of everybody.

The chapters are arranged alphabetically by country. Within each chapter you'll find lots of subdivisions to help you find the information you need in the least amount of time. Here are the topics discussed, with some general rules to follow:

MEETING PEOPLE

Greetings: It's essential to know how to say hello — and say it properly. In Asia remember to slow down when you greet people or make introductions. Many Asians are miffed by the hurried greetings of Westerners, and conclude that Westerners are cold and aloof. When someone hands you a name card, take the time to really look at it and mentally note the person's name and title. Proper use of names and titles is very important in most Asian cultures.

It's also important to know how to address a letter properly. English is the international language of business, so you'll seldom need to have letters translated. And although a letter is a good way to make yourself known, you need to know that most Asian people prefer face-to-face communication. (That's why letters tend to go unanswered in Asian countries more than anywhere else.)

Conversation: Making conversation is the key to getting along well. Your choice of topics can either impale you or mark you as an astute observer of culture. A Westerner who asks a Pakistani Muslim man about his wife, for example, or calls a Korean man by his given name, won't be made welcome. (In either case it would be safer to ask about the education of the family's children.)

At least in the beginning, keep your conversation general and impersonal and be careful to follow the lead of the locals. If you're asked how many children you have, ask the same question in return.

Never use sarcasm, even in joking. People who don't speak English as a first language will take your words literally.

Avoid disagreeing openly with locals (unless you're in Australia or New Zealand). In most Asian cultures disagreement must be very subtle to avoid offense or embarrassment. Even in Australia and New Zealand, be sure to disagree only on an intellectual — not a personal — level.

Phrases to Know: I've provided a few key phrases for each country, with phonetic pronunciations, to help you communicate some of your most important needs. Trying to learn at least a little of the local language will more than pay off in your traveling, bargaining, and creating a good impression. You'll be amazed at how many doors open when you show you care enough to learn how to say "Hello" and "Thank you" in the native language.

You'll find references to excellent phrase books for some of the countries. A good book on the whole region to take along is Charles Jamblin's *Languages of Asia and the Pacific: A Traveller's Phrasebook* (Angus and Robertson, London, 1984, $19.95).

CURRENCY

Wherever you travel it's helpful to know what the unit of currency is, what denominations are available, and how the currency relates to the American dollar. I'll also suggest where to find the best exchange rates and how to avoid exchange rip-offs. (In general you'll find the best exchange rates at banks and the worst rates at airports.) Several Asian nations have black markets for hard currencies, but playing this game is very, very risky.

ETIQUETTE

Every culture has rules of public conduct. You're at a great disadvantage if the rules are very different from those of your own culture, and the risk of offense is great.

General manners: Minor mistakes might not be held against you, but many Asians are unforgiving if you commit a major faux pas or insult someone, even inadvertently. Rather than telling you what you've done wrong, they'll simply fail to return your phone calls and avoid any other contact, leaving you in the dark. It's to your benefit to understand general manners as well as you can.

In general Asians are more reserved than Westerners. They don't like to be touched, and they're less outgoing with new acquaintances. They're rarely demonstrative. There are great differences between Asian cultures, however — the Filipinos are quite outgoing in many ways, while the Japanese hide their feelings and personalities behind a wall that's very difficult to break through.

Body language: Body language can be extraordinarily subtle yet carry profound messages. In most Asian countries using one finger to point at people or beckon them is even ruder than it is in the West. (Instead gesture with your whole hand or with your head.) Touching someone's head (especially a child's) is taboo in so many cultures that it's best to break this habit before you set foot in Asia.

Asians are especially conservative about public contact between the sexes. Displays of affection such as hand-holding and kissing — even between husband and wife — will meet with disapproval. In Islamic cultures many women are kept away from men outside their families; close contact with a foreign man can mean trouble.

Dress: Unless you're "doing" Tokyo's fashionable Roppongi district, stick with conservative dress (both in color and in coverage). Scanty or flamboyant clothing will trigger ridicule — or even anger — and you'll feel out of place among the dull gray and blue suits. You'll also contribute to the widespread Asian belief that Westerners are eccentric.

Temples (and mosques, shrines): Etiquette is especially important in places that people regard as sacred. Two American missionaries were jailed in Thailand after their photo, taken while they were standing atop a sacred statue of Buddha, was published in a Bangkok newspaper. I've provided information on what to wear and how to behave in the places of worship you're most likely to visit.

Private homes: Most Asian homes aren't open to casual acquaintances; space is at a premium, and the cramped conditions are not considered appropriate for entertaining honored guests.

Instead entertaining takes place outside the home, usually in restaurants. Consider any invitation to a home a great honor. In most Asian cultures it's customary to remove your shoes before you enter a home. To be polite many hosts invite guests to leave their shoes on, but if the family members remove their shoes, be sure to do the same.

Personal gifts: Asian cultures, like Western cultures, have rules governing what to give as a gift and when and how to present it. I'll cover most of the situations you're likely to encounter. Many gift-giving taboos are related to religion, especially in Islamic cultures. In other cases taboos are based on superstition or symbolism (for example, the Chinese like to give gifts in pairs because odd numbers signify loneliness or separation).

Tipping: It's important to understand the rules of tipping — how much to tip, and to whom. Throughout much of Asia tipping is not the custom; some peo-ple even regard it as an insult. Unfortunately it's becoming increasingly expected in tourist areas as foreigners, unaware of local wage levels, continue to over-tip.

Most tourist hotels automatically add a service charge to lodging and restaurant bills, making further tipping unnecessary. As a rule, in places where tipping is not expected, leave service people and taxi drivers the small change from the transaction.

FOOD

Asian cuisines, from fiery Thai to mild Cantonese, are for the most part absolutely delicious; you won't want to miss them. You can't be blamed, however, for retreating occasionally to the familiar golden arches of the McDonald's hidden among Hong Kong's neon signs, or to one of Tokyo's basement Shakey's Pizza Parlors.

Meals: It's very helpful to know the times of day that meals are served and what kinds of foods to expect.

Meals can vary quite a bit from one country to another.

Where to Eat: You also need to know where to find the things you want to eat. You can find every kind of eating establishment in Asia, from fine restaurants to food stalls in night markets. The food stalls offer delicacies unavailable elsewhere, as well as an ambience long remembered (sometimes intensely remembered for an excruciating few days while your system recovers from a local "bug").

In most places — especially markets — be careful about where you eat. Look to see whether the plates are soaking in filthy dishwater, the cook has dirty hands or an unhealthy appearance, or the food attracts flies.

If you want to venture outside the hotels to get Chinese food (and you should), take along James McCawley's *Eater's Guide to Chinese Characters* (University of Chicago Press, Chicago, $5.95), which will help you to decipher Chinese menus.

Foods to Try: I'll give you information on the foods you might want to seek out (and others you might want to avoid). In general stay away from dairy products, raw vegetables, and cold foods, all of which can harbor harmful bacteria. (Japan is an exception; the standard of hygiene is extremely high, so feel free to eat or drink anything you want.) But don't worry — there are plenty of safe, delicious specialties to choose from.

Table Manners: Once you find great food to eat, you'll want to know how to eat it without making a fool of yourself (especially at a banquet, business dinner, or other important occasion).

Practice using chopsticks before you go to Asia. The "chopstick zone" stretches from Japan's Hokkaido Island to the pockets of Chinese immigrants in Malaysia and Indonesia.

The "right-hand zone" stretches from Muslim Pakistan to Muslim Indonesia. There's no need to practice eating with your hands before you go; just follow the lead of your fellow diners. Always remember, especially in Islamic areas, never to use your left hand to eat or pass food (it's traditionally used to clean yourself after you use the toilet, so it's considered unclean).

bucket of water of Indonesia's *losmen*. You'll find Western-style toilets primarily in hotels and tourist areas. Carry tissue with you everywhere. In East Asia don't be surprised if the rest rooms are coed.

ACCOMMODATIONS

Hotels: Most tourists and business people frequent Asia's international hotels, which (except for their extremely helpful staff) are a mirror image of Western hotels.

To experience uniquely Asian hostelry, you'll have to seek out an expensive Japanese inn (*ryokan*), a modest Korean *yogwan,* or one of the cheap but clean Chinese hotels scattered throughout Asia. For a real adventure rent a room (for your luggage) at a moderately priced tourist hotel, then spend the night down the street at a $5 Chinese hotel among the clattering mah-jongg tiles and the hacking and coughing of early-morning risers.

Rest rooms: In many Asian countries you'll find yourself face to face with a squat-type toilet, perhaps like none you've ever seen before, with no toilet tissue in sight. These toilets can range from the porcelain pits of Japan to the simple hole in the floor and

TRANSPORTATION

Public transportation: Public transportation is readily available throughout Asia. It's often very crowded, however, and confusing for visitors who can't speak the local language. I'll help you to travel fearlessly by bus, taxi, train, and subway.

Driving: Driving in many Asian countries is a terrifying experience. I've included tips on how to rent a car (or a car and driver), important traffic regulations, and what to do in case of an accident.

BUSINESS

In the 1970s Asia surpassed Europe as the United States' largest trading partner. Every year more Westerners visit Asia to conduct business. Unfortunately too many of them arrive with the attitude — readily discernible to the locals — that their Western goods and services are inherently superior to those of Asia and that the locals are lucky to have the opportunity to buy their products. Nothing can do more to kill a deal than the ethnocentrism that many Asians see in Westerners.

Business hours: There's no such thing as standard business hours. The days and times that people work vary with climate, religion, and cultural factors.

Business customs: The formalities covered in this section might seem trivial, but they are the substance of business in Asia. Whether you're meeting potential business partners, negotiating across a conference table, or trying to make a good impression at dinner, keep in mind that in Asia form tends to be more important than substance. Actions are judged by the methods with which they are accomplished; even a completed objective is not considered successful unless you used the proper method to achieve it. You might think it necessary to disagree with a Thai contact, but by humiliating him in front of his co-workers (which is surprisingly easy to do, even inadvertently), you'll create more problems than you'll solve.

The most important fact of doing business in Asia is that you need to establish a relationship of trust between individuals before you can begin business dealings. Asian business people (most of them men) want to find out what kind of a person you are before risking a business relationship with you. You'll usually be tested during small talk at your initial meeting, at lunch or dinner, or over drinks after work. Entertainment is a large part of this testing process, so I've included a separate section telling you what to expect.

TELEPHONES AND MAIL

Telephones: You'll find great variation in both the availability and the ease of use of public telephones — from Japan's green phones that accept credit cards to Pakistan's nonexistent public phones. Most public phones either cut you off automatically after three minutes or cut you off if you don't insert more coins just before your three minutes are up.

Many hotels impose a heavy surcharge if you make overseas calls from your room, so you might want to call from a post office or telecommunications office. In most cases your call will be placed quickly; in some countries you can even charge calls on your own telephone credit card.

Mail: You'll also find great variation in the efficiency and reliability of mail service. I've offered tips on where to find mailboxes and how to avoid postal hassles.

LEGAL MATTERS

Customs and immigration: Different countries have different visa requirements and various restrictions on the amounts and kinds of money or belongings that you can bring in or take out. I've provided the basics, but be sure to check before you travel — these regulations can be quite complex and can change at any time.

Other restrictions: Most travelers would have enough sense not to climb on religious statues, but how many people know that it's illegal to buy liquor in some areas of Pakistan, or to take photographs of Taiwan's beaches (lest the mainland Communists obtain the photos to plan amphibious landings)? I'll point out at least some of the ways you can stay out of trouble.

SAFETY

Crime: In general you're safer walking around alone at night in Asian cities than in North American cities, but there are still hazards to watch out for. Pickpockets are a problem on crowded buses, for example, and in some areas transvestites target inebriated travelers for robbery. As in any country in the world, keep an eye on your valuables and use hotel lockboxes.

Health: There are also important health considerations to traveling in Asia. In most countries water is unsafe unless it's been boiled. In some places you must beware of diseases that people in Western countries don't even stop to think about.

SHOPPING AND ENTERTAINMENT

Shopping: One of the highlights of a trip to Asia is bargain-hunting in markets or small shops. But you need to know the rules — where and how to bargain, where not to bargain, and what good deals and scams to watch out for.

Entertainment: I haven't attempted to list all the types of entertainment you can find in each country. Instead I've selected certain important customs or types of entertainment that might not be covered in a standard guidebook.

HOLIDAYS

You might want to plan your trip around a country's holidays — either planning to be there for a special celebration, or avoiding making a business trip when government and business offices are closed. Many Asian holidays are Buddhist, Hindu, or Muslim observances that are based on either the lunar or the Islamic calendar; their dates in the Western calendar vary from year to year. Check with overseas tourist offices or consulates to find out holiday dates before you travel.

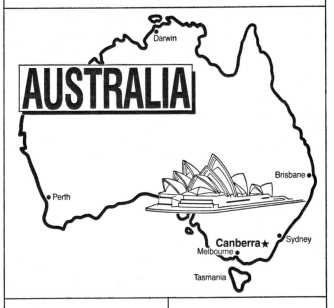

When Captain Cook stumbled upon the Australian continent in the late 1700s, he found it populated by dark-skinned native peoples who became known by the generic term "aborigines." These peoples were soon outnumbered by British immigrants — in the beginning most of whom were convicts and military personnel. By World War II Australia's population was almost exclusively of British descent. Today, however, only six in ten "Aussies" are of British descent; a growing number are of Greek, Italian, Yugoslavian, Dutch, and Southeast Asian extraction. Whatever their origins Australians are polite, friendly, and generally informal people.

A strong streak of egalitarianism pervades Australia. Aussies strongly resent signs that people consider themselves better than others.

MEETING PEOPLE

- Australians are outgoing and rather easy to get to know. Although many are of British descent, don't expect them to be as reserved as the British. They're almost as quick as Americans to move to a first-name basis.

GREETINGS

- Australians shake hands when they greet each other, except that women don't usually shake hands with other women. Close male friends sometimes pat each other on the back. Women friends often kiss in greeting.

- "G'day" is a very informal greeting, and Australians tire of hearing it from tourists. Your normal "hello" will be welcome.

- If you see a friend at a distance, feel free to wave, but don't yell.

- At a social function your host will probably introduce you to the other guests, but it's also acceptable to introduce yourself.

Names and titles. Address people initially by their title (Mr., Mrs., Miss) and last name, but expect them to move to a first-name basis quickly. (Wait for them to make the move, however.)

Correspondence. For formal or business letters, Australians use the salutation ''Dear (title) (surname)'' followed by either a comma or a colon.

CONVERSATION

- Good conversation subjects: Hobbies, Australian sights to see, professions, and sports such as cricket, rugby, and tennis. The America's Cup is an enjoyable topic for discussion as long as you don't gloat.

- Subjects to avoid: Labor unions, religion, and personal questions. It's easy to talk to Australians about almost anything (they're seldom confrontational), but two touchy subjects are the relationship between aborigines and modern Australian society, and control of the kangaroo population.

- Australians are very easygoing but take sports, religion, and politics very seriously. If a controversial topic like politics comes up, listen and ask questions but don't argue.

- It's unwise to compare Australians to Britons or Americans, or to comment on how similar the cultures are. Australians prize their unique identity and don't want to be considered "Americanized."

- In Australia accents are related more to social class than to region, so don't comment on someone's accent.

- What Americans call "koala bears" are actually "koalas." Australians find the repeated use of "koala bear" irritating.

- If you're turning down another helping of food, don't say "I'm stuffed." It means you're pregnant.

PHRASES TO KNOW

- Australian English is similar in much of its vocabulary to British English, so remember that an elevator is a lift, an auto hood is a bonnet, and a truck is a lorry.

- There are many unique

terms, however, that are true "Australianisms." It's unwise for visitors to try to use them in normal conversation. Judging acceptable usage and relative informality is difficult, and judging incorrectly can leave a bad impression.

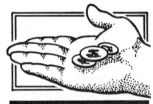

CURRENCY

- The unit of currency is the Australian dollar (A$), which is divided into 100 cents. One U.S. dollar is worth about 1.4 Australian dollars (August 1987 rates). Coins come in denominations of 1, 2, 5, 10, 20, and 50 cents and one dollar. Notes come in 2, 5, 10, 20, and 50 dollars.

- You can exchange currency at banks and hotels. Banks offer better rates.

- You can get a slightly better exchange rate on American traveler's checks than on American currency. Traveler's checks in U.S. dollars must be exchanged at banks; few shops will accept checks that aren't in Australian dollars.

ETIQUETTE

- In Australia you can usually get by using conservative North American manners. There are some differences you should note, however; they're outlined below.

GENERAL MANNERS

- When you talk about yourself, downplay your knowledge or accomplishments. Australians don't respect people who boast ("skite"). Even if you know a lot about a subject, be modest and let your expertise speak for itself.

- It's impolite for a man to wink at a woman, even in jest or in an effort to be friendly.

BODY LANGUAGE

- Men should not be too demonstrative with other men. Most Australian men don't react well to hugging or shoulder-holding.

- The American hitchhiking gesture — the clenched fist with the upraised thumb — is obscene.

DRESS

- Temperatures vary widely across the continent and from one season to another. Check on local temperatures before you come, and bring a varied wardrobe. Don't forget that Australia is in the southern hemisphere, so the seasons are reversed from those in North America.

- Australians usually dress informally. To avoid looking like a tourist, dress conservatively and avoid extreme styles and colors — at least until you see what fits in.

- Beach attire is just about "anything goes" — even bikini tops on some beaches. Wear a hat to protect against the intense sun.

MEN: For business wear a conservative jacket and tie; during hot weather you'll probably be invited to remove your jacket. If you're invited to a meal in a home or a restaurant, wear a jacket and tie (many of the nicer restaurants require them). If it's a backyard barbecue, dress informally. Jeans or shorts are fine for casual wear. For very formal occasions wear a black tie.

- In hot weather don't be surprised to see Australian men coming to work in khaki shorts ("stubbies"), which are usually worn with long socks. With a tie and a short-sleeved shirt, stubbies are considered dressy.

WOMEN: For either business or a meal in a home or restaurant, wear a skirt and blouse or a dress. Jeans or shorts are fine for casual wear. For a backyard barbecue dress informally. For formal events wear a cocktail dress.

- Australian women wear skirts more often than pants (especially in hot weather); few women wear pantsuits.

PRIVATE HOMES

- Australians seldom drop in on each other without notice. If you're going by someone's home, call first to see if it's all right to visit.

- People will usually wait until they know you before they invite you to

their home for dinner.

- When you visit a home, you'll probably be served coffee, tea, or beer.

- If you're invited for dinner, it's polite to bring flowers, wine (Australian or imported), or chocolates.

- The toilet (informally the "loo") is often located in a small room separate from the bath and washbasin.

- If you're staying with a family, it's polite to offer to help prepare meals and clean up.

- When you leave just say a simple, friendly "thank you." Australians don't like obsequious behavior.

PERSONAL GIFTS

- You'll be fine if you stick to North American customs for giving gifts.

- Good choices are wines, folk crafts, and packaged foods from your home region. Teenagers appreciate college T-shirts.

TIPPING

- Tipping is not the custom in Australia; however, service people in tourist areas have come to expect a small tip.

- Hotels and restaurants: Hotels and restaurants don't add service charges. Don't tip waiters and waitresses (they're paid fairly well, and Australians don't want to institutionalize tipping). Tip people only if they provide some service beyond their normal duties, and make it a small amount.

- Porters: Tip either one dollar or a little more than the set charges posted at train and ship terminals.

- Taxi drivers: Round off a fare in the driver's favor.

FOODS

MEALS

Breakfast: 7:30 to 8:30 A.M. The usual fare is bacon and eggs, bread, jam, and tea or coffee. Baked beans on toast are also popular, as are pork or lamb chops and steak.

Lunch: Noon to 2:00 P.M. Lunches vary widely because there are so many ethnic eateries. Some common choices are fish, pizza, Chinese noodles or fried rice, and thin sandwiches.

Afternoon tea: 4:00 to 5:00 P.M. This is a break during which tea and snacks are served. If a family invites you to "tea," it might mean either the afternoon tea or a light evening meal. Ask what time you're expected.

Dinner: 6:00 to 7:00 P.M. This is the main meal of the day (families occasionally call it "tea"). The main dish is usually a meat such as lamb, chicken, or beef. It's usually accompanied by vegetables (squash, potatoes, beans) and a salad. Typical desserts are puddings and cakes.

WHERE TO EAT

- Australia has plenty of restaurants, from chains similar to those in America to family-run ethnic eateries. Be sure to try a variety of foods.

- Many restaurants post their menus at the entrance.

- If you see a restaurant advertised as "BYO," it means that it isn't licensed to sell alcoholic beverages. You may, however, bring your own (usually a bottle of wine, not a six-pack of beer). They'll serve your wine for a small "uncorking" fee.

- If you want to drink in a restaurant after 10:00 P.M., you must order food with your drink.

- Try the friendly pubs for drinks and snacks. They're usually open from 10:00 A.M. to 10:00 or 11:00 P.M. or later, depending on the region. Although they're not labeled as such, some pubs are for men only (the only way to tell is to peek inside). Some pubs have a separate lounge for mixed-sex drinking.

- For inexpensive meals go to delicatessens. Their sandwiches, salads, and cold cuts are quite reasonable.

- Milk bars are small dairy stores with soda fountains. Most of them also sell newspapers and convenience foods.

- "Take-out" or "carry-out" food is called "takeaway."

FOODS TO TRY

- Australia has attracted settlers from all over the world, so you can sample many ethnic cuisines.

Hungarian, French, Indian, Chinese, Japanese, Italian, and German dishes are available everywhere.

Specialties. Fish and seafood are popular around the coasts. Try John Dory (tastes like halibut), *barramundi* (on the North Coast), Sydney Rock Oysters, and Victorian yabbies (taste like small lobsters).

- Try carpetbagger steak, a tenderloin of beef stuffed with raw oysters and grilled over charcoal. Lamb is also very good and very popular.

- The Vegemite sandwich is an Australian institution. Vegemite is a strong-smelling yeast spread that's quite good for you but is — at best — an acquired taste.

- Pancakes on the dinner table might surprise you, but they're usually eaten at dinner rather than breakfast.

- If you want jelly, ask for "jam." (Australians might look shocked if they see you spread it on peanut butter; it isn't a normal mixture here.)

Beverages. Australian water is safe to drink.

- Coffee is available for every meal. Coffee with

milk is called "white coffee."

- Tea, as in most British-influenced countries, is extremely popular. Expect it to be served with milk and sugar.

- Australians love beer and serve it chilled with many meals. Aussie beer is stronger than American or European beers.

- Wine is also popular. Australia has many domestic wines that are well worth trying.

TABLE MANNERS

- In general Australian table manners are very similar to those in North America. If you remember to eat the way your mother taught you, you probably won't embarrass yourself.

- If a fast-food restaurant is crowded and all the tables are taken, ask to share one with someone else. At other restaurants wait until a table is available.

- Patrons often pay a cashier rather than a waiter, even at finer restaurants. Ask the waiter who to pay when you receive your bill ("docket").

Utensils. Hold your knife in your right hand and your fork in your left. Use the knife to push food onto the back of the fork. (Note that when you eat this way, you don't need to set your knife down and switch the fork to your other hand, as you do when you eat American-style.)

- Spoon soup away from you, not towards you.

- To indicate that you're finished eating, place your knife and fork side by side on your plate.

Dining with others. Always arrive on time (or even a few minutes early) for a dinner engagement.

- If you're the guest of honor at a dinner, you'll be seated to the right of your host. Wait for your host to invite you to be seated.

- While you're eating keep your elbows off the table.

- The person who invited the others or suggested the meal often picks up the tab for everyone. In informal situations friends or acquaintances often agree to split the bill.

ACCOMMODATIONS

Hotels. Many buildings with signs that say "hotel" are actually just pubs. Both "hotel" and "pub" can mean either a place to get a drink or a place to get accommodations. A "private hotel" is one that doesn't have a license to serve liquor.

• Private hotels and guesthouses provide accommodations at reasonable rates. Guesthouses are similar to bed-and-breakfasts, with meals included in the fee. Like private hotels, most guesthouses don't have liquor licenses, so you can't get liquor with meals.

• "Morning tea" means tea and cookies. "Continental breakfast" includes cereal, toast, butter, and fruit. If you want something hot as well, ask for a "cooked breakfast," which includes bacon (or sausages) and eggs.

• Hotels often provide free electric teakettles ("jugs"), tea, and instant coffee in your room.

• As a hotel guest you can get a drink in most hotel bars anytime; non-guests might have restricted drinking hours.

• To experience Australian farm life, check with a travel agent about farm holidays, through which you can stay with a farm family for a few days. In some places you stay in the house with the family; in others you stay in a separate cottage. Meals are usually included in the price.

Rest rooms. Rest rooms are of the modern type. In some places the toilet is in a separate room from the bath and wash basin.

TRANSPORTATION

PUBLIC TRANSPORTATION

• Public transportation is overloaded during the Christmas holidays (mid-December to early February), in mid-May, and during the last week of August and the first week of September. Be sure to make reservations for travel during these times well in advance.

Buses. Local buses are uncrowded and easy to take. When you get on tell the conductor your destination and he'll tell you the fare (based on the distance) and help you find your stop. You'll need small change, but not exact change. Keep your ticket until you get off.

- If you plan to do a great deal of long-distance bus travel, the two major bus companies (Greyhound Australia and Ansett Pioneer) offer special travel plans that you must purchase outside the country. Check with a travel agent that knows Australia.

Taxis. You'll find taxis both in front of hotels and on the street; you can either hail them or phone for them. All taxis are metered.

- If you take a taxi by yourself, get into the front seat with the driver — another way Australians show their egalitarianism.

Trains. If you plan to travel extensively by train,

buy a Austrailpass from a travel agent before you arrive in Australia. It's good for unlimited travel for a specified length of time and covers everything except sleeping berths and meals.

Other transportation. Australia is a huge country, so traveling cross-country by jet can save a lot of time. Domestic airlines offer special bargain passes for tourists that can chop 40% off the normal fare. Check with a travel agent.

DRIVING

- Renting a self-drive car is a simple matter if you have a driver's license from home. You'll need third-party insurance; it's usually included in the rental charge.

- Driving is on the left, as in Britain.

- Wearing safety belts is required by law. Small children must either wear safety belts or be in a car-seat restrainer.

- Drivers can be quite aggressive. Don't expect freeway drivers to make room for motorists trying to enter from an on-ramp.

- Australia's drunk-driving laws are some of the

toughest in the world. A blood alcohol content as low as .05 can mean mandatory jail time.

- At an intersection vehicles approaching from the right have the right-of-way. Trams also have the right-of-way.

- If you encounter a traffic circle ("roundabout"), go clockwise.

- If you're in a very minor accident, exchange names and other information and report the incident to the police. If you're in a more serious accident, stay there until the police arrive.

- If you travel into the outback, use a four-wheel-drive vehicle. The roads are quite rough and can easily damage other cars. Traveling in the outback can be extremely dangerous without an experienced guide. Towns and service stations are few and very far apart. To get to the outback, you can take a plane or train and rent a four-wheel-drive vehicle once you get there.

BUSINESS

BUSINESS HOURS

Business offices: 9:00 A.M. to 4:30 or 5:00 P.M. Monday through Friday.

Banks: 9:30 A.M. to 4:00 P.M. Monday through Thursday, and until 5 P.M. on Friday. Many city banks have branches that keep longer hours.

Government offices: 9:00 A.M. to 4:30 P.M. Monday through Friday.

BUSINESS CUSTOMS

- The best time of year for business trips to Australia is between March and November. The peak tourist season for both Australian and foreign vacationers is December through February; hotels are very crowded. The weeks around Christmas and Easter are also very hectic, and many businesses close.

- Start making appointments by telex or phone a month before you leave home.

- Australian business people are easy to approach. They aren't suspicious or class-conscious. They'll almost always answer your inquiries, and executives will gladly try to meet with you to discuss business. Feel free to ask for an appointment with anyone in a company.

- Business people are also very pragmatic. They usually emphasize profit over market share.

- In negotiations Australians usually concentrate on major issues and concepts rather than on small details. In a presentation it's important to make a cogent delivery of your concept without digressing into details.

- In general Australians open negotiations with proposals very close to the acceptable terms, rather than with large, built-in fallback positions. Don't waste time on prolonged haggling.

- By law employees receive four weeks of vacation every year.

Business etiquette. Have a business card ready to present when you're introduced, but don't be surprised if your counterpart doesn't have one. Some business people don't.

- Australia is an egalitarian society. Don't give orders or try any "one-upmanship." Always speak to people — even subordinates — as equals.

- Although Australians are informal and friendly in business, they value directness. If they don't like something, they'll tell you that (politely) and expect you to do the same. Taking a stand is respected. In negotiations they're often quite pointed in their comments. React openly and with good humor and be candid about your strengths and weaknesses.

- Connections and introductions play an important part in getting business. Take every opportunity to establish connections and find out who knows whom.

Appointments and meetings. Many executives start work around 8:30 A.M. and leave at 4:30 P.M. Don't ask for appointments close to those times.

- Shake hands with everyone both before and after a meeting.

• At a first meeting don't launch directly into business. Talk briefly about your trip, sports, or your favorable impressions of Australia.

Business gifts and entertainment. It's not customary for business people to exchange gifts at the first visit or meeting.

• Developing a friendly relationship is important for business success. If you have an opportunity to dine or party with Australian business people after hours — take it.

• Your counterparts will probably invite you out for drinks to get to know you before you do business. Don't talk about business over drinks unless your companions bring the subject up. Be sure to buy ("shout") a round of drinks in turn. If you plan to leave early, buy the first round.

TELEPHONES AND MAIL

Telephones. You'll find public pay phones ("telephone boxes") on streets and in pubs, shops, and restaurants.

• For local calls wait until you get the dial tone, then deposit 20 cents and dial. Local calls have no time limit.

• In an emergency, dial 000.

• For domestic long-distance calls, use the gray-green STD (Subscriber Trunk Dialing) phones. Dial the number directly and pay the amount the operator indicates.

• Make overseas calls from your hotel room or a post office. (Check to see what the hotel surcharge is before you call.) Direct dialing is available in most hotels, and you can also make reverse-charge or person-to-person calls.

• On most hotel phones you dial "0" to get an outside line and "9" to get the hotel operator. Many hotels add a 30- to 60-cent service charge when you make local calls from your room, so calling from the pay phone in the lobby might save you some money.

Mail. Mail ("post") boxes are painted red.

• You can buy stamps at newspaper stands.

LEGAL MATTERS

Customs and immigration. Visas are required for all travelers except New Zealanders. You'll need to obtain your visa before you arrive.

• You may bring in any amount of currency, either foreign or Australian, but there are restrictions on the amount of Australian money you may take out.

Other restrictions. If you plan to travel cross-country, note that you're not permitted to take vegetables, fruits, or plants across state lines.

SAFETY

Crime. Street crime is rare but on the rise, especially in urban areas. Women traveling alone should use taxis after dark and avoid making eye contact in some of the less-safe city neighborhoods, such as Kings Cross in Sydney. All travelers should exercise a normal degree of caution.

Health. The water is safe to drink throughout Australia.

• Medications and toiletries are easy to obtain. Just remember that a pharmacy is called a "chemist."

• Bring a hat and sunscreen. The Australian sun is intense — in fact, Australia has one of the highest skin cancer rates in the world. And if you venture into the outback, be sure to get expert advice and take lots of water.

SHOPPING AND ENTERTAINMENT

Shopping. Except in designated tourist areas, trade laws prohibit most stores from being open longer than 9:00 A.M. to 6:00 P.M. Monday through Friday (sometimes until 9:00 P.M. on Thursday or Friday), and 8:00 A.M. to 1:00 P.M. Saturday. Convenience stores, restaurants, and supermarkets keep longer hours.

- Sales tax varies depending on the kind of goods you buy. It can be as high as 32% on items such as watches, shampoo, and consumer electronics.

- Bargaining is not practiced in stores — don't even try.

- Sizes are in metric measurements, as they are in Europe.

- A bill is called a "docket."

- At supermarkets customers unload their own carts and in many cases bag their own groceries.

Entertainment. Private social clubs (sometimes called "sports clubs") usually admit men with overseas passports for a small admission fee. Women must be escorted by men. In New South Wales most of these clubs have slot machines.

HOLIDAYS

Official holidays: New Year's Day (January 1), Australia Day (January 26), Good Friday (April), Easter (April), Easter Monday (April), Veteran's Day (April 25), Queen's Birthday (second Monday in June), Christmas (December 25), Boxing Day (December 26).

- Labor Day varies from state to state. In South Australia Labor Day is the second Monday in October; in New South Wales it's the first Monday in October; in Western Australia it's the first Monday in March; in Queensland it's the second Monday in May; and in Victoria it's the second Monday in March.

KEY PHRASES

North American English	Australian English
Thank you	Ta (informal)
It'll be OK	She'll be right
An Australian	Aussie (pronounced "ozzie")
An English person	Brit or (derogatory) pom, pommie
Good friend (male)	Mate
Young woman	Sheila (rude)
Afternoon	Arvo (very informal)
Bad, defective, or ill	Crook
Ball-point pen	Biro
Car trunk	Boot
Cookie	Biscuit
Druggist or pharmacy	Chemist
Flashlight	Torch
French fries	Chips
Truck	Lorry
True, genuine	Fair dinkum
Try something	Give it a burl
Your turn to pay	Your shout

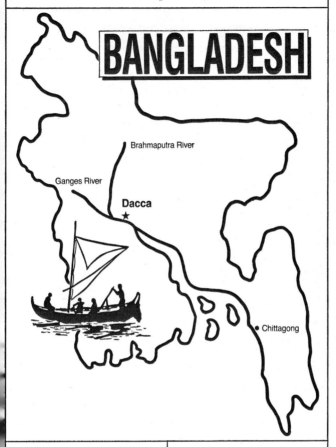

BANGLADESH

Brahmaputra River

Ganges River

Dacca
★

● Chittagong

Few travelers fall in love with Bangladesh, but almost all travelers agree that a visit to this nation of 87 million people is interesting and worthwhile.

Formerly part of Pakistan, and known as East Pakistan until the 1971 civil war, Bangladesh is a pre-

dominately Muslim nation where life has never been easy. The country has been racked for decades by poverty, natural disasters, coups, assassinations, and corruption. The nation is draped across the delta formed by the Brahmaputra and Ganges rivers, and travelers often encounter roads and railroads closed by flooding.

On the positive side historic Dacca, the bazaars, the riverboats, the Bengali people, and the low cost make Bangladesh a unique destination that few outsiders have visited. (If you like to embellish your experiences a little, no one will be the wiser.)

MEETING PEOPLE

GREETINGS

- If you're a Western man introduced to a Bengali man, shake hands and say, *"A-Salam mu Alaikum"* (peace be with you). The polite response is *"walaikum-as-salaam"* (and also on you).

- Western men introduced to Bengali women (or Western women introduced to Bengali men) should nod rather than shake hands.

- Many people of Hindi descent (about 14% of the population) also use the *namaste* gesture. Place your palms together as though praying and nod slightly (see Greetings in India chapter).

Names and titles. When you address people use the titles Mr., Mrs., or Miss. Use last names unless you're invited to do otherwise.

- Hindu Bengalis add the prefix *Sri* before a man's last name. When they address a woman, married or single, they use the prefix *Srimoti* before her last name. For older men or women, they use the respectful prefix *Srijukto.* Foreigners aren't expected to use these titles since English titles are so widely used and understood.

- Occasionally you might hear the older term *Babu* (Mr.) used after a man's last name.

Correspondence. For formal letters use the standard English format with the salutation "Dear (title) (name)," (for example, "Dear Mr. Huq,").

- Bengalis often place the recipient's address in the lower left corner.

CONVERSATION

- Good conversation subjects: Most business

people enjoy talking about foreign travel and their professions. Intellectuals appreciate some familiarity with the works of the great Bengali poets Rabindranath Tagore and Nazrul Islam.

- Subjects to avoid: Any criticism of the country or its government. Bengalis relish politics and take it seriously.

PHRASES TO KNOW

- Bengali (also called Bangala) is the national language of Bangladesh and is also spoken by about 35 million people in the West Bengal area of India. Bengali is written in its own version of the Sanskrit alphabet. It places less emphasis on inflection than does English. In earlier times many Bengalis spoke English; today, fewer do.

CURRENCY

- The Bengali unit of currency is the *taka,* abbreviated "Tk." The *taka* is divided into 100 *poisa*s.

One U.S. dollar is worth about 30 *taka* (August 1987 rates). Coins are issued in 1, 5, 10, 25, and 50 *poisa*s. Notes are issued in 1, 5, 10, 20, 50, 100, and 500 *taka*.

- No active black market exists for hard currency.

- To convert U.S. currency go to the U.S. Embassy's cashier, commercial banks, or hotel cashiers. Rates are most favorable at banks.

- Each time you change money, use the currency declaration form you were given when you entered the country. The form will be checked when you depart.

- When you depart you may reconvert up to either 500 *taka* or 25% of the total foreign currency you converted while you were in the country. The Bank of Bangladesh has a $50 limit on the amount of U.S. currency that it will give a departing traveler. *Taka* are hard to convert outside Bangladesh, so be careful not to have too many left when you leave.

ETIQUETTE

GENERAL MANNERS

- Poverty is everywhere, and so are beggars. If you give a needy person a few coins, be discreet or you'll draw a crowd that just won't quit. Watch out for some young people who demand money rather insistently.

- Muslim customs are usually followed in Bangladesh (over 80% of the population is Muslim).

- In rural areas people see very few foreigners, so you might draw a crowd. If you find yourself the center of attention, don't stop to talk to the crowd — they might get out of hand. Just smile and keep walking.

- Before you take photographs of people, get permission. Many people (especially older people) don't wish to be photographed.

- Any show of anger or frustration will result only in not getting your way. Persistence and a smile will achieve much more.

BODY LANGUAGE

- Use your right hand for eating (even with utensils) or handing an object to someone. Bengalis use their left hands for cleaning themselves after they use the toilet, and consider the hand unclean.

- The thumbs-up gesture is very obscene in Bangladesh.

DRESS

- Cotton clothing is recommended because of the heat and humidity. During the monsoon season (mid-June to mid-October) have an umbrella handy.

MEN For business wear a shirt and trousers or, for a first meeting, a lightweight suit. Business suits are fine for formal occasions.

WOMEN Legs are considered provocative, so wear pantsuits or moderate-length dresses in public. For formal functions wear long dresses, short cocktail dresses, or long skirts and tops.

- Bengali women wear *saris* (see India).

TEMPLES AND MOSQUES

- Before you enter a mosque or temple, remove your shoes and hats. If you're barefoot and you see other people washing their feet before they enter, do the same.

- Wear conservative clothing. Women should cover their arms and legs. Men should wear long pants, not shorts.

- Before you take any photographs inside, ask permission.

(For more information on mosques, see the Indonesia and Malaysia chapters.)

TIPPING

- In Bangladesh, as in India, the line between "tipping" and "bribing" is blurred. Often you must tip not just to reward people, but also simply to get things done. A "tip" to the station porter, for example, will get you a train seat when no seats are available.

- If you are going to use a service repeatedly during your visit, a tip will ensure that the standard of service will be kept up.

- Hotels and restaurants: Major hotels and restaurants add a 15% service charge to food and beverage bills; add an additional 5% if service is exceptional. At restaurants that don't add a service charge, tip 10-15% for good service.

- Taxis and rental cars: Taxi drivers don't expect to be tipped, since fares are bargained. Tip rental car drivers 10% of the bill.

- Porters: Railway and airport porters expect one *taka* per bag.

FOODS

MEALS

Breakfast (*nasta*): 6:00 to 8:00 A.M. Breakfasts are light — often just tea and spiced rice.

Lunch (*moddhanno bhoj*): Noon to 2:00 P.M. Typical fare might be *nan* (bread), *biriyani* (rice with chicken or a rice-and-chicken curry), *dahl* (lentils), and water.

Dinner (*noiso bhoj*): 7:00 to 9:00 P.M. Dishes are similar to those at lunch. A typical dinner might include a meat *kebab,* curried fish in yogurt sauce (*dahi maach*), rice, and water, coconut milk, or sweet tea.

WHERE TO EAT

- Western food is available at all tourist hotels and in many of the finer restaurants.

- Dacca is loaded with Chinese restaurants, most of them run by non-Chinese. Take a look inside. If the restaurant is run by ethnic Chinese, the dishes will probably be smaller but better.

- Most restaurants (except those in hotels) close by 9:00 P.M.

- Bars are scarce in Bangladesh. Almost the only ones you'll find are in the large hotels. Licensed wine shops sell a variety of drinks at prices much lower than those in the hotels.

FOODS TO TRY

- Bengali cuisine shows both Moghul (*kebabs*) and southern vegetarian influence. Much of the food is similar to that found in India — vegetables, *dahl* (lentil soup), *chappati* (unleavened bread), and chilies. Bengali yogurts, however, are always sweetened.

- Rice is the staple. It's eaten with a variety of curries.

Specialties. Three rice dishes you can find anywhere are *biriyani* (rice with mutton, beef, or chicken), *pulao* (a meatless dish of spices and rice), and *baht* (plain rice).

- Try the chicken *kebabs* served with *nan* (bread) or Persian rice. Also good are the smoked *hilsa* fish, *shami kebab* (fried minced meat), and *koftes* (meatballs in gravy).

- Bengalis like sweets. Good sweets to try are *sundesh* (a milk-based dessert), *zorda* (sweet rice and nuts), and *halva.*

- Fruits available when they're in season include mango, watermelon, banana, pineapple, papaya, jackfruit, orange, and guava.

- In the Chittagong Hill Tracts area, you might or might not want to try a dish called *napi*. It's made from the decomposed fat of snakes, deer, and fish.

Beverages. Water isn't safe unless you know it's been boiled. Don't put ice in your soft drink unless it was made from boiled water (get used to drinking your soft drinks hot). Milk and yogurt might also present health risks.

- The national drink seems to be the sweet, milky tea called *chai*. Coconut milk (safer than animal milk), *lassi* (a yogurt drink), and soft drinks are also common.

- Coffee is usually available only in hotels and finer restaurants.

- Local alcoholic drinks include *tari*, a fermented coconut-based beer, and "Kesare rose," a liqueur made from date molasses. Kesare rose is mixed with boiled water and costs about 10 *taka* per bottle.

TABLE MANNERS

Utensils. Except in better restaurants, Bengalis eat with their fingers. Use only your right hand for eating (for more information see India chapter).

Dining with others. Men and women often dine separately. At a home the women often eat after the men.

- Always go into the washroom to wash up both before and after a meal. Don't visit the washroom during the meal.

- Never transfer food from one person's plate to another's, even between spouses. Food that has been on your plate is considered unclean.

ACCOMMODATIONS

Hotels. You'll find international-standard hotels only in the cities of Dacca and Chittagong. You must pay your bill in a convertible foreign currency, such as U.S. dollars or British pounds.

- Elsewhere, most hotels are of low quality and feature such amenities as bedbugs and unsanitary toilets. Look for motels managed by the national tourist board (Bangladesh Parajatan Corporation). They're the best you'll find outside the cities.

• The electric supply is 220-volt, 50-cycle AC, and fluctuates tremendously. The fluctuations can ruin appliances that don't have a surge protector. Buy one at a travel shop before you leave home.

Rest rooms. Except in hotels and finer restaurants, rest rooms are of the squat type and seldom supply toilet paper (carry some with you).

TRANSPORTATION

PUBLIC TRANSPORTATION

• If you want to board a bus, train, or boat, don't hesitate to push and shove along with everyone else. Bangladesh is the most densely populated nation in the world, and pushing and shoving is a way of life.

Buses. Local buses have destination signs and route numbers in Bengali script and no English route map to help you out.

• Long-distance express buses run from 6:00 A.M. to 3:00 P.M., and again from 8:30 to 10:30 P.M. They are very cramped by Western standards, but some do feature television. You must book your seats in advance on some buses, so go to the station early.

Taxis. Taxis are usually black and yellow and are not easy to find (especially in Chittagong). Look for them at tourist hotels.

• Taxis don't use their meters; you must bargain the fare before you get in. Within Dacca you'll pay about 60 *taka* for a cab during the day and about twice that amount in the evening.

Trains. People traveling by train are usually more sociable than those on other forms of transportation. You can buy first-class tickets (ask for the tourist discount), but board quickly — it seems as though people sit in whatever class they want. Trains rarely run on schedule.

Riverboats. Riverboats are a common (and pleasant) way to travel throughout the country. Both the government and private corporations run ferries and launches along

Bangladesh's numerous rivers and waterways.

- Tourists can book first-class berths at the Bangladesh Inland Waterway Transport Corporation (BIWTC) office in Dacca, across the street from the Biman Airways office. First-class passage on BIWTC's "Rocket" launches (some of which are paddlewheel steamers) features two berths, a sink, a fan, and a communal toilet and shower. On overnight voyages you can sit on the deck watching the stars and sipping tea. Meals cost about 20 *taka* in the dining room.

Other transportation. Those garishly painted and tinseled rickshaws you see are an inexpensive way to get around town. Negotiate the fare before you get in. Expect to pay 2-5 *taka* for a short journey.

- The domestic flights of Air Biman, the national carrier, can get you around Bangladesh quickly and are even cheaper than first-class train travel. The air fares are subsidized by the government.

DRIVING

- Driving is not recommended for foreigners. The streets are very congested with vehicles, rickshaws, pushcarts, animals, and pedestrians. The roads are rough and narrow, and the only available maps are too inaccurate to be of any help. You might prefer to rent a car with a driver.

- If you really want to try it, you can hire a car at most tourist hotels for about 40 *taka* per hour plus 5 *taka* per kilometer.

- Driving is on the left, as in Britain.

BUSINESS

BUSINESS HOURS

Business offices: 9:00 A.M. to 6:00 P.M. Saturday through Thursday, with a lunch break between 12:30 and 1:30 P.M.

Banks: 9:30 A.M. to 4:30 P.M. Saturday through Wednesday, and 9:00 to 11:00 A.M. Thursday.

Closed Friday. Foreign bank hours are 9:00 A.M. to 1:00 P.M. Saturday through Thursday, and 9:00 to 11:00 A.M. Friday.

Government offices: In Dacca 7:30 A.M. to 2:00 P.M. Saturday through Thursday. Outside Dacca 9:00 A.M. to 5:00 P.M. Saturday through Thursday. Friday is a holiday.

BUSINESS CUSTOMS

• The best time to visit Bangladesh is during the cool, dry season from mid-October through February.

• Many Bengali business people like to meet visitors at the airport, so cable your arrival time several days in advance.

Business etiquette. Business people usually exchange name cards when they're introduced. Almost all business people read English, so translated cards aren't necessary.

• Vague replies to your proposals or questions often mean "no." Bengalis, including business people, are reluctant to give a flat "no" as an answer.

Appointments and meetings. Arrive on time for meetings. Punctuality is expected of foreigners, but don't be surprised if your counterpart is late or doesn't show up. Leave gaps in your itinerary so you can reschedule.

• At a meeting you'll be offered sweet, milky tea. Don't refuse the offer. Drink it slowly unless you want more (empty glasses are automatically refilled).

Business gifts and entertainment. It's a good idea for visiting business people to host small luncheons or dinners for Bengali agents and contacts. Spouses are not often included in such gatherings.

• Visitors are usually entertained in hotels and clubs. Spouses are not often invited.

TELEPHONES AND MAIL

Telephones. Public telephones are frequently out of order, and breaks in connections are common.

• International telephone service is usually adequate (once you get through). Completing the connection might take several hours, so book with the hotel operator well in advance. Calls to the U.S. average US$ 7.80 for the first three minutes. Bangladesh imposes a 10% excise duty on overseas calls.

Mail. The mail service is inefficient. Don't try to send parcels out of the country — too many get lost.

LEGAL MATTERS

Customs and immigration. Transit visas good for 72 hours are usually granted when you arrive at the airport. You can also get 7-day visas. You can extend both visas easily by going to the Special Branch Office on Kakrail Road and the Immigration Office in Dacca.

• When you enter the country, customs usually records electronic gear, cameras, and typewriters. If you don't take them with you when you

depart, you'll have to pay duty.

• To enter the country you'll need an International Health Certificate for typhoid and cholera. A yellow fever vaccine is required if you've been in an infected area within the previous 14 days.

• Many border crossings along the Indian border are closed or can be crossed only on foot. Stick to the main border crossings. The border with Burma has been closed since the 1950s.

Other restrictions. Most regions of the Chittagong Hill Tracts District in far eastern Bangladesh are closed to foreigners. Tribal clashes make travel there unsafe.

SAFETY

Crime. The crime rate is rather low in Bangladesh. Pickpockets exist but aren't as common as in some nearby countries.

• The problem of *baksheesh* (bribes or "tips") is not as serious as it is in

India. (At least, people aren't as aggressive about it.)

Health. Drink hot tea or soft drinks from well-known bottlers. Never drink water, even in hotels and restaurants, unless you know it's been boiled for ten minutes or treated with purification tablets.

- Don't eat fresh salads, uncooked foods, or ice cream or other dairy products. Drink coconut milk or green coconut water instead of animal milk, and peel all fruit before you eat it.

- Meat is rarely inspected, so make sure it's well cooked.

- Bangladesh is host to infectious hepatitis, rabies, cholera, typhoid, diphtheria, polio, tetanus, and malaria, so get immunized before you arrive. Ask your doctor for anti-malaria tablets.

- Treat cuts promptly with antiseptic. The hot, humid weather promotes infection.

SHOPPING AND ENTERTAINMENT

Shopping. Shop hours are 9:00 A.M. to 8:00 P.M. Monday through Friday, and 9:00 A.M. to 2:00 P.M. Saturday. Some shops close for the lunch hour, and some close all day on Friday.

- Bargaining is the rule in Bangladesh. Begin by offering about half the quoted price.

- Good buys are brasswork, jute products (but remember that jute carpets have a short life-span), silk *saris*, jewelry, leatherwork, ceramics, and metal sculptures.

Entertainment. Nightlife is very limited in Bangladesh. You can find bars in the tourist hotels; they open at 6:30 P.M.

- Americans with passports in hand can enter the Friday night disco at the U.S. Embassy Marines' Club.

HOLIDAYS

Official holidays:
Martyr's Day (February 21), Independence Day (March 26), Bengali New Year (April), May Day (May 1), Buddha Purnima (May), Shad-e-Qadr (July), Eid-ul-Azha (variable), Eid-ul-Fitr (September), Durgah Puja (October), Muharram (October), Revolution Day (November 7), Victory Day (December 16), Christmas Day (December 25), Eid-e-Milad-un-Nabi (variable).

- Muslim and Buddhist religious holidays vary according to the lunar calendar. The Muslim calendar is ten days shorter than ours, so Ramadan and all the other Muslim festivals come at a different time each year.

- The Muslim Ramadan is a month in which people fast between sunrise and sunset to observe the Koran's revelation. Eid-ul-Fitr, which celebrates the day the Koran was revealed to the Prophet Mohammed, is observed at the end of Ramadan.

- Durgah Puja is a holiday celebrating the birth of the Hindu goddess Durgah (the wife of Shiva).

KEY PHRASES

English	Bengali	Pronunciation
Good morning	Namaskar/ A-Salam mu Alai-kum	Nomosh-karr/ Ah Sa-la-mu-a-lai-kum
Good afternoon	"	"
Good evening	"	"
Good night	Namaskar/ Khoda hafej	Nomosh-karr/K'hohda hahfez
Goodbye (leaving)	Asi/A-Salam mu Alaikum	Ahshee/As Sa-la-mu-a-lai-kum
Goodbye (staying)	Asun nomoskar/ Asun khoda hafej	Ahshoon no mosh-karr/ Ahshoon k'hoda hahfez
Please	Anugroho kaye	Ohnu-gro-ho ka-ye
Thank you	Dhonnobad	D'honno-bud
Excuse me	Ami dukhito	Ahmee dook'heeto
Don't mention it	O kotha bolben na	Oh kott'ha bol ben nah
Yes	Ha	Hahn
No	Na	Nah
I understand	Bojhi	Bohj'hee
I don't understand	Bojhi na	Bohj'hee nah
How much?	Koto dam?	Kottoh dahm?
Does anyone here speak English?	Map korben, ek-hane Engraji bolte pare, emon keu ache?	Map Koorrben, ek-hahneh Ing-grah-jee boll-teh pahreh, emmon kyoo a-cheh?
Sir	Mosai/Janab	Moe-sigh/Jha-nhab
Mr.	Janab	Jha-nhab
Madam, Mrs., Miss	"	"

If you can get away from the tour groups, factory and commune tours, and banquets, you can see the real China — the spontaneous side of this tightly-regulated nation of one billion people. The Chinese government still encourages visitors to book expensive tours through the China Travel Service and a few other approved agencies, but it's beginning to let tourists travel individually. This option is only for the patient, however — language barriers, red tape, and the need for local travel permits all present significant obstacles.

The People's Republic of China is still searching for its future. Over the past four decades it has undergone many mini-revolutions and changes in direction, encouraging free thinking for a while and then penalizing nonconformists. This is an especially important time for China and a unique opportunity for foreigners to see a nation undergoing dramatic change.

MEETING PEOPLE

- The Chinese people are very friendly to foreign tourists and seem fascinated by Westerners, especially Americans.

GREETINGS

- When you greet someone, a nod or slight bow will usually suffice, but shake hands if the Chinese person offers a hand first. Don't hug or kiss anyone.

- If you greet a group of Chinese, direct your first greeting toward the oldest or most senior person.

- If you're with a group entering a room for introductions, line up according to seniority, with the most senior person or leader at the head of the line. The Chinese will be arranged similarly. The senior people greet each other first.

- If you're with a tour group or delegation, people might greet you with applause when you arrive for a meeting or a visit to a factory or neighborhood. Return the applause.

Names and titles. Almost all Chinese names have three parts (for example, Lee Fang Wang). The first is a one-syllable surname, or family name. The second is a generation name, shared by brothers, sisters, and often cousins of the same family and generation. The third is the person's individual given name. Unfortunately, it's almost impossible to tell men's from women's names.

- Some Chinese put their names in Western order on the English side of their business cards — thus confusing everyone. One clue is the hyphen sometimes placed between the generation and given names.

- Close friends and family members often call each other by their generation and given names (Fang-Wang). You, however, should use only the surname with Mr., Mrs., or Miss (Miss Lee).

- Most Chinese women keep their maiden names and some indicate their marital status to Westerners by using the title

"Madam" (abbreviated "Mdm."). Westerners may call them Mrs.

- The Chinese sometimes address foreign women, no matter what their marital status, by their first names (Miss Mildred).

- The Chinese often use the prefixes *lao* (old) and *xiao* (little; pronounced "show" as in "shower") when they address friends and family members. Don't use these nicknames yourself.

Correspondence. Use the person's surname and title (for example, address Guo Fang Wang as Mr. Guo). Some Chinese business people prefer to use their initials in English translation (F.W. Guo). Use the salutation, "Dear Mr. Guo."

CONVERSATION

- Good conversation subjects: China's beauty and culture, life in your home country (but don't make comparisons), and families.

- Subjects to avoid: Politics, comparative wealth, Taiwan, sex, the Cultural Revolution, or any other aspects of China's recent history. Don't make derogatory remarks about China or your own country, and don't joke about Chinese politics or leaders, or about sex.

- The Chinese might ask you very personal questions such as, "How many children do you have?" or "How much money do you make?" These are the types of questions they ask each other. If you don't want to answer seriously, say something like, "I earn enough to feed my children" and smile.

- When you speak about the People's Republic of China, don't call it "Red China," "Communist China," or "Mainland China." Try to avoid speaking about Taiwan, but if you must, refer to it as "Taiwan" rather than "Free China" or the "Republic of China."

PHRASES TO KNOW

- China has many regional dialects, but Mandarin (the dialect of Beijing) is the national language, taught in schools everywhere. The Chinese system of romanizing characters is *pinyin;* signs often show *pinyin* as well as Chinese characters.

CURRENCY

- The Chinese unit of currency is the *renminbi* (People's money), abbreviated "RMB." One U.S. dollar is worth about 3.7 *renminbi* (August 1987 rates). The *renminbi* is also called the *yuan* or, in everyday speech, the *kuai*. The *yuan* is divided into 100 *fen* or 10 *jiao*. Coins are circulated in values of 1, 2, 5, and 10 *fen*. Notes are issued in .10, .20, .50, 1, 2, 5, and 10 *yuan*.

- You can exchange traveler's checks and most foreign currencies at hotels, Friendship Stores, or the Bank of China. Take your currency declaration form (obtained at customs) with you, and keep the exchange receipt for each transaction. You will be issued Foreign Exchange Certificates (FECs) that are good at most tourist places but are not accepted elsewhere.

- If possible change a large amount of money immediately after you arrive. The Police Bureau might keep your passport for a while, and you can't exchange currency without it.

- A black market exists for both hard currency and FECs. Occasionally people will approach you near tourist hotels and offer to buy your FECs at a very favorable rate. No matter what rates you're offered, however, don't exchange currency with unauthorized people or swap your FECs for *renminbi* with a local. The local might be severely penalized, and you might be deported.

- Only large hotels and Friendship Stores accept credit cards; don't be surprised if they charge you an extra 4% to 6% for using them. Restaurants accept only cash.

- Foreign visitors often pay higher prices than residents do for items and services. Foreigners of Chinese ancestry, however, can usually get the local price or at least a discount. The government endorses this three-tiered pricing system by incorporating it in train and airplane fares.

ETIQUETTE

GENERAL MANNERS

• Some Chinese will seem nervous when you talk with them alone. It's because such meetings are reported to the neighborhood police, who will question them about it later.

• People — especially children — outside of the largest cities and tourist attractions might stare at you if they haven't seen many foreigners. Don't get offended. If you draw a crowd, just smile, greet them politely, and continue on your way.

• If children shout *"gweilo"* or *"guizi"* at you, they're calling you a "foreign devil." Smile and show them that foreigners aren't all that bad.

• Chinese don't like to say no, so try to phrase your questions so that they don't require a yes-or-no answer. For example ask, "What is this material?" rather than, "Is this made of real leather?" Try not to say no yourself; instead, just say "It would be difficult" and the Chinese will know what you mean.

• If you need to criticize someone, do it only in private.

• Being late isn't fashionable. Always be on time or a few minutes early to any appointment or engagement.

• Displays of affection between the sexes — even between spouses — are frowned upon. Flirting with locals will meet with embarrassment or even violence. Young Chinese men are sometimes belligerent towards a Western man seen with a Chinese woman. Most Chinese don't wear wedding rings.

• If people applaud you at a banquet or other social functions, return the applause.

• Before you take anyone's photograph, ask permission.

• If you wish to smoke, offer cigarettes to the other men in your group. Chinese women rarely smoke or drink. Western women are sometimes offered cigarettes and alcohol and should feel free to accept.

BODY LANGUAGE

• The Chinese dislike being touched by people they don't know, and prefer a smile to a pat on the back or similar gesture. Be especially careful to avoid physical familiarity with older people or people in important positions.

• Chinese point with an open hand rather than with one finger, and beckon someone with the hand facing palm-down.

DRESS

• Dress modestly. Don't wear designer clothes, expensive jewelry, flamboyant accessories, or bright or revealing clothing.

• Many Chinese wear short-sleeved, open-necked shirts. Except in summer officials wear them under dark jackets with high necks.

MEN For business and banquets wear a sports coat and tie. You might be able to take off the jacket during a banquet; take your cue from your hosts. In the summer (especially in southern China) you may omit the jacket and often the tie. A safari suit is comfortable and suitable for informal business meetings, sightseeing, and summer banquets.

WOMEN Wear modest dresses or pantsuits for business and formal dresses for banquets. Use little makeup and jewelry. Don't wear high heels, shorts, or halter tops.

PRIVATE HOMES

• Foreign visitors are rarely invited to a private home unless the authorities have approved the visit in advance. Unless you are of Chinese ancestry, you may not stay overnight with a Chinese family.

• If you are invited to a home, be prompt or even a little early when you arrive, and make the first move when it's time to leave.

• Don't give a gift on your first visit; it could be interpreted as a bribe. Instead, wait until your third or fourth visit. On the other hand it's a good idea to have a gift handy in case you're presented with one. A good choice is a small present you can give "for the children."

- Conduct yourself with restraint, and refrain from loud, boisterous speech and behavior. Don't wander around the house unaccompanied — bedrooms and kitchens are considered private.

- Toilets are of the squat type.

PERSONAL GIFTS

- If you give a gift — no matter how small — to someone in a group, either give a gift to everyone or present the gift to the group as a whole.

- To be polite Chinese usually refuse a gift at first, so persist until they either accept or indicate that accepting would be "inconvenient."

- Good choices for children are Frisbees, baseballs, and picture books — but not money. Adults appreciate cigarettes, sweets, imported whiskey, and T-shirts from overseas universities.

- People might ask you to get them expensive presents from the West because they don't know the value of things outside China. If that happens just say that "It would be difficult"; you might also explain that the item is very expensive.

TIPPING

- Until recently tipping has been not only forbidden, but also a potential insult — something a superior does to an inferior. To improve service standards, however, China now permits guides, drivers, translators, and other service people to accept tips. Rules on tipping tend to change, so inquire about current government policy.

- If someone does you a special favor, reciprocate with a small present such as a ballpoint pen, a souvenir pin, cigarettes, or sweets. Tour guides welcome foreign books written about China, since these books often cover topics not included in their training.

FOODS

MEALS

Breakfast (*zaocan*): 6:00 to 8:00 A.M. Typical fare varies by region. In the South, look for either *dim* *sum* or rice *congee* (porridge) with peanuts, thousand-year-old eggs, and pickles. In the North, expect fried bread dipped in soy milk. In Shanghai, you might find gelatinous rice balls with sugar inside. Hotels serve Western-style breakfasts.

Lunch (*wucan*): 11:00 A.M. to 2:00 P.M. A typical meal might be curried chicken, mushrooms and greens, steamed buns, clear soup, steamed rice, and fruit. Noodles are a quick alternative.

Dinner (*wancan*): 5:00 to 7:00 P.M. This is the main meal of the day, and the variety is tremendous. Most dinners feature meat and fish dishes, a vegetable dish, steamed rice, and a clear soup.

WHERE TO EAT

- Many restaurants close between meals, so to avoid disappointment get information from your hotel. And dine early — restaurants often run out of selections later.

- For Western meals or an English-speaking staff, your best bet is a tourist hotel. (A favorite of foreign visitors is the romantically named Beijing Air Catering Services Restaurant.) Hotels that have only one restaurant often serve Western breakfasts and Chinese lunches and dinners. Boiled eggs in Western breakfasts are often overdone; ordering scrambled eggs is safer.

- Many hotel restaurants have both ala carte and fixed menus; the latter are usually shown only to tour groups. Ask to see the fixed menu (*fen fa*) — it usually offers a varied meal at a lower cost.

- To eat at the better local Chinese restaurants, you'll need reservations, which you can arrange through your hotel. Most better restaurants don't accept either reservations or customers after 7:00 P.M.

- Most fine restaurants charge a fixed price (usually 30 to 100 *yuan* per person) and select the menu from available ingredients.

- Unfortunately, price gouging sometimes occurs, so find out the price before you order. In some cases you pay when you order. If you see others paying for tickets, do the same before you order.

- Government managed

restaurants usually have poor service and surly service people. Some of these restaurants expect customers to get their own drinks.

- In most of the better government-run restaurants, you'll be seated in a separate area from the locals, usually upstairs. Don't object and try to sit where you aren't wanted — you'll make everybody uncomfortable, but you won't change any policies. Most private restaurants don't have these separate seating arrangements.

- For inexpensive eating (usually one to three *yuan*), try the private restaurants frequented by locals and the food stalls. Don't expect the highest sanitation standards, however. If the tea is hot, use it to scald your utensils.

- Before you buy from a food stall, make sure the food is fresh and hot, the server is clean, and the utensils are washed in hot water. You might want to carry your own chopsticks. A recent gamma globulin inoculation is recommended.

- Noodle and bun shops are fast and cheap. They're very popular with the locals and might be uncomfortably crowded at lunch.

- Vegetarians should try the Beijing Sucai Restaurant, which serves roast duck, fish, shark's fin soup, and other dishes — all made from vegetables. Try the mock abalone with fresh vegetables (*su shih ching*). In other restaurants beware of meat sauces that are often poured over vegetables. Other special diet foods (salt-free or diabetic) are very hard to find.

FOODS TO TRY

- Chinese cuisine varies greatly from one region to another. Most family meals are based on rice, potatoes, barley soup, corn meal, steamed buns, and other grain dishes. Dishes made with pork, chicken, mutton, or fish are also popular, as are various fruits and vegetables when they're in season. There are few dairy products.

- You don't need to know Chinese to order, even in restaurants without English menus. Either point at something that looks good on somebody else's table, or have someone write the name of your favorite dish on a card you can carry around. If you really want to explore the menu, get a copy of James D. McCawley's *The Eater's Guide to Chinese Characters* (University of Chicago Press, Chicago, 1984, $5.95).

• Be sure not to eat ice cream or any other dairy products or cold foods except in the tourist hotels. To avoid intestinal parasites stay away from fruits full of surface water, such as watermelons.

Specialties. Cantonese cuisine features many foods that are either steamed or stir-fried at a high temperature in a little peanut oil to preserve the natural flavors. Dishes tend to be sweet. Try the roasted goose, prawns in ginger sauce, and wintermelon soup. Dessert is often a sweet cake followed by fruit. *Dim sum* is a lunchtime favorite that consists of little dumplings and other small portions selected from a cart pushed around to the tables. At banquets watch out for dishes made from monkey, civet cat, and dog.

• Shanghai cuisine features longer cooking in sesame oil, which softens the vegetables and enables them to absorb sauce. Look for sweet-and-sour carp, red-cooked meat (meat cooked in soy sauce, sugar, ginger, and spices), and hairy crab.

• Mandarin (northern) foods are generally oilier and saltier than the other regional cuisines. Mandarin cuisine is famous for fried or steamed meat and vegetable dumplings (*zhaozi*) and Peking duck (*Beijing kao ya*). To eat Peking duck, place the flat bread on your plate, scoop up the *hoisin* sauce with a scallion, brush the sauce on the bread, and place the scallion, duck skin, and meat together at one end of the bread. Roll the contents up in the bread and eat it with your fingers.

• Sichuan (western) cuisine is highly spiced with hot peppers and oil. Noodles (hotly spiced) are included in most meals. Other dishes to try are hot bean curd, spicy chicken in peanut sauce, and hot prawns with peanuts.

• Fujian (eastern coast) cuisine features lots of seafood and soups. Many dishes are sweet and include pineapple and coconut. Spring rolls and suckling pig are favorites.

- In the South try pomelo (a sweet fruit with a thick rind) or *lichee*s (a sweet, grape-like fruit available in May and June).

- The hundred- (or thousand-) year-old eggs served at breakfast are actually no older than a few months. The eggs are placed in a lime bath, buried in mud, and cooked slowly by a chemical reaction that turns them dark.

Beverages. Don't drink water or eat ice unless you know the water has been boiled.

- Tea is popular everywhere and is served with all meals. Other drinks are beer (Tsingtao is the most famous), local soft drinks, Coca-Cola, and expensive fruit juices. You can buy Coca-Cola only with foreign currency.

- Chinese vodka and brandy are quite good. Also try *maotai,* a liquor made from sorghum and wheat yeast and aged five or six years. It's very potent, so use the tiny goblets provided with it.

TABLE MANNERS

- Address waiters, waitresses, and other service people as *tong zhi* (comrade; pronounce *zhi* like the "ger" in "gerbil"), not as "waiter," "boy," or similar terms. Don't snap your fingers or clap to get their attention.

- Except in hotel dining rooms and expensive restaurants, seat yourself.

- Most restaurants are simply too crowded to provide private seating, expect to share a table with other diners. If you're seated in a private dining room, expect to pay more for the food.

Utensils. Chopsticks are used for all meals (see Utensils in the Taiwan chapter for information on how to use them).

- When you serve yourself from communal dishes, don't use the ends of the chopsticks that you put in your mouth.

- Watch how your Chinese friends eat. Cup the bowl of rice in your hand, hold it close to your mouth, and scoop in the rice using your chopsticks.

- To eat long noodles pick up a few with your chopsticks, put them partway in your mouth, and slurp. Slurping is perfectly acceptable when you're eating noodles and soup. The long noodles might be inconvenient, but they symbolize long life.

- Put any bones, seeds, or other rejects on the table or in the special dishes provided, not in your rice bowl.

- When you finish eating place your chopsticks neatly on the table.

- Diners are often given a hot or cold towel for wiping their hands before the meal.

- When you use a toothpick, cover your mouth with one hand.

Dining with others. If your Chinese friends invite you to an expensive restaurant, they might ask you to make the reservations. Some restaurants make reservations only for officials and foreigners.

- Tables are usually round, and communal dishes are placed in the center so people can help themselves. When you order get one dish for each person, one more dish for good measure, and rice or buns. Soup might come at any point in the meal.

- In a home all the dishes will be served at once. The host will begin the meal by placing portions on the guests' plates. It's polite to sample every dish.

- Make conversation during the meal, but not about business.

- If you're the guest make your move to leave shortly after the meal finishes.

- The host (whoever invited the others or suggested the meal) always pays for everyone.

Banquets. Most banquets begin about 6:30 or 7:00 P.M. and last two or three hours. Always be on time or, preferably, a few minutes early — the food is usually ready at the specified time.

- The host usually sits opposite the entrance door, with guests seated to the right and left in order of seniority. The host starts the meal by placing food on the guests' plates with serving chopsticks.

- Soon after the meal begins, the host will toast the guests. Don't drink until this occurs. After a short interval, respond to the toast by emptying your glass and turning it upside down.

- It's impolite to drink alone, so people usually offer toasts to those sitting near them or to the whole table. After the first toast, however, sips are sufficient. Nondrinkers may toast with water, juice, or soft drinks.

- You'll be expected to participate in numerous toasts. There's no stigma attached to being tipsy as long as you don't become boisterous and bother others — your hosts might appear to enjoy you as much as you're enjoying yourself, but they'll greet you coolly the next time you meet.

- At a formal banquet have a short, friendly speech prepared to respond to your host's toast and speech. If you're the guest of honor, follow the host's lead and reciprocate appropriately. If the host follows the toast and speech by visiting other tables in your party and toasting guests, then you should do the same.

- If you receive applause, be sure to return it.

- Dishes are served in several courses, with soup coming at either the beginning or the end of the meal, and rice served throughout. Beer is drunk during the meal, and tea afterward.

- Refusing food is impolite. If you don't want to eat something, pretend to eat it by pushing it around your plate with your chopsticks and then hide it among the other foods. Eat less of each dish as the meal progresses.

- Don't linger past 10:00 P.M.

ACCOMMODATIONS

Hotels. Make your hotel reservation before you arrive. The China International Travel Service (CITS, or Luxingshe) has offices in Western countries that can help. Your travel agent can contact either CITS or some of the new hotels operated jointly by Western hotel chains and the Chinese.

- A few hotels, such as the Beijing Hotel, do not permit foreigners to book directly. You'll have to depend on CITS or a Chinese contact to make your reservations.

- Many hotels have stringent no-show deadlines, so to avoid losing your room, consider paying for your first night in advance.

- If you walk into an unpretentious hotel and try to book a room, don't be surprised if they refuse. Many small hotels are either reserved for Chinese, or don't want the hassle of doing business with foreigners.

- Tourist hotels have a service desk on every floor. It is staffed twenty-four hours a day by someone responsible for emergency help, accepting laundry, placing phone calls, ensuring safety, and making sure that no Chinese accompany foreigners to a room unreported.

- Some hotels require you to leave your passport or travel document with them during your stay.

- Hot water availability is unpredictable in some hotels and restricted in others to certain times of the day. Take your hot shower whenever you can.

- Many hotels now provide ice made from boiled water, but be sure to ask.

- China's newest hotels have their own telephone exchanges, which makes telephone calls a bit easier.

- Message delivery has not been a strong point at many hotels. Improve your chances of receiving messages by asking people to use your room number when they contact you.

- If you like to read in bed, bring a reading light that attaches to the book. Hotel lighting is often poor.

Rest rooms. Look for public rest rooms in hotels and restaurants. Those in restaurants and public areas (parks, for example) are usually of the squatting type and are often unclean. Always carry toilet tissue with you.

TRANSPORTATION

- The China Travel Service (CTS) can make your transportation and tour arrangements. Your local travel agent might be able to assist.

PUBLIC TRANSPORTATION

- Avoid the rush hours from 6:00 to 8:00 A.M. and 5:00 to 6:00 P.M.

- Taxi drivers and ticket takers are very honest about making change. If you haven't figured out Chinese money yet, just offer a handful of change and they'll take the right amount. Make sure you carry change, though — they don't carry much.

- Queues for buses and subways quickly disintegrate into masses of pushing and shoving people when a bus or train pulls up. If you want to get on, just push and shove along with everyone else, and smile.

Buses. Buses are inexpensive but crowded (especially on Sunday). The local routes are marked on maps. Fares (5 to 10 *yuan*) are based on distance, so make sure you can pronounce your destination. Pay the ticket-taker near the rear door. City buses run until 11:30 P.M. or midnight.

Taxis. You can find taxis at tourist hotels, at train stations, and in front of some government offices. You won't see them cruising for fares. Taxis don't have meters; instead, they charge by an unfathomable formula that factors in the time, distance, and type of car. At the end of the trip, the driver will hand you a slip of paper with the fare printed on it (usually 2 to 7 *yuan*).

- Taxi drivers often refuse to wait for you to finish a meeting, to take you back to your hotel. If you have appointments, arrange for a car and driver.

Trains. Long-distance train travel can be rewarding but exhausting. You can buy tickets from CITS either before you arrive in China or (for less money) after you arrive.

- Soft-class berths are the most comfortable way to travel by train. They have two upper and two lower sleeping spaces, a table lamp, an overhead fan, and overhead storage for suitcases. Compartment doors can be closed but not locked. A steward will give you a dining car menu soon after you get on board. Give him your order and he'll call you to the dining car when your meal is ready.

- Hard-class berths crowd six people into each

compartment and provide no door for privacy (although people tend to respect your privacy anyway). CTS won't make hard-class reservations for foreigners.

- Keep your ticket handy. You'll need to show it when you depart and sometimes during the trip.

- If you're with a tour group, your luggage will be stored at one end of the car, unavailable to you during the trip. Keep a toiletries bag and a change of clothes with you.

- The rest rooms and washrooms are often filthy. Try to get a compartment in the middle of the train and away from the rest rooms — it will be less noisy, less bumpy, and less smelly.

Subways. Beijing is the only city with a subway. Like the buses, it's inexpensive and crowded, and the fare (5 to 10 *yuan*) is based on distance. It operates between 6:00 A.M. and 9:00 P.M., and has only one line.

Other transportation. Rental bicycles are hard to come by, but if you plan to stay a while, consider buying a bike and reselling it. If you buy one take it to the police and register it for a nominal fee. There are designated areas for bicycle parking, some of which are policed by attendants who will give you a ticket and charge you for parking when you return. Be aware that any vehicle larger than the bike has the right-of-way, and will take it.

DRIVING

- Self-drive rental cars are not available in China. This is a blessing. Driving is made very confusing by many pedestrians, bicycles, slow-moving vehicles, and horse-drawn carts. Night driving is an adventure — vehicles dash through the streets with their lights off, switching them on only to warn other vehicles at the last possible moment.

- You can hire a car and driver either through your hotel or (before you go to China) with National Car Rental. The daily rate averages 60 to 100 *yuan*. You'll be charged for cancellations.

- If the car you are riding in has an accident, stay there until the police arrive. If you're found at fault (even a passenger can be at fault for distracting the driver), you'll either pay a fine or pay damages calculated by using a standard formula.

BUSINESS

- To visit China on business, you must obtain a written invitation from a Chinese trading corporation. For help in obtaining an invitation, contact either a U.S. Department of Commerce International Trade Administration office, found in most state capitals and large cities, or a People's Republic of China embassy. Once you have the invitation, you can obtain a visa from a Chinese mission or the China International Travel Service (CITS or Luxingshe).

- Joining a business delegation to China is often the quickest way to make contacts in your industry and obtain an invitation to return by yourself for negotiations. It's also a good way to scout the sit-uation and overcome culture shock before you get down to business. To find a delegation check with your trade association or the Department of Commerce.

BUSINESS HOURS

Business offices: 8:00 or 9:00 A.M. to noon, and 2:00 to 5:00 P.M. Monday through Saturday. Everything stops for the two-hour lunch break. In the North office hours are usually shorter during the coldest months (December through February).

Banks: 10:00 A.M. to noon, and 2:00 to 6:00 P.M. Monday through Saturday.

Government offices: Same as business offices.

BUSINESS CUSTOMS

- Arrange your visit well in advance by telex, representative, or — as a last resort — mail. The Chinese will want to know all about your company before they reply, so shorten the process by providing background information and references up front.

- If you come to China at another organization's invitation, expect them to direct your schedule.

- The Chinese might be reluctant to negotiate with anyone but high-ranking members of your organization, assuming that lower-ranking people don't have decision-making powers.

- Contract negotiations will be more detailed, technical, and time-consuming than in any other Asian nation. Don't assume anything — even the obvious — or leave any ambiguities in the contract. To the Chinese signing a contract means that the parties have established a relationship and can expect favors of each other.

- If you want to communicate with your home office, you can send telexes and cables from most tourist hotels and telecommunications offices, but you might be expected to punch your own tape.

Business etiquette. Most Chinese officials now offer business cards when you meet them, and you should offer them one. If they don't offer you one, it might be because their work unit doesn't supply employees with cards.

- Use name cards with a Chinese translation on one side. You can get these made quickly in Hong Kong, but be sure to specify that they're for use in mainland China — the character style differs from the traditional style used in Hong Kong and Taiwan.

- If the person's title is on the name card, address him or her by that title.

- At every encounter your Chinese counterparts will be studying your temperament and sincerity. If they don't like you, they'll do business with someone else.

- To succeed you must be patient and persistent. Quiet persistence and high principles are virtues in China.

- Try to send the same representative on each trip. The Chinese tend to place their trust in the individual as much as in the company.

- Don't ignore the senior person in a Chinese negotiating team — even if the person doesn't speak English. Even if you're communicating through interpreters, look at and address the senior person from time to time.

- Whenever your Chinese counterparts are speaking, don't interrupt them. Delay your comments until they're done.

- Avoid using maps, flags, or any references to politically sensitive countries such as Taiwan or the Soviet Union (with which the People's Republic has boundary disputes).

Appointments and meetings. The best times for meetings are 10:00 A.M. and 3:00 P.M. Appointments before 9:00 A.M. are unusual, and breakfast meetings are almost unknown. Don't ask for a meeting on a Friday, when many officials are out of their offices. Allow more time for meetings than you would in the West.

- Arriving late for a meeting is very rude. Missing it altogether is a deliberate affront.

- Shake hands with everyone at a meeting in order of seniority, both when you arrive and when you leave. The Chinese will line up in order of rank, and so should you and your team.

- At the meeting you'll be shown to a seat. The ranking Chinese will sit either in the middle or at the head of the negotiating table, facing the door at meals.

- Early negotiating sessions will take place around a coffee table in a room set aside for greeting visitors. The senior member of your team will sit to the right of the leader of the Chinese team.

- Meetings begin with tea and conversation. Don't launch right into the business discussions. During the tea, try to make favorable remarks about China.

- Wait for your host to ask you what you would like to talk about, then spell out your business clearly. Always defer to your host.

- During meetings make sure subordinates on your team don't interrupt your team leader or enter the conversation without permission.

- Don't say anything in English you don't want everyone to hear. There are usually people who understand English present, even though they might not let on.

- Be friendly and sincere. The atmosphere of every meeting is more important to the Chinese than to Westerners. Once a bad atmosphere is created, it is almost impossible to change.

- Avoid jokes. They usually don't translate well.
- If the Chinese leader suggests that you must be tired or busy, it's probably a hint that it's time to end the meeting. Remember that people often leave their offices at 4:00 P.M.

Business gifts and entertainment. Government officials and employees are not supposed to accept anything more than token gifts. If you give a valuable gift (for example, a television set or computer), present it to the organization as a whole.

- For individuals give imported liquor, ballpoint pen sets, calculators, or products typical of your home (and preferably with your company's logo on them).
- Present gifts in private unless they're meant for the whole group.
- If you consummate a business deal during your visit, give a banquet. If your hosts give you a banquet, reciprocate with an equivalent one.
- If you are treated to a banquet, don't assume that it means negotiations are going well or nearing the end. Banquets are a traditional custom, and they permit Chinese negotiators to enjoy delicacies they can't have every day.
- If you arrange a banquet, make reservations at least twenty-four hours ahead of time. Your hotel can help you; just tell them how much per person you want to spend. Let the chef decide the menu. There will be a charge if you cancel.

TELEPHONES AND MAIL

Telephones. There are few public phones. Look for them in hotels, Friendship Stores, or near yellow metal signs that depict a phone.

- Local calls are free, but are frustrating to make because the phone systems in most cities (including Beijing) are so antiquated. If you get through let the phone ring for a long time before you give up. Once you connect you may need to shout to be heard.

- The Chinese answer the phone with *"wai"* (pronounced "why"), which means hello.

- Very few Chinese have telephones, and an office usually has only one. You might have to wait while the person who answers it finds the person you're calling. Keep talking while you wait, though — you might be disconnected if you're silent.

- Avoid making local calls from noon to 2:00 P.M. These are the *xiuxi,* or rest hours, when many people take naps.

- Because the phone system is unreliable, cablegrams are often used for domestic communications. Unlike international cables, they're reasonably priced.

- Cables to the U.S. cost about a dollar a word, so telephone calls are less expensive. Some hotels and the telecommunication offices have telex capabilities, but do not provide assistance in typing or sending telexes.

- Make international calls from either your hotel or the telecommunications office. There is no international direct dialing. Since international connections sometimes take an hour or more, you might want to call from your hotel and wait in your room. Just fill out the form the hotel provides and give it to the desk on your floor. Don't try calling between noon and 2:00 P.M., however — hotel operators leave for lunch.

- The hotel will add a service charge for international calls; be sure to find out how much it is before you book your call. To avoid the service charge, you can try to get through to Beijing's international telephone office at 337431.

- You might want to call home collect. Collect calls to the U.S., for example, cost about 50% less than if you charge them locally. International credit cards are also accepted.

- Time your international calls yourself. After you hang up the operator will call you to ask whether you're finished. Be sure to confirm how many minutes were used and what the charge will be. There is a minimum charge of three minutes.

- If you're expecting any calls, give the callers your room number. Western names are often difficult for the Chinese to interpret.

Mail. Most tourist hotels either have a branch post office or accept mail to be posted.

- To mail parcels containing anything except printed matter, go to the main post office and fill out a customs form.

LEGAL MATTERS

Customs and immigration. Visas are required. It's a good idea to obtain a letter of confirmation from the CITS (Luxingshe) or an invitation from someone in China, especially if you're traveling on business. Hong Kong travel agents can arrange independent tourist (non-tour-group) visas good for a month. A transit visa is good for visits of up to a week. Cities you want to visit must be stamped on the visa.

- Pornographic materials, books critical of socialism, and large batches of religious books might be confiscated at customs.

- Declare any items such as cameras, radios, and calculators when you enter. If you leave China without them, you'll have to pay duty. You'll have to turn in your declaration form when you leave the country, so don't lose it (or any other forms that customs gives you). You might be delayed if all your forms are not in order.

- It's illegal to take Chinese currency into or out of the country. When you leave, the currency control desk will check your currency declaration form and your currency exchange receipts to make sure that the amount you exchanged equals the amount you declared when you entered.

- When you leave by air, your luggage will be x-rayed, so don't leave undeveloped camera film or anything else sensitive to x-rays in it.

Other restrictions. Don't photograph police officers, military personnel, airports, ports, anything else of military significance, or some museums, and don't photograph anything from the air. Be careful about taking pictures of scenes of poverty — officials and locals might get upset, even to the point of blocking your view.

• Don't risk drawing police attention to your Chinese friends by exchanging packages or papers in public places. Chinese don't even like to show foreigners to police stations lest they be seen and later questioned.

SAFETY

• Be very careful crossing streets — pedestrians never seem to have the right-of-way. Watch out for the large, chauffeured cars of officials that speed through the streets expecting everyone to get out of the way.

Crime. The incidence of street crime in China is low but growing. Watch out for pickpockets on buses, and don't wander around alone after 10:00 P.M.

Health. Boil water before you drink it, and don't use any ice unless you know it was made from boiled water. Also avoid ice creams, dairy products, and cold foods outside the main

tourist hotels. If you plan to patronize food stalls, get a gamma globulin shot just before you arrive in China.

• To avoid intestinal parasites don't eat watermelons or other fruits that contain lots of surface water. Human waste is used as fertilizer.

• Some people consider China's medical care to be the best in the third world. Bring medications with you, however — exact equivalents for Western medicines are hard to find.

• Mosquitos are a problem in some rural areas. Bring your own insect repellent — the local mosquito coils might give you more of a headache than the mosquitos do.

• Dengue is a problem in some areas, so use your mosquito repellents. Typhoid and infectious hepatitis are sometimes problems.

• Hospitals don't store O-negative blood. (That type is absent in China.)

• Women should bring a supply of sanitary napkins or tampons; they're hard to find.

SHOPPING AND ENTERTAINMENT

Shopping. Shop hours are 9:00 A.M. to 7:00 P.M. every day of the week. A few shops close for lunch.

- Chinese merchants will give you the right change. Don't ask them to keep the change; it will embarrass them.

- Bargaining is not the norm; don't try to bargain for any products except antiques. Instead just ask whether any discounts are available. If the answer is no, don't persist.

- If you buy an antique, make sure it has a red wax export seal. If it doesn't, take it to the Bureau of Cultural Relics (or some Friendship Stores) and ask them to attach one. Antiques more than 120 years old cannot be exported. Have the purchase recorded on your currency declaration form and keep all receipts.

- Friendship Stores, which

are for foreign visitors only, are located in most of the cities frequented by tourists. They are the most convenient and least crowded places to find a full range of Chinese products.

- If you go shopping with any Chinese, don't buy local products. Your Chinese friends might feel obligated to buy them for you, and most Chinese have little money to spare.

Entertainment. Entertainment is limited if you're not fond of dining out, banquets, or factory or commune tours. However, don't miss the national opera, theater groups, and ballets of Beijing. Either your hotel or Luxingshe, the government tourist office, can make arrangements for you.

HOLIDAYS

Holidays: New Year's Day (January 1), Chinese New Year (three days in January or February), Labor Day (May 1), and Chinese National Day (October 1 and 2). Offices and businesses often close for one or two days on either side of these holidays. Provinces and cities also have their own holidays.

Unofficial holidays: Other holidays feature celebrations and special programs, but offices and businesses remain open. These include International Working Women's Day (March 8), Youth Day (May 4), Children's Day (June 1), Communist Party Founding Day (July 1), and People's Liberation Army Day (August 1).

- The Chinese New Year is celebrated as the Spring Festival, and its date varies with the lunar calendar. Unlike in Hong Kong, fireworks are not permitted in most areas of China. The Chinese like to wear new clothing and shoes on the first days of the new year. Private businesses often close for up to two weeks around this holiday.

- Chinese National Day celebrates the founding of the People's Republic of China in 1949. Large military parades are held in Beijing, and hotels are booked solid.

KEY PHRASES

English	Mandarin	Pronunciation
Hello	Nin hao ma	Neen how mah
Good morning	Zao	Dzow
Good afternoon	Nin hao	Neen how
Good evening	"	"
Good night	Wan an	Wahn ahn
Goodbye	Zaijian	Dzigh jyen
Please	Qing	Ching
Thank you	Xie xie	Syeh-syeh
You're welcome	Bu xie	Boo syeh
Excuse me	Duibuqi	Dwei boo chi
Don't mention it	Mei shenme	May Sh'ma
Yes	Shi	Sher
No	Bu shi	Boo sher
I understand	Wo dong	Waw dawng
I don't understand	Wo budong	Waw boo-dawng
How much?	Duoshao qian?	Dwaw-shaw ch-yen?
Does anyone here speak English?	Shei hui shuo ying wen?	Shay hu-way shwo ying win?
Sir, Mr.	Xian sheng	Syen-sheng
Madam, Mrs.	Tai tai	Tigh tigh
Miss	Xiaojie	Shyow-jyeh

- To pronounce *pinyin* note the following:

Pinyin	English
g	k
j, q	ch
r, zh	j
x	sh
c	ts
i	ee
ai	eye

- Business people will find the book-and-tape set *Business Chinese 500* (Foreign Language Press, China, about $6.00) invaluable. You can order it in the West.

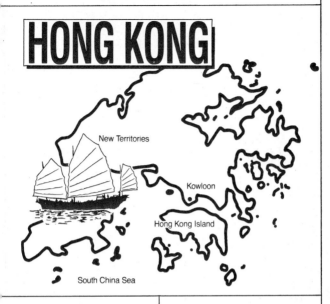

HONG KONG

New Territories

Kowloon

Hong Kong Island

South China Sea

Hong Kong has lost some of its luster as the shopping capital of the East since other cities — Seoul, Singapore, and Bangkok — have moved in with competitive prices and goods. Still, no other city can rival Hong Kong as a palace of consumption. The formerly robust mood of the British colony has been subdued by the knowledge that China will take over in 1997, when Britain's lease runs out. Corporations have begun leaving, and families are placing family members overseas to prepare the way for escape before the Chinese government moves in.

It's not too late, however, to relish the markets that clog the streets, the floating restaurants in Aberdeen Harbor, and the surliness of the city's merchants. If you're looking for historical reminders of the colony's past, you'll have to look hard, since most of the lovely old colonial buildings have been razed and replaced by gleaming glass and concrete towers. But if you spend your time bargain-hunting and sampling the various Chinese regional cuisines, you'll leave satisfied — and with extra luggage.

You'll be cheating yourself, however, if you spend all your time in the city of Hong Kong. Take a breather, hop a ferry to one of the outlying islands such as Cheung Chau, and enjoy a quiet hour on a hill overlooking the South China Sea.

The musty Portuguese colony of Macau is only a short jetfoil ride from Hong Kong. For gambling or for walking the streets of a 1930-ish colonial outpost, Macau can't be beat. Macau reverts to Chinese control in 1999, two years later than Hong Kong.

MEETING PEOPLE

GREETINGS

- Most men and women of Hong Kong understand and welcome an English-language greeting and a handshake. Older Chinese sometimes clasp their hands together about throat level and nod in greeting.

- When you visit a family, always greet the eldest members first. Greet the youngest members last and ask them about their schoolwork. Education is highly respected in Chinese society and an important topic of conversation.

- At a social function feel free to introduce yourself as you wish.

Names and titles. A Chinese person's name has three parts. The surname is written first, followed by a generation name and a given name. Thus, Chan Yun-Lei would be Mr. Chan. Many Hong Kong Chinese have adopted English given names for their children.

- Titles are used as they are in the West. Put Mr., Mrs., Miss, or professional titles such as Doctor before the surname.

Correspondence. Address letters using Western salutations, but remember to use only the person's surname ("Dear Mr. Wang:").

CONVERSATION

- Good conversation subjects: Chinese restaurants and cuisine, families, hobbies and special interests, schools, and favorite travel destinations.

- Subjects to avoid: Politics in the People's Republic of China, the 1997 Chinese takeover of Hong Kong, very personal questions, and comparative living standards.

- Although the Hong Kong Chinese talk loudly (especially when bargaining) and ask personal questions of visitors, they do not like Westerners to do the same.

- The Queen's English prevails in this British colony. American usage is understood, but apartments are called flats, lawyers are solicitors, the mail is the post, the elevators are lifts, and so on.

- You can express almost any story or concept by using a Chinese anecdote. You'll be able to communicate ideas very effectively if you do a little research and use examples from Chinese culture.

PHRASES TO KNOW

- Hong Kong has an English educational system, so English goes farther here than it does elsewhere in Asia. Officially, however, Hong Kong is bilingual (English and Cantonese). Learning a few words of Cantonese, the Chinese dialect spoken by most of Hong Kong's inhabitants, will please the Chinese and bring smiles to their faces.

- Cantonese, like Mandarin Chinese, is a tonal language that requires saying words with the correct tones to avoid confusion. This takes years of practice. These short phrases can often be understood even without the correct tones:

CURRENCY

- The unit of currency is the Hong Kong dollar (HK$), which is divided into 100 cents. One U.S. dollar is worth about 7.8 Hong Kong dollars (August 1987 rates). Coins are issued in denominations of 5, 10, 20, and 50 cents, and HK$ 1, 2, and 5. Notes are available in HK$ 10 (green), 50 (blue), 100 (red), 500 (yellow), and 1,000 (orange).

- If you're stuck with unexchangeable Asian currencies, bring them to Hong Kong, where you can change virtually any currency.

- The money changers at the airport don't give good rates, so change just enough to get you to your hotel. Most hotels will exchange currency, but banks and money changers offer the best rates. Be sure to compare — the rates vary even from bank to bank.

- Private money changers (found mostly in the Tsimshatsui area of Kowloon) often tack on commissions. Some add a commission to the quoted rate after they've taken your money.

ETIQUETTE

GENERAL MANNERS

- Many people in Hong Kong seem rude to Westerners, giving rise to the colony's reputation as one of the rudest places in Asia. Show your appreciation when people treat you courteously.

- The Chinese think Westerners are aggressive and arrogant, so be careful not to speak loudly or look aggressive, particularly if you're a woman.

- Hurting someone's feelings is a breach of courtesy. If you must criticize or correct someone, do it tactfully and in private. To the Chinese, it's more important for things to appear all right than to actually be all right.

- When you meet elderly people, always treat them with deference. Greet them first, offer them your seat, express interest in their health, and don't smoke in their presence.

- If someone compliments you, politely deny it. The Chinese appreciate compliments and offer them often, but consider it impolite to say "thank you" in response.

- If someone has an appointment with you, allow them a half-hour "courtesy time." Punctuality is respected, however, so be on time for appointments yourself.

- The Chinese often use *"gweilo"* (foreign devil) to mean "foreigner," although they usually don't mean it rudely. Try to ignore this habit. If you must respond you can say, *"Ngoh mhai gweilo. Ngoh hai sai yahn"* (I am not a foreign devil. I am a Westerner.).

- Eating food in the street is impolite.

- Telling the resident British to "have a good day" sometimes irritates them.

BODY LANGUAGE

- The Chinese don't appreciate physical contact. Don't pat people on the back, kiss or hug them in greeting, or put an arm around their shoulders. Don't be surprised to see friends of the same sex holding hands, however. It's perfectly acceptable.

- When people in Hong Kong talk, they usually stand closer together than North Americans do.

- To beckon people extend your arm, palm down, and flutter your fingers. Never use the one-fingered beckoning gesture of the West — only animals are called with this gesture.

- Point with your open hand, not with your index finger.

- When you sit put your hands in your lap and keep your feet on the floor. Women may cross their legs.

- Winking at someone is considered rude.

DRESS

MEN Standard business attire in the hot months is a washable, tropical-weight suit plus necktie. For informal occasions such as barbecues or forays to casual restaurants, wear an open-necked shirt or safari jacket. Men sometimes wear shorts on the street. For formal dinner parties wear a dark dinner suit and black bow tie.

WOMEN For business wear a dress or suit in muted colors. Women rarely wear shorts on the street. For informal occasions wear a dress or a blouse and skirt. For formal dinner parties wear a cocktail dress, evening suit, or long gown, depending on the occasion.

- For any Chinese social function, particularly a wedding, don't wear blue or white. They're the colors for mourning.

TEMPLES

- When you visit a temple, wear modest clothing. Men should wear long pants and remove their hats. Women should wear long skirts or pants and a top with sleeves.

- Temples are usually open to visitors, with no admission fee. It's polite to drop coins into the offering box near the entrance.

- You may wear shoes around the temple courtyard, but remove them when you enter any building.

PRIVATE HOMES

- Before you visit someone, call ahead. Don't just drop in without an invitation.

- For a first visit to someone's home, take a gift (fruit or candy) for your hosts. Chinese custom frowns on making a first visit empty-handed.

- Most people in Hong Kong don't remove their shoes when they enter a home, but take your cue from the residents.

- Taking a tour of your host's kitchen is inappropriate. So is offering to help in the kitchen (many families have servants who cook and clean).

- Your hosts will usually offer you tea, warm water, or a soft drink. It's polite to accept.

- If you see a household object you like, don't praise it too highly or your host will feel required by custom to give it to you.

- If you make a local phone call, don't offer to pay. Local calls are free.

- If people tell you they live in a mansion, don't be overly impressed. Apartment buildings are called "mansions" in Hong Kong.

PERSONAL GIFTS

- If people give you gifts, don't open them in their presence. (This custom ensures that they won't lose face if a gift is not "good enough" for you.) Use both hands to give or receive a gift.

- Good choices for gifts are handicrafts from your home region, Scotch, brandy, or packaged foods. Teenagers appreciate T-shirts from overseas colleges. Don't give electronic items, which are available locally at low cost.

- For the sake of any superstitious Chinese friends you might have, don't give clocks (the Cantonese word for clock has funeral connotations), books (gamblers take this as a wish for them to lose), or blankets (they stifle the recipient's prosperity).

- If you send flowers to a Chinese person in the hospital, don't choose white or red. White is a color of mourning and red symbolizes blood.

TIPPING

- Hotels: Hotels add a 10-15% service charge. The service personnel might never see it, however, so tip them 10-15%. (You might ask the assistant manager at the lobby desk whether the service people receive the "service" charge.)

- Restaurants: Restaurants and nightclubs also add a 10-15% service charge to your bill. Friendly service is so rare in Hong Kong, however, that a tip to a smiling waitress is always in order, even on top of a service charge.

- Taxis: Taxi drivers don't

expect more than the small change, but tip them 10% of the bill if they helped with your luggage. If you take a taxi to or from the airport, tip HK$ 1 to HK$ 5.

- Porters: Porters expect HK$ 3 per bag (HK$ 1 at the airport).

- Barbers and beauticians: Tip 10%.

- Doormen, washroom attendants, and other small services: Tip HK$ 1.

FOODS

MEALS

Breakfast (*jouchaan*): 6:00 to 7:30 A.M. A typical breakfast is either fried bread and soy milk, or *congee*, a porridge made from rice. Some people enjoy *dim sum* for breakfast. Hotels and fast-food restaurants serve Western-style breakfasts.

Lunch (*ngaanjau*): Noon to 2:00 P.M. Cantonese often have *dim sum,* more commonly known as *yum cha.* Tea is the usual beverage.

Dinner (*maahn faahn*): 6:30 to 8:00 P.M. This is the main meal of the day. A non-banquet meal might consist of a fish dish, steamed rice, a vegetable dish such as mushrooms and bamboo shoots, and a clear soup. Desserts are seldom eaten.

WHERE TO EAT

- You'll find every conceivable type of cuisine among Hong Kong's 30,000 eateries, from American to Chinese, Korean, Indian, or Russian. For help in making decisions, get the Hong Kong Tourist Association's free publication, *The Official Guide to Shopping, Eating Out, and Services.*

- You'll also find every version and regional type of Chinese cuisine. Hong Kong is in the Canton (Guangzhou) region, however, and many people consider its Cantonese restaurants to be the best in the world.

- For the least expensive restaurants, look outside the Central District and the touristy southern tip of Kowloon.

- To save money ask for set meals at restaurants. They tend to be the best bargains.

- The area east of Nathan Road in Tsimshatsui is crowded with ethnic restaurants. The Chinese and Russian establishments are usually the least expensive. Look for the Russian restaurants above bakeries.

- For lunch go to one of Hong Kong's cavernous *dim sum* restaurants. *Dim sum* (more commonly known as *yum cha*) is a lunch tradition best sampled from 11:00 A.M. to 2:00 P.M. in the restaurants of the Central District (although restaurants serve *dim sum* from 7:00 A.M. to 3:00 P.M.). Go early and sit in the middle so you can get a waiter's attention. Waiters wheel carts around to the tables, offering small servings of dumplings, seafoods, sweets, and other tidbits. Diners choose the dishes they want and the waiter adds up the tab by counting the number of dishes on the table. Green tea is served during the meal.

- For vegetarian Cantonese food try the Wishful Cottage or the Vegi Food Kitchen on Hong Kong Island.

- The street stalls are an inexpensive, quick alternative to sit-down restaurants. Chinese food is usually well cooked, so parasites are rarely a problem. Do, however, observe how the proprietor washes the dishes and whether the stall attracts flies. There aren't any menus, so point to what you want and smile. Pay when you order so you don't get overcharged after the food is prepared.

- Hong Kong's fine European restaurants, many of which are in the tourist hotels, often require a coat and tie in the evening as well as advance reservations.

- At some of Hong Kong's fast-food chain restaurants, you buy a ticket for the food from a cashier and then hand it to the food servers.

FOODS TO TRY

- Most of Hong Kong's Chinese are from the neighboring province of Canton (Guangzhou), so Cantonese food is the Crown Colony's ethnic specialty. For an introduction pick up the *Visitor's Guide to Chinese Food in Hong Kong,* free at the Hong Kong Tourist Association offices.

- Cantonese dishes often include fish, pork, chicken, or vegetables. The emphasis in Cantonese cooking is on maintaining the freshness and flavors of the ingredients, usually through steaming or stir-frying. A wide variety of fruits is also available.

Specialties. Some Cantonese specialties are shark's fin soup (expensive), roast pig, abalone, pigeon, *congee* (rice porridge), and a dish known as "dragons duel tiger" that's made from wild cat and snake. Be sure to try sweet-and-sour pork, egg foo yong, crabmeat omelet, chicken with cashew nuts, and beef with oyster sauce. Expect the fried rice to be served at the end of Cantonese dinners. Fruit- or almond-flavored jelly is the usual dessert.

- If you visit a Chinese restaurant featuring Chiu Chow cuisine, you might want to try the expensive bird's nest soup (made from a real bird's nest) or shark's fin soup, both considered delicacies. Chiu Chow meals always begin and end with a serving of Iron Buddha tea, a strong, well-fermented tea.

- Typical *dim sum* or *yum cha* dishes are shrimp dumplings (*ha gaau*), spring rolls (*chun gyn*), meat-filled steamed buns (*cha-sui bao*), and vegetable-filled dumplings (*sui-maai*). Also try the *ma yung bau* (steamed sesame buns), *ma tai goe* (fried water-chestnut sticks), *woo kok* (fried taro puffs), or *pai kwat* (steamed spare ribs).

- Noodle dishes can be meals in themselves. They're often listed on the back of the menu.

- Chinese dessert soups are served at the end of a meal and, unlike other soups, are thickened and quite sweet. Many are made from sweet corn, red beans, or exotic ingredients such as swallow's nests and coconut juice.

- Thousand-year-old eggs are duck eggs soaked in a lime-and-soda solution for several days, a process that turns the egg whites dark green. Eat them with slices of pickled ginger.

- Fortune cookies are an American invention. Don't wait for them at the end of your meal in Hong Kong.

Beverages. Tap water is usually safe to drink, although unpleasant (ice cubes are safe, too).

- Tea and beer are the beverages most often served with casual Chinese meals. Men often drink beer with a meal, while women usually drink only tea. (In fact, Chinese women rarely smoke or drink.) No one's surprised, however, to see a Western woman drink during a meal.

- Clear tea is served with all meals in Hong Kong. The teapot is usually left at the table for diners to help themselves. If you would like more tea, put the teapot lid on upside down to signal the waiter. Don't add sugar or milk to Chinese tea unless you want to attract attention.

- Three basic types of black tea are served: Oolong, a semi-fermented tea from southern China; keemun from northern China; and orange pekoe. Jasmine and green (unfermented) teas are also served during meals.

- Other beverages include a Chinese rice-based wine (*shiuhing*), a sweet herbal wine (*ng ka pay*), San Miguel beer, and Tsingtao beer (from China). *Maotai* and *go leung* are drinks that have an alcohol content of up to 70% — so watch out! Brandy is the most popular alcoholic drink in Hong Kong.

- There are no restrictions on the hours for selling or serving liquor.

TABLE MANNERS

- Wait to be seated at restaurants. Don't be embarrassed if restaurants seat you with other diners. Often, they don't have enough room to give people private tables.

- To get the waiter to bring your bill, either motion as though you were writing the bill yourself or say, *"mai don"* (check).

- Either ask the waiter or check the bill to see whether the restaurant adds a service charge. Most small establishments don't, so leave a tip. Also check for errors in the bill — they always seem to be in the restaurant's favor.

Utensils. Chopsticks are the eating utensils used at every meal. To use them brace one chopstick firmly between the joint of your thumb and the end of your ring finger. Then put the second chopstick between the tip of your thumb and the ends of your index and middle fingers. Hold the lower chopstick still while

you move the upper one in a pincer-like movement. For the best leverage, hold them in the middle or slightly higher.

- When you put chopsticks down, rest them either on your porcelain chopstick rest or on the side of your plate. Never stick them into your food. The Chinese, like most Asians, will be shocked if you leave chopsticks sticking upright into the rice — that's the way joss (incense) sticks are used at religious ceremonies and in communing with ancestors.

- You'll usually be given a plate, chopsticks on a chopstick rest, a small saucer for dipping sauces, a bowl, and a porcelain soup spoon. Napkins are rare, but you'll sometimes be given a hot towel for washing your hands before the meal.

- Tables are usually round, with communal dishes placed in the center, often on a lazy Susan. Turn the lazy Susan to your neighbor after you serve yourself.

- When you serve yourself from one of the communal dishes, pick up the food with either your porcelain spoon or the large ends of your chopsticks (the ends you aren't putting in your mouth). Don't pick over the serving dishes looking for the best pieces. Put the portions you select either on your plate or in your rice bowl before you eat them.

• To eat rice, hold your rice bowl close to your mouth and use your chopsticks to scoop the rice into your mouth.

• Knives aren't available at most Chinese meals, so eat large pieces of food by raising them to your mouth with your chopsticks, biting off a small piece, and returning the rest to your plate.

• Chinese soups are clear (except for dessert soups) and unthickened. They often contain dumplings, seafood, noodles, or other morsels that you may pick out with your chopsticks. Use the porcelain spoon for the broth.

• When you finish your meal, either lay your chopsticks across your rice bowl or place them neatly on the table.

• When you use a toothpick, cover your mouth with your free hand.

Dining with others. Chinese seldom invite

each other out for just drinks. A meal should be included in the invitation.

• Chinese seating plans, like those in the West, have relaxed over the years; it's no longer customary to seat couples according to a rigid hierarchy. Nevertheless, it's still a courtesy to seat a guest of honor facing either the door or the serving area. Guests of honor are usually seated opposite each other, with the host to the left of the female guest of honor, and the hostess to the right of the male guest of honor.

• Your host will place delicacies on your plate. You should reciprocate, using the large ends of your chopsticks to pick up the food.

• Fish is normally served whole at a Chinese meal, with the head pointed at the guest of honor. The guest of honor uses chopsticks to divide the fish, then lets everyone help themselves. Don't turn the fish over — a superstition links this act with turning over the fisherman's boat at sea.

• When you serve yourself, don't take the last bit of food on the serving plate. Taking it would imply that the host didn't provide enough food for the guests.

- Your host will try to refill your bowl with more rice and other food until you politely refuse.

- If you encounter bones, shells, or other rejects in your food, put them either on the table or on the plate provided for this purpose. Don't put them in your rice bowl or on your own plate. Dirtying the tablecloth with bones and stains is quite normal.

- The Chinese often smoke between the many courses of a dinner.

- Belching, loud sipping, and similar noises are perfectly acceptable signs of enjoyment at a Chinese dinner table. The English, however, don't care for them.

- At the end of a dinner, the guest of honor should rise and thank the host on everyone's behalf.

- To express thanks or acknowledge service at a meal, tap the table quietly three times with the middle finger of a lightly-clenched fist. This gesture represents a kowtow, or traditional Chinese bow, and the Hong Kong Chinese will

appreciate it.

- After a meal don't linger for conversation. Serving oranges signals that the meal is finished, and guests should begin to leave soon afterward. Guests can either eat the oranges or take a couple with them as they leave. Oranges and other golden fruits symbolize good fortune to the Chinese.

Banquets. A formal banquet lasts almost two hours and is preceded by about ten minutes of drinking tea and talking. Cold appetizers are served first, followed by eight to twelve courses. Soup is served either midway through the meal or at the end.

- It's very rude to be late for a banquet.

- If you're toasted as the guest of honor, join in the toast by smiling, raising your glass with the others, making eye contact, and drinking. Then raise your glass to those toasting you and express your thanks. Don't clink your glasses together. *"Yam boui"* is Cantonese for "cheers." *"Yam sing"* or *"Gan bei"* is a challenge to drain your cup. By custom you need to drain your cup only on the first challenge; after that sips are sufficient.

- A banquet host visits and drinks a toast with the guests at each table.

- At banquets the rice is used only as a filler. Eating large amounts of it implies that the host has been stingy.

- At the end of a banquet, you might be served a very strong tea in a small cup. Take your cue from the other guests, but it's traditional to drink only a sip of this tea and pour the rest onto the serving tray to symbolize the bond between the diners.

ACCOMMODATIONS

Hotels. During the peak travel seasons of April through May and October through November, make reservations well ahead of time. Many hotels are fully booked.

- During the off season (June through August) don't hesitate to bargain for rooms in less expensive hotels. Even the best hotels run specials; ask for them.

- Look for less expensive hotels on the Kowloon side of the harbor, but stay away from the cheap hotels in the Mongkok area of Kowloon — that's where most of the brothels are. If the entryway exhibits a seedy plushness or a barstool, you can bet your luggage won't be welcome.

- Guesthouses offer inexpensive rooms. Most of the guesthouses are in the Chungking Mansions building on Nathan Road, across the street from the Hyatt Regency. Guesthouses range from very spartan places with no air conditioning to places similar to regular hotels. Shop around for accommodations and feel free to ask for a discount. Remember, those with plush entryways usually offer rooms by the hour.

- A 10% service charge and a 5% tax are usually added to hotel bills.

Rest rooms. You can find public rest rooms (most of them Western-style) in hotels, bars, and all transportation terminals. They're often marked with the initials "WC," for water closet. If there is an attendant, tip HK$ 1.

TRANSPORTATION

- The airport has no public address system; flights are announced only on the screens. Carry-on luggage restrictions are strictly enforced.

- For local travel try to avoid the rush hours from 7:00 to 9:00 A.M. and 4:00 to 7:00 P.M.

PUBLIC TRANSPORTATION

- Public transportation is very congested during holidays.

Buses. Public buses have destination boards in English, but the bus maps are hard to read. Buses operate until about 11:00 P.M.

- Bus stops are marked by rather misleading red signs that say, "All Buses Stop Here." Actually only those buses whose route numbers are listed below the sign stop at that spot. Buses with route numbers between 100 and 200 cross the harbor via the Cross-Harbor Tunnel.

- When you board a bus, drop the correct fare into the red coin box at the entrance. There's usually a standard fare for the route regardless of where you get on or off. You'll find the fare posted near the bus doorway or on the coin box.

- Red-and-cream-colored minibuses ply unmarked routes all over the colony. The destination is displayed in the front window. The drivers will stop for passengers almost anywhere. When you want to get off, just ask the driver to stop (*"hai nido ting"* in Cantonese). As you get off, hand the driver the fare that was posted on the plastic card in the front of the bus when you got on (usually HK$ 1 to HK$ 4). Unlike the fares on larger buses, minibus fares vary with the distance traveled. Exact change is not required.

- Green and cream minibuses are fixed-route, fixed-price buses that are easier for visitors to use.

Taxis. Taxis are numerous and easy to catch — just flag one down on the street or wait at a taxi stand. Taxi stands are everywhere and usually have orderly queues. The only times taxis are hard to find are during rush hours and at the shift change (around 4:00 P.M.).

- The fare shown on the meter is in Hong Kong dollars. Expect to pay HK$ 2 extra to go through Aberdeen tunnel and HK$ 20 to go through the Cross-Harbor Tunnel between Kowloon and Hong Kong Island. The tunnel charges are not shown on the meter. There should not be an extra charge for more than one passenger. Some taxi drivers don't know the English names of hotels, so carry a note with your destination written in Chinese.

Subway. The Mass Transit Railway (MTR) connects the Kowloon peninsula with Hong Kong Island. This subway is very safe and clean, and runs from 6:00 A.M. to 1:00 A.M. Signs are in both English and Cantonese. Station announcements are also in English and Cantonese but are hard to understand.

- You'll enter and exit through automatic turnstiles fed with pre-coded plastic cards. You can get the cards from machines (which do not give

change) at the station entrance. The tickets are valid for only ninety minutes after you buy them.

- Eating, drinking, and smoking are prohibited both in the subway stations and on the trains. Luggage is not allowed on the subway.

Ferries and jetfoils. The Star Ferry crosses from the clock tower in Kowloon to Central Hong Kong in ten minutes, for only 70 cents (first class). Just insert change in the turnstile at either the first- or the second-class entrance (be careful not to go through the turnstile marked for children). The last ferries depart at 11:30 P.M. Don't smoke on the ferry.

- Ferries, hovercraft, hydrofoils, and jetfoils also take passengers to the outlying islands and to Macau. Most of these terminals are located west of the Star Ferry, in the Central District. The jetfoils offer a smoother ride than the hydrofoils. Jetfoils to and from Macau are crowded on Sundays, when Hong Kong residents spend the day gambling in Macau's casinos. The Macau-Hong Kong jetfoils operate between 7:00 A.M. and 2:00 A.M.

- When a group travels by ferry, the first person to reach the ticket window or turnstile customarily buys tickets for the entire group.

Other transportation. An electric, double-decker tram runs along the north side of Hong Kong Island. The tram is much slower than the subway, but its upper deck offers one of the best tours of Hong Kong (for only 60 cents) and it runs until midnight. Watch your head — the tram ceilings are only 5′ 11″ high. Enter from the rear and exit from the front, dropping the exact fare into the box as you exit.

- The quickest way to the top of Hong Kong Island is via the Peak Tram — a funicular (cable) tram that takes a steep, straight route 1,350 feet up to the peak, from which you can take a bus to the south side of the island. The view from the peak is well worth the trip. Catch the tram across the street from the U.S. consulate.

- The bright red rickshaws by the Star Ferry terminal are rarely used by residents. They're also disappearing, since no more licenses to operate them are being issued.

Before you board one, bargain for the fare.

DRIVING

- You can rent a self-drive car at the airport and at tourist hotels; a subcompact is about HK$ 200 per day. Traffic congestion and parking difficulties, however, make driving frustrating.

- You can use an International Driver's License in Hong Kong for up to one year.

- Traffic moves on the left, as in Britain.

- If you ride in the front seat, you must wear your seat belt.

- Parking is prohibited wherever there are no signs expressly permitting it. Parking tickets cost about HK$ 140.

BUSINESS

BUSINESS HOURS

Business offices: 9:00 A.M. to 5:00 P.M. Monday through Friday. Some offices close for lunch from noon to 2:00 P.M. Many offices are open on Saturday mornings, but the atmosphere is informal, so schedule serious meetings for a weekday.

Banks: 10:00 A.M. to 3:00 or 4:00 P.M. Monday through Friday, and 9:00 A.M. to noon Saturday.

Government offices: 9:00 A.M. to 1:00 P.M. and 2:00 to 5:00 P.M. Monday through Friday, and 9:00 A.M. to 1:00 P.M. Saturday.

BUSINESS CUSTOMS

- The best times for business visits are October, November, and from March through June. Local business people vacation during the summer months. Avoid visits during the two weeks before and after Christmas as well as the week before and after Easter. Also avoid the two weeks before and after the Chinese New Year, which takes place in January or February and lasts ten to twelve days.

- You'll need advance appointments for all business and government visits. Begin arranging your meetings by telex or cable a month before your arrival.

- Chinese business people drive hard bargains, but live up to them. Negotiations tend to be slow and methodical. Be prepared to negotiate every detail and then discuss "compromises" (discounts) at the end of the negotiations. Don't expect to get everything done in one trip. The relationship between individuals is important, so bring the same people to negotiate each time.

- The Chinese are conservative and respect tradition, and are unlikely to jump at new concepts or products. New ways are highly suspect until proved. Family-owned businesses are especially conservative.

- If your company is opening an office in Hong Kong, make sure you consult a geomancer, or *"fengshui"* man, about facilities, moving dates, and other arrangements. Many Chinese are very superstitious, and workers and clients will feel much better if you engage a professional *fengshui* man. Ignoring this custom is asking for trouble from spirits and might lead locals to doubt your future success — creating a self-fulfilling prophecy. Ask any business person where to find a good *fengshui* man.

Business etiquette.

Business cards are essential. Cards with English on one side and a Chinese translation on the other are appreciated. Exchange cards when you're introduced, and take a moment to study the other person's card before you put it away.

• To the Chinese, not knowing or failing to understand something — or making a mistake — causes a loss of face. Avoid public confrontations, accusations, or anything else that might cause a loss of face — otherwise, the resulting humiliation will ruin your relationship.

• A Chinese business person will lose face if you refuse an invitation to lunch or dinner. If you can't go at the proposed time, at least suggest an alternate date. (Most business deals seem to be made over dinner, so you can't afford to refuse.)

• "Yes" means "I heard you" and does not necessarily mean that the speaker agrees with you. Listen for a clear statement of agreement. Many Chinese don't like

to give a flat "no" for an answer, and will try to get their message across by saying something like, "It would be difficult."

Appointments and meetings.

Most local business is conducted by telephone, since phone calls are free. You can often arrange meetings on short notice by phone.

• When you make appointments remember that many offices close for lunch from noon to 2:00 P.M., and that executives often take very long lunches. Business meetings are often scheduled for dinner, however, and Chinese business people work and entertain well into the evening.

• In scheduling appointments most people allow a half-hour courtesy time for late arrivals. Punctuality is respected, however, and business people are usually on time.

• In your schedule allow extra time between meetings to get from one place to another. Traffic is congested, especially in the Central District.

• When you arrive for a meeting, be sure to greet each person present, beginning with the most senior.

• During meetings you'll be served tea. Don't touch yours until your host begins to drink. If the host lets the tea sit untouched for a long time and then only sips it, it means the meeting is finished.

Business gifts and entertainment. At a first meeting with business people, it is good form to present small gifts. Good choices are consumables (such as packaged fruits, candies, and special liquors), pen sets, books for children, or products local to your area. Present the gifts wrapped, with both hands.

• If you bring a gift — or even a sample product — don't package it in blue (a color of mourning). Gold, red, and green are preferred.

• Customers and clients usually exchange gifts at both Christmas and the Chinese New Year. Consumables such as bottles of Scotch or boxes of fruit make excellent gifts. Don't offer presents to civil servants, however — it's illegal for them to accept.

• Business is often conducted over lunch or dinner. Hong Kong businessmen like to invite visitors to luncheon meetings at their private club's restaurant. Wear a coat and tie to these luncheon clubs. (If you're invited to a Chinese dinner in the summer months, however, you need not wear a coat.)

• When Hong Kong business people entertain associates or visitors, they almost always invite them to restaurants or private clubs rather than to their homes. Banquets or dinners with eight to twelve courses are common.

• If you're treated to dinner or a banquet, make sure you reciprocate. Chinese business people appreciate invitations to banquets at one of the colony's best international hotels. (Be sure to make arrangements with the hotel several days ahead of time.)

• Chinese businessmen rarely include their wives in business entertaining. Don't bring your spouse along for a business dinner unless specifically invited to do so. If spouses are invited, don't discuss business.

• Before and after you conclude a deal, considerable business entertaining will take place. Spouses are not welcome in most cases; however, if the host is the company chairman or president, he may bring his wife.

TELEPHONES AND MAIL

Telephones. There are few public phones, since calls from private phones are free. Most businesses and restaurants will let you use their phones without charge.

- Public phones are usually gray, red, or pink, and can be found in hotels and transportation terminals. Local calls from public phones are HK$ 1 for the first three minutes.

- In an emergency dial "999." You don't need a coin.

- Phone numbers are prefixed by area codes: "5" for Hong Kong Island, "3" for Kowloon, and "12" for the New Territories. Use these prefixes only when calling from one area to another — for instance, from Kowloon to Hong Kong Island.

- Most Hong Kong Chinese answer the phone with a loud *"wai!"* It isn't a demand to know why you're calling; it's just their way of saying hello.

- International direct dialing is available in most tourist hotels. It's quite inexpensive, since you're charged by the second rather than by the minute. To avoid the hotel's 10% service charge for calls, go to the Cable and Wireless offices in several of the shopping centers attached to hotels.

Mail. Mailboxes are cylindrical, four feet high, and painted red.

- Most hotels will package and mail parcels for you, for a small fee.

LEGAL MATTERS

Customs and immigration. Citizens of most countries don't need visas for stays of under thirty days. Canadians may stay up to three months without a visa.

- There are no restrictions

on the amount of foreign currency you may bring into Hong Kong. Personal effects are allowed in duty-free.

- When you leave you'll have to pay a departure tax of HK$ 120 at the airport.

Other restrictions. Hong Kong's drug laws are tough and make no distinction between possession and trafficking. If you're coming to Hong Kong from Bangkok, be prepared for a thorough inspection at customs.

SAFETY

Crime. Beware of pickpockets in Causeway Bay, on ferries, and on Nathan Road. Japanese tourists, renowned for carrying large wads of cash, are favorite targets.

- If you visit the rougher bars, go in pairs and take only enough money for a few drinks.

- Female travelers should be extremely wary of people who offer them an enormous sum to model

or serve as an escort. Local pimps have reportedly used this ruse — with alarming frequency — to intimidate foreign women.

- Fraudulent travel agencies take advantage of Hong Kong's reputation as a center for cheap airfares, cheating passersthrough by selling nonexistent seats or using bait-and-switch tactics. Patronize only those agencies that are Hong Kong Tourist Association members.

Health. Tap water is unpleasant but drinkable (although some people suggest drinking the tap water only in hotels). Wash or peel fruit before you eat it. Anything freshly cooked is safe.

- The church-sponsored hospitals provide excellent medical care.

- Imported pharmaceuticals and toiletries are readily available and reasonably priced.

SHOPPING AND ENTERTAINMENT

Shopping. Shop hours are 10:00 A.M. to 6:00 P.M. in the Central District, 10:00 A.M. to 9:30 P.M. in the Causeway Bay and Wanchai areas, 10:00 A.M. to 7:30 P.M. in Tsimshatsui East, and 10:00 A.M. to 9:00 P.M. in Tsimshatsui, Yaumatei, and Mongkok. Most stores are open every day, although they might keep shorter hours on Sunday. The Japanese department stores close one day a week.

- Many Western residents and middle-class Chinese shop in the Causeway Bay area, which has several Japanese department stores.

- Bargaining is expected in most types of stores, but don't start bargaining for an item unless you plan to buy it. If your offer is accepted, you are obligated to buy. Let the salesperson state the first price, then haggle firmly but politely.

- It's impolite to bargain in department stores or up-scale stores.

- The Chinese department stores feature products from the People's Republic of China. The prices are clearly marked; don't try to bargain. These stores are scrupulously honest, so they're good places to buy jade and gold jewelry.

- Many places charge a 5% to 7% surcharge for using a credit card, even though it's against card company rules. Settle the method of payment before you start to bargain.

- The scams and rip-offs perpetrated by Hong Kong merchants are many and ingenious. The rule is to trust no one and patronize only those shops that display the Hong Kong Tourist Association's emblem (a Chinese junk). A few things to watch out for:

Make sure that the serial number on the guarantee matches the number on your purchase, and that the guarantee is worldwide.

Ask whether the attachments to your product are included in the price. Often merchants leave out parts such as connecting cords and camera cases, then sell them to you later (at a high price) to make up for the discount they gave you earlier.

Before you walk out the shop door, double-check your receipt and purchase to make sure nothing's been switched.

Check all silk for stains and imperfections. Some shops carry damaged goods.

Beware of watches with Swiss- or Japanese-made cases but with movements made in Hong Kong.

The electric current is 200-volt, 50-cycle AC. When you buy electronic items, be sure they're suitable for your home country.

Hong Kong law requires that gold be accurately stamped with the carat content. Items that are 18-carat gold have a ".750" mark to indicate their 75% gold content. Always ask for a receipt and a certificate of authenticity.

Watch out for fake pearls. One way to check a pearl is to rub it against your teeth. If it's gritty it's real; if it's completely smooth it's a fake. (Some jewelers object to having customers chew on their necklaces.)

Jade is also subject to fakery. To determine whether the jade is real, try the water test. A drop of water on jade will stand out like a bead; on an imitation it will spread.

Entertainment. Kowloon's bars and hostess clubs often become raucous after midnight. Most of the bars and massage parlors are around the Chungking Mansions and Tsimshatsui. Bars in the Wanchai District of Hong Kong Island tend to be rougher, especially during visits by military fleets. Watch for padded bills, especially in the Wanchai area.

• Women are welcome at a few of Hong Kong's many topless and hostess bars. Men are expected to drink with the establishment's women.

• The Japanese nightclubs (identifiable by their Japanese names) feature female companionship, primarily for Japanese male tour groups. They are within stumbling distance of the international hotels of Kowloon and cost about US$ 15 per hour, plus drinks ($3-$5), plus a cover charge, plus a hostess "nomination" charge.

HOLIDAYS

• A Chinese society with British rulers, Hong Kong is well supplied with holidays from both the East and the West.

Holidays: New Year's Day (January 1 and 2), Chinese New Year (January/February), Ching Ming Festival (Good Friday, Easter Sunday, and Monday), Dragon Boat Festival (June), Bank Holidays (July 1 and first Monday in August), Liberation Day (August 25), Mid-Autumn Festival (September), Chung Yueng (October), Christmas (December 25), and Boxing Day (December 26).

(Holidays listed without exact dates are based on the lunar calendar and vary from year to year.)

• The Chinese New Year is the most important holiday on the lunar calendar. Signs covering the sides of skyscrapers proclaim *"kung hei fat choy"* (good fortune to you), and the Chinese put on new clothing in celebration. Visitors will see Lion Dances and other celebrations in shopping centers, parks, and hotels.

• The Ching Ming Festival celebrates the coming of spring. During this holiday the Chinese visit their family graves to tidy them and, after the work is done, usually hold a picnic at the gravesite.

• Liberation Day, on the last Monday in August, celebrates the colony's liberation from Japanese occupation in 1945.

• The Mid-Autumn Festival celebrates a 14th-century call to revolt against the Mongols. During the full moon of this festival, people gather in parks to gaze at the moon, enjoy moon cakes, and display a wide variety of lanterns.

• During the Chung Yueng Festival, in mid-October, your Chinese friends might disappear into the New Territories' mountains. Ever since the Han Dynasty, the Chinese have moved to high ground on this day to avoid disaster.

- During the New Year, Dragon Boat, and Mid-Autumn festivals, look for performances of Cantonese opera in the large shopping complexes and on the street.

KEY PHRASES

English	Cantonese	Pronunciation
Good morning	Jou sahn	Dyoh sahn
Good afternoon	Ngh-on	Ng-awn
Good evening	"	"
Good night	Jou tau	Dyoh tow
Goodbye	Joigin	Dyoy-geen
Please	Mh-goi	Mm-goy
Thank you	Dojeh	Daw dyeh
Excuse me	Deui-mh-jyuh	Der-mm-dyoo
Don't mention it	Mh-hou haak-hei	Mm-hoh hahk-heigh
Yes	Haih	High
No	Mh-haih	Mm-high
I understand	Ngoh mihngbaahk	Ngaw ming bahk
I don't understand	Ngoh mh-mihng-baahk	Ngaw mm-ming bahk
How much?	Geido?	Geigh daw?
Can you speak English?	Neih wuih mwuih gong ying mahn?	Neih wooih mwooih gong ying-maHn?
Sir, Mr.	Sinsaang	Seen-sahng
Madam, Mrs.	Taaitaai	Tie tie
Miss	Siuje	See-oo-jeh-eh

PRONUNCIATION

Pronounce a, e, i, o, and u as ah, eh, ee, aw, oo.

aa = long a	b = p
au = ow	d = t
ou = owe	g = k
oi = oy	j = ch

- Cantonese is a seven tonal language and the tone with which a syllable is pronounced can effect the meaning. Learning the tones requires listening to a native speaker and the novice Cantonese speaker can probably improve his or her chances of being understood by speaking as rapidly as possible.

Visitors to India leave either enraptured or appalled; no one remains indifferent. From its exotic Taj Mahal to its erotic Hindu sculptures, India mesmerizes both those who just pass through and those who choose to linger. You'll feel intense admiration, but you'll also feel shock at the horrors of poverty and frustration with the ever-present *baksheesh* (bribes or "tips").

India is confusing for the culturally sensitive visitor. It has countless ethnic groups, fourteen major languages, and over 200 minor languages. People and customs vary tremendously throughout the country.

India is also confusing for travel and doing business. Travel is difficult; conditions are crowded, and *baksheesh* is an integral part of getting anywhere.

Indian bureaucracy is unrivaled for its ability to stop action in its tracks. I once sat in Singapore for a week waiting for an Indian visa that never came. The local Indian High Commission dismissed the inconvenience with, "There wasn't room in the passport to stamp the visa, anyway." Despite its obstacles, a visit to India is well worth the time and effort.

MEETING PEOPLE

GREETINGS

- Most Indians greet each other with the *namaste* gesture (bending gently with palms together below the chin). They rarely shake hands. Men don't touch women in either formal or informal situations.

- Indian men and very Westernized Indian women often offer handshakes to foreign men and sometimes to women. A Western woman should not initiate a handshake with an Indian man; instead, she should wait for him to offer one. If he does not, she should nod and smile. Most Indian women will shake hands with foreign women but not men.

- Hindus, Muslims, and Sikhs are greeted differently — although you might find a person's religion difficult to determine. Many Indians wear Western clothing, so clothes only sometimes provide a clue (see Dress). Another clue is the person's name (see Names and Titles).

- After you offer the *namaste* gesture, say *"Namaskar"* or *"Namaste"* to Hindus, *"Salam alaikum"* to Muslims, and *"Sat Sri Akal"* to Sikhs. If this is too confusing, just say "Good day" or "Pleased to meet you" — most people you are likely to meet speak English.

- When greeting or saying goodbye to Muslims, use only your right hand for the *salam* (*namaste*) gesture — the left hand is considered unclean.

- In North India a woman might cover her head with the end of her *sari* (the traditional wraparound dress) before she makes the *namaste* gesture. The traditional way to greet elders in this region is to touch the person's feet with your right hand and then touch your own forehead, but foreigners aren't expected to do this. Sometimes the gesture is abbreviated to bending.

- People of the opposite sex never touch (except to shake hands), hug, or kiss when they greet each other, unless they're old friends. Women often hug each other when they meet.

- If you run into Indian acquaintances around noon, they will ask whether you've eaten yet. It's just a greeting. To be polite, say yes.

- You might be greeted with a garland of flowers placed around your neck. Make the *namaste* gesture to the person who gave it to you and then take the garland off to show your humility.

- At a party you'll be introduced to only a few people; you're expected to introduce yourself to the rest.

- Indians usually ask permission before they take leave of others.

Names and titles. Names often indicate whether people are Hindu, Muslim, or Sikh. Common Muslim names for men are Khan, Ali, Mohammed, and Hussein; Muslim women's names often end in Begum or Han. Common Hindu names are Gopal, Krishna, Ram, Lal, Prakash, and Vijay. All 13 million Sikhs share the surname Singh (but not everyone named Singh is a Sikh).

- Actually, the Sikh name "Singh" (lion) is more a symbol of courage and brotherhood than a surname. A Sikh may be named something like Gurdip Singh s/o Bhopinder Singh (the "s/o" means "son of," so Bhopinder Singh is his father). Gurdip is his individual name. Friends would call him Gurdip, and business associates would address him as either Mr. Gurdip Singh or Mr. Singh. Sikhs are generally called Sardars (leader), so his full formal name would be Sardar Gurdip Singh. All Sikh women have the name "Kuar," but if a woman marries she is addressed as "Mrs." plus her husband's full name. Recently, Sikhs have been adding a third name indicating the home village of their clan.

- Hindus often add *sahab* or *ji* after a person's name

to show respect (for example, *Palmer-sahab* or *Carmen-ji*). *Shri* (Mr.), *Shrimati* (Mrs.), and *Kumarii* (Miss) are also used before surnames.

- Never address people by their given names unless they ask you to or you are close friends.

- Indians sometimes call each other by their initials. A man might be known as "SK" without anyone knowing what the letters stand for.

- Use people's titles, such as Professor or Doctor, when you address them.

- Indians often use familial nicknames such as "uncle" or "mother" and might give you one when you become a friend. Don't hurt their feelings by refusing.

Correspondence. For most purposes you can prepare business letters in the English style using the salutation "Dear (title) (surname),".

- Hindus in southern India usually use only the given name in the salutation, indicating formality by adding titles such as Mr. or Mrs. Hindus in northern India use only the surname and title. If you're in doubt, note how the person signs a letter to

see whether you should use the given name or the surname.

- When you're writing to a Sikh, if "Kaur" is in the name, address the letter to Miss Kaur. If "Singh" is in the name, address it to Mr. Singh (a married woman would be Mrs. Singh). Some Sikhs have a third name, written last, that they use as a surname.

- For Muslims use the Muslim naming system in salutations (see Pakistan).

CONVERSATION

- Good conversation subjects: Families, education, Indian food, the cinema (especially the prolific Indian cinema), and India's beauty and culture. Ask for recommendations on restaurants and points of interest.

- Subjects to avoid: Religious strife, relations with Pakistan, poverty, salary, and sex. Most Indians don't appreciate having topics like snake charmers, wife-burning, or other negative images brought up.

- Indians often ask for your home address to show their friendliness. They don't intend to drop in on you; it's just that they don't like to think of a parting as permanent — even if they just met you in passing.

PHRASES TO KNOW

- Hindi and English are India's official languages. Hindi, with slight variations, is the first language of 450 million Indians, most of them in the North. India has many regional languages, however, and there's much resistance to making Hindi a national language. An inquiry from your Hindi phrase book might go unanswered in southern India even if the other person understands Hindi quite well.

- English is more widely spoken in southern India than in other regions; the primary native language in the South is Tamil.

- In general English is the most useful language to use throughout the country.

CURRENCY

- The Indian unit of currency is the *rupee,* abbreviated "Re" (singular) or "Rs" (plural). Each rupee is divided into 100 *paisa.* One U.S. dollar is worth about 14.6 *rupees* (August 1987 rates). Coins are available in 1, 2, 3, 5, 10, 25, and 50 *paisa,* and 1 *rupee.* Notes are circulated in denominations of 1, 2, 5, 10, 20, 50, 100, and 1,000 *rupees.*

- In markets people might occasionally quote prices in *annas,* although this unit of currency is no longer used. A *rupee* used to be divided into 16 *annas.*

- If you need to exchange money quickly, change it at your hotel, where the line is short. If you need to change a lot of money, try a bank; they offer better exchange rates but are slow and often open only for the morning.

- Keep your exchange receipts. You'll need them to change *rupees* back into your own currency.

- People often try to unload torn or worn-out notes on tourists; don't accept them. Many merchants won't accept them either, particularly in West Bengal and Assam. Notes in large denominations might be equally hard to use.

- Change from a purchase isn't counted back to you, as it is in the West. Instead, you'll be handed a lump of change that's difficult to count with people in "line" behind you shuffling impatiently. Hold your place for a moment and look expectant, and you might be handed more change.

- International credit cards are accepted by tourist hotels, fine restaurants, airlines, and department stores. The bills often take several weeks to get back home.

ETIQUETTE

- Indians are very tolerant of foreigners' unfamiliarity with Indian ways and will forgive most social errors. Nevertheless, they respect visitors who know something about Indian customs.

GENERAL MANNERS

- Whenever you walk somewhere you'll be plagued by beggars. Either take a taxi to avoid them or, if you walk, avoid making eye contact and try to fake a look of indifference. Looking at impoverished people is considered to humiliate them, and you'll be expected to pay if you indulge your curiosity. (Use the same look of indifference when you walk away from taxi drivers who demand an overpayment.)

- If you give a beggar money, you'll be surrounded immediately by other beggars and marked as an easy target for days, particularly if you're staying in the area. Some beggars near tourist hotels are professionals; India's real poverty lies off the tourist trail. But don't be rude to beggars, no matter how frustrated you feel.

- You'll also be pestered by touts offering to show you a monument, find you a hotel, or carry your belongings. Some hotels and shops pay touts a commission to bring you to them; once you're there, they'll pressure you to part with your money. If you don't want a tout's services, look determined and say "No, thank you" very firmly.

- If someone extends a hand to you on the street — beware. A common trick is to slap religious bracelets on tourists' arms and demand donations. This practice is especially common around temples, so put your hands in your pockets.

- Indian bureaucracies move extremely slowly. If a bureaucrat tells you that what you want "can't be done," be polite but persistent.

- If you have trouble communicating or getting results, don't get angry.

Instead, repeat your request with a big smile. You'll get much better results.

- When Indians are invited to a social function, they're too polite to say no. Instead, they usually say "I'll try." Vagueness is the polite way to say no.

- ''Thank you'' and "please" are not used as often in India as they are in the West. Using them frequently seems comical to Indians.

- When a host and guests go out, the host insists on paying for everything. The guests might reciprocate by giving gifts such as specialty foods (fruits or sweets) from other areas of the country or gifts for the host's children.

- At social gatherings guests are often adorned with garlands of flowers. Remove your garland immediately, as an expression of humility, and carry it in your hand.

- Single and married Indian women wear a *bindi,* or red dot, on their foreheads. If the dot is accompanied by white powder on the upper forehead, it signifies that the woman is married and that her husband is alive (widows don't wear a *bindi*). Some women wear a black dot to counteract the evil eye. Other women wear various *bindi*s for cosmetic purposes; they have no traditional meaning.

- Unless you're among urban or educated people, don't praise children. Many Muslims and Hindus believe that such praise might draw the attention of the evil eye. (But don't do the reverse and insult the children.)

- Before you take anyone's photograph, ask permission. Some Indians don't like having their pictures taken. (Film developing in India is poor, so have your film developed at home.)

- If you smoke don't smoke around elderly Indians unless they invite you to do so, and don't offer cigarettes to Indian women, almost none of whom smoke. The Sikh religion prohibits smoking, so don't smoke around Sikhs or in their homes or offer them cigarettes. In the Punjab area don't smoke on buses or in other crowded areas; the local Sikhs might get upset.

- When you see garlands of flowers displayed at bazaars, don't sniff or handle them.

- Whistling is very impolite. Women, especially, should never wink or whistle.

BODY LANGUAGE

- Indians usually maintain an arm's length distance between them when they talk. If people back away from you, you might have invaded their private space.

- Public displays of affection between the sexes are inappropriate. So is informal physical contact like back-slapping or arm-grabbing. But don't be surprised to see Indians of the same sex hugging or holding hands.

- When you eat, hand something to someone, touch someone, or handle merchandise or money, use only your right hand. Indians traditionally use their left hands for cleaning themselves after they use the toilet, and consider them unclean.

- "Yes" is often indicated by a smile and a jerk of the head, a gesture that can also mean "I don't know." Indians prefer vagueness to yes or no answers.

In southern India "yes" or "I understand" is indicated by moving the head quickly from side to side. If people do this while you're speaking with them, it means they understand what you're saying.

- Indians believe that the head is very sensitive. Don't touch an older person's head. And never pat a Hindu child on the head — it's considered easily harmed.

- The feet are considered very unclean. If either your feet or your shoes touch another person, apologize.

- Grasping your ear expresses remorse or honesty.

- Beckon someone by turning your hand palm down and fluttering your fingers. Don't use one finger. Because of the nation's colonial past, Indians are sensitive to being summoned rudely by Westerners.

- Point with your chin or your whole hand, not with one or two fingers.

DRESS

- Wearing leather (belts, shoes, handbags) might offend people, especially in holy places. Hindus don't kill cows, and Jains refrain from killing any animal or insect.

MEN Wear a suit and tie for business appointments (except during the summer, when you can omit the coat) and formal functions. For informal occasions wear a bush shirt and pants. If you visit a temple, feel free to wear short-sleeved shirts but make sure you wear long pants.

WOMEN For business or dinner invitations, wear conservative pantsuits or dresses. For casual wear dresses, skirts, slacks, and blouses are fine. If you visit a temple, wear clothing that completely covers your arms and legs; you don't need to cover your head or face.

- Revealing clothing will make you the center of attention and cause you to be "bumped" in crowds and propositioned. Bikinis are permissable only at hotel pools and beaches; cover up with a T-shirt elsewhere.

NATIVE DRESS Hindu men usually wear Western-style clothing. Hindu women usually wear the long, colorful dresses called *saris*, although many younger women adopt Western-style dress.

Western women may wear *sari*s for casual functions, but they're inappropriate for business. If you choose to wear one, have an Indian woman show you how to put it on correctly (otherwise it might fall apart).

- Many Muslim men wear a beard and a black fez of Persian lamb skin. Hindus (except Saddhus and Sikhs), rarely grow beards.

- Sikh men wear a beard, a steel bracelet, and a turban used to bind up their hair, which they are forbidden to cut. The color of the turban is a matter of personal taste except that the Akalis wear powder blue, and the Namdari wear white. Sikh women wear a long shirt reaching to their knees and a *shalwar-kameez,* wide trousers fastened at the knees.

TEMPLES AND MOSQUES

- Before you enter a temple or mosque, remove your shoes (stockinged feet are usually permitted). Step over, not on, the threshold.

- If you go in barefoot, wash your feet before you enter to be polite.

Water is provided at the entrance.

- Taking leather goods (shoes, handbags) into Hindu temples might arouse animosity. Hinduism and some other Indian religions prohibit the use of leather in temples and kitchens.

Before you enter a Jain temple, be sure to remove all leather items to respect the Jains' reverence for life. Inside temples of the Jain Digambara sect, be prepared to see naked male *munis,* who fear that wearing clothes risks killing an insect in the folds.

- Traditionally, women who are menstruating do not enter a temple.

- It's polite to put a small contribution in the donation box at the temple entrance.

- Indians usually take offerings of coconuts, flowers, and fruit to the temple to show their dedication. Women cover their heads when they enter the most sacred places.

- When you're inside a temple, don't touch statues or paintings.

- If you visit a temple during services, be very quiet and look to see whether people are segregated by sex. If they are, follow their lead.

- Visitors are usually not allowed into a temple's inner sanctum. Watch for signs designating the points beyond which you may not go.

- Temple visitors are offered saffron powder, holy water from the Ganges River, and sometimes food (coconuts and bananas) as *prasad* (blessings from the Lord). Don't refuse these gifts. If you don't want to eat them, take them with you.

- Before you take photographs inside a temple, get permission.

PRIVATE HOMES

- Some Indians can't invite you to their homes because of religious, financial, or spacial limitations. Among people you feel comfortable visiting, you may drop in unannounced but make sure it's between 5:00 and 8:00 P.M.

- If you're a dinner guest, be a few minutes late unless it's an official function.

- If you're invited for a meal, bring a box of European chocolates or Indian sweetmeats as a gift. Flowers are also suitable. Roses and marigolds symbolize prosperity, but don't choose frangipani blossoms (they're used only for funerals).

- Most traditional Indians don't wear footwear in their homes, so remove your shoes before you enter unless you see the family wearing shoes. Even if you do wear shoes inside, don't wear them into the *puja* (worship room) or the kitchen. (Some Indian women prepare food on the kitchen floor, so they must keep it clean.)

- You'll probably be entertained in the family room. Don't take a tour of the house, peeking into every room. The kitchen is considered private, so don't enter it uninvited.

- In many homes you'll be invited to sit on mats on the floor. Men should sit cross-legged, and women should sit with their knees together to either side.

- Except in urban and educated households, men and women usually segregate in a home, as they do in most other situations.

- If you are a man invited to an orthodox Muslim home, your wife might be welcome, but don't be surprised if you don't see any other females — not even the host's wife. Many orthodox families don't permit women to be seen by men outside the family. Don't ask about the women if you don't see them.

- You'll probably be offered tea or coffee with sugar and milk added, or perhaps fruits or sweets. To be polite refuse these refreshments at first, then accept them when they're offered again.

- Religious paintings and statues are common in Indian homes. To be courteous don't stare at them without making the *namaste* gesture (see Greetings).

- If you stay in a home as a guest, observe the following customs:

You'll be smothered with attention, and your every move will be planned by family members who want to show you around. Refusing their guidance will hurt their feelings.

If the family has servants, don't order them around or be abrupt with them. It would irritate everyone.

During your stay ask to take a bath every day (your hosts will expect you to).

In a traditional home if someone leaves the house, don't say "goodbye"; it's considered a bad omen. Instead, say "Go and come back." If you're leaving say, "I'm going and will come back," and be sure not to leave in a group of three. (In urban and educated households this custom has given way to saying "goodbye.")

- If Indians return to the house to get something they forgot, they sit down and do something (such as drink some water) and then prepare to leave as though it were the first time. Leaving without proper preparation is believed to bring bad luck.

- When guests leave, the hosts arrange for their transportation (providing they have a car) and accompany them to the gate or beyond.

PERSONAL GIFTS

- If you visit a family you know well, bring crafts from your home area, wall calendars, radios, jeans, and small electronic items. Give liquor only to Westernized, non-Muslim men. Women appreciate cosmetics. If you give money to the family children, give an odd number of *rupees,* especially 5, 11, 21, 51, or 101.

- Wrap gifts in yellow, red, or green; they're lucky or happy colors. Don't wrap them in white or black, which are unlucky colors.

- Gifts are not opened in the presence of the person who gave them. If you receive one, set it aside until the person leaves.

TIPPING

- Unfortunately tipping in India is often more of a bribe (*baksheesh*) to make sure something gets done than a gesture of gratitude. Occasionally people might throw a tip to the ground if they think you didn't tip them enough — but notice that they always pick it up.

- People who approach you on the street to offer you help might expect a tip if you accept, but don't try to tip someone who is obviously just being friendly.

- Hotels: Many hotels tack a service charge onto your bill; nevertheless, give your maid or room boy 2-5 *rupees* for each day you were there — and give it to them per-

sonally, or they might never see it. Ignore all the other people who magically appear when you leave and claim to have done you a service.

In some areas (especially Delhi) hotels don't add a service charge to the bill, so tip 10% in the restaurant and 5% for other services.

- Restaurants: Tip 10% if a 10% service charge hasn't been added to the bill.

- Taxis and rental cars: Tipping taxi drivers is not customary for Indian customers, but foreigners are expected to tip 10% of the fare. If you had to bargain for the fare, don't tip. Tip rental car drivers 10-20 *rupees* for a full day of driving.

- Porters: Tip 2 *rupees* for each bag. If the airport has a baggage charge per piece, you don't need to tip the porter.

On trains you might need to tip the porter either to get a seat on a "sold out" train or to get a better seat than the one you've been assigned.

- Tour guides: Tip 10-20 *rupees* per full day if the service is good.

- At temples and mosques

it's customary to give 10-25 *paisa* to the shoe guardian.

- If you stay in a home with servants, quietly tip each one 3-4 *rupees* per day. Be discreet; some hosts might be offended if they knew you tipped their servants. Never give servants gifts. It equates them with the family, insulting the family and embarrassing the servants.

FOODS

MEALS

Breakfast (*naashtaa*): 6:30 to 8:00 A.M. In the South breakfast is light — usually only coffee. In the North the usual fare is *chappati* bread, sweets, and tea. Hotels serve Western-style breakfasts.

Lunch (*dopahar kaa khaanaa*): Generally noon to 2:00 P.M. Typical fare varies by region. *Chappati* with a curry dish and tea or soft drinks is very common.

Dinner (*saam kaa khaa-*

naa): 7:30 to 9:00 P.M. (after dark). The main meal of the day, dinner often consists of either a *thali* feast (see Specialties) or a curry dish with several side dishes of vegetables and yogurts. Tea is usually served after the meal.

WHERE TO EAT

- Indian restaurants rarely post menus in the window, and some have no menus at all. If you don't know what kind of food a restaurant specializes in, just pop in and ask.

- Restaurants often offer a combination of Indian, Continental, and Chinese cuisines. In general, the Continental dishes are poor.

- Tourist hotel restaurants serve foreigners mild or watered-down Indian dishes. In other restaurants ask for a dish to be served "mild" if you don't like the hot spices typical of Indian food.

- Coffeehouses and snack bars serve snacks and drinks throughout the day. Try them for sandwiches, *samosas* (filled, deep-fried pastries), soft drinks, fresh juices, and coffee.

- Train-station restaurants have both Indian food at

reasonable prices and poor Western food at higher prices. Hygiene is fairly good, and the rapid turnover means that the food doesn't sit around drawing flies.

• *Dhabba* are basic Indian restaurants that serve inexpensive dishes. Order meat and fish "well done" in these often-unsanitary eateries.

• In small restaurants the meal is cooked where you can watch it. The *dahl* (lentils) are usually free, but you pay for the bread and rice.

• Some small restaurants serve half-dishes upon request. If you order that way, you can try a wider variety of dishes. The price should be half that of a regular dish.

• If you're really hungry try the all-you-can-eat buffet lunches in the tourist hotels. They're often quite reasonable except for extras such as drinks.

FOODS TO TRY

• Regional cuisines vary enormously, especially from north to south. The North has been influenced by Muslim culture, and its cooking is often Moghul-style, featuring lots of meat, grains, and breads. The South is more vegetarian and features rice and hot curries. The only thing all Indian cuisines have in common is the inspired use of spices.

• The basic foods of most Indian meals are rice, *chappati* (unleavened bread), *dahl* (lentils), condiments, and two or three vegetable side dishes for dipping the bread. Common condiments are green chilies, chutney, and coriander leaves.

• Meals often begin with a soup, frequently a thin curry. The remaining dishes are usually served all at once rather than in courses.

• Hindus eat no beef (the cow is sacred). Many Hindus are vegetarians, as are all Jains and many Sikhs (especially women). "Beef" on some menus means water buffalo, not cow.

• Muslims eat no pork or shellfish.

• Yogurt and other dairy products are usually safe to eat in tourist hotels and fine restaurants, but they're risky if you get them from smaller restaurants or street vendors.

Specialties. Wheat bread

(*roti*) is the staple food in the North; rice is the staple in the South. Curried dishes (eggs, fish, meat, or vegetables in a spicy sauce) are perhaps India's most popular food.

- Curry is what makes Indian food so distinctive, and its taste can vary depending on the proportions of the twenty-five or so spices used to make it. The curry is mixed with various fried (in *ghee,* clarified butter) meats and vegetables and is always served with rice. Many curries contain peppercorns and can be very hot. Reaching for water won't put out the fire, but yogurt or fruit will give quick relief.

- Indian breads are varied and delicious. Try *chappati* (flour and water fried like a pancake), *poori* (deep-fried *chappati*), *dosa* (lentil flour and water), and *nan* (oven-baked). *Masala osa* is a *dosa* wrapped around curried vegetables.

- *Dahl* is a thick lentil soup served free with many meals or (with *chappati*) as a meal in itself. The *chappati* is used to scoop up and eat the *dahl.*

- Side dishes are served with every meal. The most common are *dahi* (curd or yogurt), *sabzi* (curried vegetables), *raita* (curd mixed with vegetables), *bhartha* (puréed vegetables), and chutney (pickled vegetables or fruit).

- *Tandoori* food is cooked in a clay oven and is popular in Moghul-influenced northern India. The food is first marinated in a mixture of herbs and yogurt and then baked. Be sure to try *tandoori* chicken.

- Other northern specialties to try are *gushtaba* (spiced meatballs in yogurt sauce), *rogan josh* (curried lamb), *dahi maach* (curried fish in yogurt sauce), and chicken *makhanwala* (cooked in butter sauce).

- In the Delhi area try Moghul-influenced dishes, which are often creamy: *biriyani* (spiced meat cooked with rice in a sealed pot), *patharka gosht* (marinated mutton cooked on a stove), and *goochi pulao* (mushrooms and rice).

- Near the coast try saltwater fish dishes, such as the *tandoor*-cooked *pomfret.* Buy fish, however, only when you know it's fresh. Inland cities like Delhi don't have fresh seafood.

Never eat fresh-water fish; it's not safe.

- In the South try *haleen* (pounded wheat in spiced mutton gravy) or *chansak* (chicken or lamb in curried lentils and rice). The Udipi Brahmin restaurants provide inexpensive vegetarian meals in clean surroundings. Look for *idli* (rice balls), *dosai* (crisp stuffed pancakes), and coconut-based vegetable curries.

- In the state of Gujarat, try a *thali* (plate meal) of the strictly vegetarian Gujarati cuisine. Vegetables, fresh curd, and pulses are poured over a platter of leaves sewn together. All this is accompanied by *chappati* and other hot breads, salads, and chutneys. Other Gujarati dishes to try are *khaman dhokla* (chickpea-flour cake), *srikhand* (*puris,* a bread, with sweet yogurt flavored with cardamom, nuts, and saffron), and *undhyu* (broad beans, eggplant, potato, and sweet potato cooked buried under a fire). *Thali* meals can be found throughout India.

- For dessert try *kulfi* (ice cream with pistachio nuts), the many rice-based puddings, *rasgullas* (balls of cream cheese flavored with rose water), *jalebi* (pancakes in syrup), and the misnamed *barfi,* which is made by boiling away the liquid in milk and then adding nut flavorings. Also try the Bengali sweets made from cheese and milk; they aren't as heavy and sticky as the Moghlai sweetmeats. Fresh fruit is also a common dessert — but be sure to peel it.

- After meals Indians serve *paan* — a mixture of betel nuts, slaked lime, and spices wrapped in a betel-nut leaf — to aid digestion. The betel nut makes it mildly intoxicating and addictive. *Paan* also stains your teeth and lips a bright red because of the red paste (*kattha*) used in it. Don't swallow *paan* if it was made with tobacco; just spit it out when you've had enough and don't be alarmed by the color.

- Sweetmeats, or candies, are an Indian specialty, but you won't usually find a wide variety in restaurants. Instead, look for a sweetmeat shop.

Beverages. Drinking unboiled water is very risky. If you aren't sure the water has been boiled, order a name-brand soft drink without ice. Some restaurants open a whole case of soft drinks at once and let them sit out waiting for customers and flies (not necessarily in that order), so ask for a bottle with the cap on.

- In the South strong coffee is the most popular beverage. In the North people prefer tea. Both drinks are always served with milk and sugar, at any time of the day. If you want your tea without milk and sugar added, ask for "tray tea."

Get freshly brewed Mysore coffee instead of the instant coffee served in most hotels and restaurants. It's widely available in the South, but in the North you might find it only in fine hotels.

- *Nimbu pani* is a cold drink of fresh lime juice diluted with soda water. Try it, but only at a hotel where you can trust the hygiene.

- Other beverages to try are coconut milk (in the South), *lassi* (a yogurt drink), and Campa Cola (India's version of Coca-Cola). Fruit juices can be pressed from any of the fruits in season; mango, sweet lime, and papaya are good.

- In Delhi try *chaas,* a thin yogurt drink flavored with green chilies, roasted cumin powder, coriander, and ginger.

- Alcohol is less popular than in Western countries, and in many states, especially those that are Muslim dominated, its consumption is banned outside of tourist hotels. In Delhi the first and seventh days of every month, as well as holidays, are "dry days" when drinks can be served only in hotel restaurants and rooms. Tourists can request an All-India Liquor Permit when they obtain their visas; it will allow them to transport and consume liquor in areas where it is normally prohibited.

- Indian-made liquor, for some unknown reason, is called "Foreign Liquor." Indian rum (for example Khoday Dark and Old Monk) is excellent and cheap. Indian gins and wines are poor. What's known as "Indian liquor" is often dangerous, illegally brewed liquor.

- For regional specialty liqueurs, try *feni* (from the Goa district), made from fermented cashew nuts, and *toddy,* a mildly alcoholic spirit popular in the South that is made from palm flowers.

- Indian beers are gassy and similar to lager. In the South Haywards and Kingfisher are popular; in the North Rosy Pelican is the favorite. Beer goes well with spicy dishes.

TABLE MANNERS

- Both before and after a meal, it's important to go to the washroom to wash up. In Hindu homes rinse your mouth as well as your hands before the meal.

- If a restaurant is packed, you may ask to share a table, except in the far North.

- Throughout most of India women can eat alone in a restaurant without being harassed. Harassment is more likely the closer you are to Pakistan.

- Indians often snap their fingers and hiss at waiters to get their attention, but Westerners should beckon quietly in the Western manner. Don't use one curled finger.

- When you receive the bill, make sure the total is correct. If it isn't, question it.

Utensils. Eating utensils are not used in India except in Westernized households and better hotels and restaurants.

- In the North eat only with the fingertips of your right hand. Getting food above the second joint is impolite. Tear off a piece of bread and then either wrap a piece of meat in it or dip it in one of the pureed vegetable dishes.

- In the South use your whole right hand — quite messy for most inexperienced Westerners — to mix curry and rice and form them into a ball, which you then eat.

- Even when you're eating with your fingers, never use them to touch or serve yourself from a communal dish, or your fellow diners will shy away from it. Instead, transfer the food to your plate with the serving spoons.

- Most meals include a flat bread such as *chappati* or *poori.* Tear it into small chunks and use them to scoop up the *dahl,* curries, and vegetables.

Dining with others. If you're invited to dinner, it will probably be in a home rather than a restaurant. If an Indian man takes guests to a restaurant, it can be a slight to both his wife and his guests.

- If you dine in a home, you're expected to arrive fifteen to thirty minutes late. It's customary to bring your hosts sweets, flowers, or fruits. Other possible gifts include Scotch whiskey (if your hosts drink alcohol), blank videotape cassettes, or camera film. Present your gift with your right hand.

- In a traditional home diners sit on either a floor cushion or a low wooden seat at a low table. If you're the guest of honor, you'll be seated first; sit wherever your host suggests (there's no particular seat for the guest of honor).

- Conversation and drinking usually come before the meal. In traditional homes and rural areas, guests usually eat first with the men, elderly people, and children, and the women eat after the guests have finished. The cook eats last. Even when the sexes eat at the same time, men usually talk to men, and women talk to women.

- If the family uses no cutlery, assure them that you enjoy eating with your hands.

- Although porcelain is becoming more popular, dinners at home are usually served on *thali*s, silver trays crowded with small bowls of vegetables, *dahl,* rice, flatbreads, and fish.

- In a home the hosts will serve you; don't serve yourself. Don't refuse an offer of food or drink if at all possible. Food is seen as a gift from God, and refusing it is being ungrateful to God. If you have dietary restrictions, inform your host discreetly before anything is served.

- Don't take food from the eating area.

- Even if you can't eat all the food on your plate, refrain from offering it to anyone else. Once you touch food it becomes "tainted." Many Hindus also make sure that their food is not touched by anyone outside of their caste or religion.

- Water is sometimes served in a communal container. Don't let your lips touch the container; hold it away from your mouth and aim well.

- To indicate that you've had enough to eat, give the *namaste* gesture by placing your palms together in front of your throat. You may leave some food on your plate.

- After the meal you'll be served *paan,* the betel-nut concoction believed to aid digestion (see Specialties).

- After you've finished, a bowl of hot water might be brought to the table for you to wash in.

- Saying "thank you" for the meal might offend your hosts (the words are interpreted as a form of payment). Instead, say that it was delicious and that you enjoyed it.

- Guests should leave about half an hour after the meal finishes.

- If someone has treated you to a dinner, return the gesture by inviting them out. Don't try to outdo their meal or take them to a more expensive restaurant — it will embarrass them.

ACCOMMODATIONS

Hotels. The heaviest tourist season is from October to March. Book your hotel rooms (and transportation) early if you travel at this time.

- Unless you bring written confirmation of your room reservation, your reservation might be denied.

- Before you register always ask whether a seasonal discount is available. Such discounts are common even at the best hotels.

- If you want a good room, request something specific and take a look at the room before your luggage arrives. If it isn't what you asked for, request another one.

- For safety's sake check to make sure the doors and windows lock before you settle down in your room. If they don't, ask for another room. Theft is not uncommon, so don't leave money or valuables in the room.

- In and around major cities, look for bungalows operated by the government. They are relatively safe, clean, and affordable. Check with the tourist offices for locations.

- If you're traveling by train, you can stay overnight in railway retiring rooms, which are just like hotels except that they're inside train stations. They're fairly inexpensive, but noisy. The rooms can range from terrible to Raj-like.

- Some hotels, even if they don't add a service charge, add a "luxury tax" to restaurant and bar bills. Inquire when you check in.

- Most hotel bills must be paid in a hard currency (U.S. dollars or British pounds), but you can pay hotel restaurant and bar bills in *rupees* when you're served. (Some hotels let you pay your bill in *rupees* if you can show them exchange receipts from banks.)

- To save time and avoid some of the everyday hassles of Indian life, ask your hotel to provide someone (for a fee) to run errands for you or stand in line for movie tickets.

- In medium- or lower-class hotels, service people might pester you to let them perform small services, such as carrying your briefcase, to get a tip. Try to select one person to do the things you actually need done and tip regularly.

- Telephone connections are difficult to obtain, so consider asking your hotel to reconfirm other reservations for you.

They might charge 10-25 *rupees.*

Rest rooms. Tourist hotels have Western-style toilets. Other hotels, train stations, and restaurants usually have Indian-style squat toilets, sometimes with one or two Western toilets included in a row of cubicles. A bucket of water often takes the place of toilet paper, so carry some toilet tissue with you.

TRANSPORTATION

- At the airport as soon as you walk out of customs, you'll be besieged by porters wanting to carry your bags. Be firm when you choose one, and the others will pounce on somebody else. While you wait in line to change money, keep an eye on the porter watching your bags.

- Most airports don't have car rentals. Before you encounter the airport taxi drivers, ask the tourist office desk how much a ride to your hotel should cost. If you look for the taxi booth outside the arrival gates, you'll find the fares to various destinations posted. In most instances you pay at the booth and get a receipt with the number of your taxi on it.

- An alternative to changing money at the airport is to go straight to the taxi stand, ask the taxi driver to pay off your porter, and then have the driver wait at your hotel while you change some money.

- When you go to or from the airport, make sure the taxi driver puts all your bags in the trunk and shuts it before you get in the cab.

- Travel to some parts of India is limited by the lack of roads and other services. You'll need permits to travel in some areas, such as the Northeast Frontier.

- Streets often have two names, one from colonial days and another from after independence. Local people usually use the former, while maps use the latter. Finding an address can be quite frustrating.

- Indians often refer to streets, cities, and other locales by initials. Thus, Mahatma Gandhi Road is "MG Road," and the state Uttar Pradesh is simply "UP."

PUBLIC TRANSPORTATION

Buses. Local buses are very crowded — so crowded, you might not be able to get off when you want to. In Bombay bus service is orderly; elsewhere, schedules are haphazard, queues are nonexistent, and buses are often dilapidated.

- In northern India buses often have seats set aside for women only.

Taxis. You can find taxis at hotels, at taxi stands, and in front of tourist information centers. The quickest way to get one is to hail it on the street. Most taxi drivers speak English.

- Before using a taxi ask at your hotel what a fare should average. Taxi stands sometimes post official fares, but you might still have to bargain. If you catch a taxi on the street and it has no meter (or the meter doesn't work), settle on the price before you get in. Even if the meter does work, the driver might show you a "fare adjustment" card at the end of your trip, explaining that the meter has not been reset to reflect new rates.

- In most areas taxis take up to five passengers with no surcharge. Just remember that most taxis are not air-conditioned; crowding can be insufferable.

- In Delhi the yellow-and-black cabs are metered but seldom air-conditioned. The drivers don't expect a tip, but they'll charge an extra *rupee* per bag for your luggage.

- Most taxi drivers, especially in the North, are Sikhs. Their religion forbids smoking, so don't smoke in their cabs.

- If you're going sightseeing or to a meeting, consider paying the driver a small fee to wait for you. That way, you can avoid any difficulty you might have in getting another taxi.

Trains. Trains have two classes, first and second. First class has two subclasses, air-conditioned and regular. Second class is divided into reserved and unreserved seats. Don't try unreserved second class unless you enjoy fighting for a seat — people even jump through the windows to get them.

- To avoid queues reserve train seats well ahead of time either at the railway station or through travel agents. Indian travel agents might need your passport to make reservations.

- If you buy your own ticket at a station, go to the tourist information window in the reservations section. You'll be given a voucher to take to another window, where you'll pay for the ticket. If you want a sleeper berth, you'll have to wait in yet another line to fill out a sleeper reservation form. Your compartment and seat number will be on your ticket.

- For overnight train trips be sure to get a sleeping berth. First-class sleeper compartments have two or four fold-up berths and usually have two toilets. Second-class compartments have up to three tiers for sleeping. Except in air-conditioned first class, you must bring your own bedding, toiletries, tissues, towels, and drinking water.

- If you plan to travel by train a lot, consider buying an Indrail Pass, which permits unlimited train travel for a specified period and also covers berth costs at night. You can buy these passes either from an overseas travel agent or at the main railway stations. If you buy them in India, you'll have to pay in U.S. dollars or pounds sterling. The real advantages to having an Indrail Pass are that you won't have to wait in long ticket lines, and that you can often get a seat even when all the regular seats are "taken."

• Train schedules for all of India are sold at station newsstands. They don't include the slow limited-express trains, which make frequent stops.

• Train stations usually have two waiting rooms, one for first-class ticket holders and another for second-class

• Train stations can wire your meal order ahead so that a tray of hot dishes is delivered to your seat at the next stop. You can order morning or "bed" tea with breakfast.

• When your train comes in, move quickly and look for your car number. Your name should be on the list posted both on the platform and outside the car.

• At each stop food and drink vendors will pester you through the windows. To be safe buy only bottled soft drinks (with the caps on) and packaged foods.

• Women traveling alone should try to sit next to other women or a family; otherwise, they stand a good chance of being harassed by men or even robbed. Some trains have cabins and cars reserved for women.

Other transportation. You can catch auto-rickshaws, which are three-wheeled motorcycles, on the street. They cost about half the fare of a taxi and are faster, as well as more dangerous — the drivers whip from one side of the road to the other to pass other vehicles. Unlike taxi drivers many auto-rickshaw drivers don't speak English.

• Cycle rickshaws are available in some cities and towns. They demand higher-than-normal fares from tourists, so you'll have to bargain.

• If you fly within India, make arrangements well in advance and try to avoid changes in your itinerary. Planes are often overbooked, and changing reservations can be a hassle.

• All five miles of India's subway system are in

Calcutta. Fares depend on distance.

DRIVING

- Rental cars always come with a driver. A full day of driving costs about Rs 400, depending on hours and distance. If you rent a car for overnight trips away from the city, give the driver Rs 20 for overnight money.

- Driving is on the left, as in Britain.

- India has one of the highest accident rates in the world. Drivers simply stare straight ahead, displaying a fatalistic attitude (you can't yield to what you can't see).

Daytime driving is dangerous enough — streets are crowded with vehicles, motorcycles, bikes, animals, and pedestrians — but at night there's the added danger of no taillights.

- Vehicles have the right-of-way over pedestrians. Drivers just plant their hands on their horns and plow through.

- If your car hits a cow or a pedestrian, don't stop if there are people around to help. Go quickly to a police station and tell them what happened. If

you stop the bystanders might harass or even beat you.

BUSINESS

BUSINESS HOURS

Business offices: 10:00 A.M. to 5:00 P.M. Monday through Friday. Many offices close from 1:00 to 2:00 P.M. for lunch. Except in Bombay some offices are open on Saturday mornings.

Banks: 10:30 A.M. to 2:00 P.M. Monday through Friday, and 10:00 A.M. to noon Saturday.

Government offices: 10:00 A.M. to 5:00 P.M., Monday through Saturday. In Delhi offices close on the second Saturday of every month.

BUSINESS CUSTOMS

- The best time to visit India on business is from October to March. Religious holidays vary from year to year, however, so check with an Indian consulate or tourist office about other dates to avoid (see Holidays). For comfort's sake, avoid trips during the rainy monsoon season (June through August).

• Many Indian companies don't have telexes, so request appointments by letter and back them up with cables. The mail can be very slow, so begin requesting appointments two months before your trip.

• When you make company contacts, go right to the top. India is a paternalistic society, and decisions are made at the top. Don't ignore middle managers, however; they can help push your proposal.

• Permits are required for most transactions. Check with the commercial section of your country's embassy in India to find out which ones you need.

• Decisions come slowly in India, and only after your counterparts get to know you, so plan to make several visits before you reach an agreement. Be patient. Indians value self-control.

• When you enter negotiations have in mind a fairly firm price. There will be little haggling; the Indians won't budge much from their initial proposal.

Business etiquette. When you are introduced always have your business cards ready to present. English-language cards are fine; it's the language of commerce in India.

• If you're given a garland of flowers at a reception or after you give a speech, accept it with gratitude but take it off immediately to demonstrate your humility.

• Indian businessmen engage in back-slapping and touching that seems excessive to Westerners. It's simply a demonstration of friendship.

Appointments and meetings. The best times for appointments with executives are 11:00 A.M. and 2:00 P.M. Top executives don't relish early morning or late afternoon meetings and might decide not to come. They also might seem reluctant to agree on a specific meeting time; it's because they don't consider time as important as Westerners do. Nevertheless, they respect punctuality.

• Middle managers and entrepreneurial business people will be happy to meet with you at any time of day.

- When you plan your trip schedule, allow gaps so that you can reschedule any meetings for which your Indian counterparts don't show up.

- If Indian business people know you and know which hotel you're staying in, they might drop by unannounced at any time, expecting to have a meeting on the spot. In the same vein, if you haven't been able to contact people to request a meeting, it's acceptable in most cases just to show up at their office and ask for one. This custom of impromptu meetings results from the difficulty of relying on the often unworkable phone system.

- Before a meeting actually starts, you might be offered a very sugary, milky tea, coffee, or a soft drink. Refusing is an affront. Drink slowly; each time you drain the glass, it will automatically be refilled. If snacks are served you are not obliged to eat them.

- While you're drinking the tea — and before you discuss business — inquire about your counterpart's family, interests,

and hobbies. Your counterpart will do the same. What might seem like very personal questions are just intended to show friendliness.

Business gifts and entertainment. If you know that your Indian counterpart drinks, bring some imported whiskey. Buy it on the airline or at a duty-free shop before you arrive; otherwise, there's a 27% tax.

- Visiting business people receive many invitations to dinners and home visits. Never flatly refuse or beg off an invitation. If you can't go, be vague and avoid a time commitment. (Just say "Yes, I'll do that" and leave it at that.)

- Most initial business entertaining takes place in restaurants. Unless it's strictly a business discussion, spouses are often invited.

- Businesswomen may invite an Indian businessman to lunch and pick up the tab without embarrassing him (although he might try to pay).

- Don't offer a Sikh business person a cigarette. The Sikh religion prohibits smoking. Alcohol is also prohibited, strictly speaking, but an offer of a drink is usually quickly accepted.

TELEPHONES AND MAIL

Telephones. Public pay phones are few, far between, and often inoperative (except in Bombay, Delhi, Madras, and Hyderabad). If you find one it will cost 50 *paisa*. You can also ask to make local calls from shops and restaurants; offer to pay the charge. Tourist hotels provide direct dialing for local calls.

• You might have to shout into phones to be heard, but no matter how frustrated you get, never slam the receiver down — repairs can take months.

• If you try to use a telephone book, you'll find that subscribers are sometimes listed under their employers (who provided their phones) rather than under their own surnames.

• Make long-distance and international calls from the post office or an international hotel (you can't direct-dial them on public phones). From hotels you can either dial direct or book your call; in the latter case getting through might take up to twenty-four hours. Check the hotel's service charges first (they can be quite high).

• Long-distance calls within India come in classes. "Lightning" class is the fastest and most expensive; other classes might take hours to get through.

Mail. Mailboxes are painted red.

• Mailing a package in India requires sewing it up in linen, then securing all the seams with sealing wax impressed with a seal (use a foreign coin). You can find people who specialize in this service outside major post offices. If you are staying in a first-class hotel, ask the bell captain to send your parcel.

• If you do mail a package at the post office, make sure the stamps are put on the package and cancelled. Stamps and packages don't always stay together.

• When you use postage stamps, don't lick them.

Post offices and stamp sellers provide water for moistening them.

LEGAL MATTERS

Customs and immigration. Visas are required and are valid for up to 90 days. You might need onward tickets and proof of finances. Try to obtain your visa well before you travel — Indian consulates in southeast Asia might take up to a week to process your application.

• It's illegal to import or export Indian currency. You must declare foreign currencies in excess of US$ 1,000.

• When you enter you must declare cameras and electronic gadgets such as radios and computers, because in some areas they're in great demand on the black market. When you depart you'll have to pay tax on items you leave in India.

• A black market for currencies also exists. You'll need receipts from all your currency exchange

transactions to change *rupees* back to your own currency when you leave.

Other restrictions. It's illegal to take photos at airports, railway stations, large bridges, and military bases. It's not safe to take photos of Muslim women, cremations, or scenes of poverty.

• In the states of Gujarat, Bihar, and Tamil Nadu, drinking is prohibited except in tourist hotels. Check with your hotel for any local regulations. If you want to be able to drink anywhere, request an All-India Liquor Permit when you apply for your visa. The permit allows you to buy and consume liquor even in states where it's otherwise prohibited.

SAFETY

Crime. Theft can be a problem. Always keep your wallet in your front pocket, your handbag tightly clutched, your passport and money in a money belt, and your valuables in a hotel lockbox. Be especially wary of pickpockets in the bazaars. Carry a lock with you so you can lock doors or lock your bags to a train seat while you're sleeping. Don't report small incidents to police; it will only result in a lot of paperwork.

- If someone offers to buy your hard currency on the street, don't accept. Some purchasers will set you up with the police.

- Bribery (*baksheesh*) is an art in India. You might need to practice it to get train seats or get permits stamped, but don't try it on the police.

Health. Never drink water unless you know it's been boiled. Don't eat unpeeled fruit or raw vegetables anywhere, since human waste ("nightsoil") is used as fertilizer. Dairy products outside of hotel restaurants are risky. Salami, ham, and pork might contain parasites if not properly cooked. Avoid freshwater fish — India's rivers are polluted with everything imaginable.

- Most toiletries are available in India, but be sure to bring special medications and tampons.

- Serious sunburn is common in southern India. Bring sunscreen with

you; good brands are sometimes hard to find locally.

SHOPPING AND ENTERTAINMENT

Shopping. Shop hours are 9:00 or 10:00 A.M. to 7:00 P.M. Monday through Saturday. Markets are open Sunday but many close on Monday. Stores often close from 1:30 to 2:30 P.M. for lunch. In predominantly Muslim Kashmir, shops close on Friday, the Muslim day of prayer, rather than on Sunday.

- In most shops and markets, including "fixed-price" and "government-approved" stores, bargaining is the rule. Don't try to bargain, however, in bookstores, grocery stores, or government-run stores. Always bargain vigorously with drivers of rickshaws or non-metered taxis, vendors, and shoeshine boys.

- Even if an object has a price on it, that doesn't

INDIA

INDIA

INDIA 115

mean you can't bargain. Start by asking the price anyway, then offer half that amount. Always check two or three shops for comparative prices.

- If you don't have time to slog around shops and markets bargaining, try the state-run craft emporia in the cities. They feature good-quality crafts at set prices. If you do have time, check the price of an item in an emporium and then try to do better by bargaining in private shops and markets.

- To get a good price, try to be a shop's first customer of the day. Merchants believe that the first customer sets the tone for the whole day; a sale is very important. Don't be the first person in if you don't intend to buy anything. You'll ruin the merchant's whole day.

- Good buys are *dhurries* (flat-weave rugs), brass, silk, carvings, jewelry, and tailored clothing. Buy jewelry in hotel shops, which will give you a certificate of authenticity. Hotel-shop prices aren't as unreasonable as they are in most countries.

- When you buy fine silk in South India, you'll pay for it by weight. If you ask you can sometimes get a 10% discount by paying in foreign currency.

- Real sandalwood is expensive. Inexpensive "sandalwood" is probably a cheaper wood with scent added. To be safe buy from government-operated or approved stores.

- Antiques are often faked. Much of the brass sold as antique, for example, was made quite recently. If you buy an antique, demand a written guarantee and make sure you can take it out of the country. Items over 100 years old cannot be exported. Real antiques are best purchased in the West (New York and London).

Entertainment. Nightclubs are often called "superclubs." Many of them serve Chinese or European food.

- Discos are also called "night spots," but are unexciting and often restrict who they admit. Discos in international hotels charge a high membership fee for locals (hotel guests pay only a small fee), so don't expect to meet many locals on the dance floor.

HOLIDAYS

Official holidays: Republic Day (January 26), Good Friday (April), Independence Day (August 15), Mahatma Gandhi's Birthday (October 2), Christmas Day (December 25).

Other public holidays fall on Hindu, Muslim, Buddhist, or Sikh festival days, and their dates vary from year to year. They include Holi (February/March), Mahavir Jayanti (March/April), Ramanavami (March/April), Good Friday (March/April), Buddha Purnima (May/June), Janmashtami (August/September), Dussehra (September/October), Diwali (October/November), Govardhana Puja (November), Nanak Jayanti (November).

About twenty-two days each year are dedicated to religious and sacred holidays. Check with the tourist offices for these varying dates.

- The Hindu festival of Holi celebrates the advent of spring. Wear old clothes or a raincoat; it's customary to shower passersby with water or colored liquid. Celebrants fast until noon and wear yellow and green to symbolize spring.

- Dussehra is a very important Hindu festival that lasts for ten days. It celebrates Rama's victory over the demon king Ravana. Ravana is burned in effigy on the last day.

- During Holi and Dussehra watch for Hindu plays and dances in the streets or near temples.

- During Diwali, people light oil lamps to show Rama the way home from exile. This festival lasts for five days, each dedicated to a different deity. It's courteous to send your Hindu friends cards during Diwali. Business people should note that the first day of Diwali begins the Indian business year.

- Muslim influenced areas observe traditional Muslim holidays, which vary greatly from year to year because the Muslim calendar is ten days shorter than ours. (See the Holiday section under Pakistan for more information.)

PRONUNCIATION

Double consonants should be pronounced double. Stress is relatively even.

a = "u" as in "cut"

e = eh

i = "i" as in "bit"

o = oh

u = "oo" as in "look"

t = th

d = th

n = ng if before k, g, or h

ai = "a" as in "bat"

KEY PHRASES

English	Hindi	Pronunciation
Good morning	Namaste (Salam)	Na-mahssteh (Sa lahm)
Good afternoon	"	"
Good evening	"	"
Good night	Namaste (Khuda haafiz)	Na-mahssteh (Khooda hahfiz)
Goodbye	"	"
Please	Mehrbaanii	Meh-hehr-bahnee
Thank you	Sukria	Shookree-a
Excuse me	Maaf kiijiye	Mahf keejyeh
Don't mention it	Koii baat nahi	Koee bahtt na-heen
Yes	Jii ha	Jee hahn
No	Jii nahi	Jee na-heen
I understand (masc.)	Mai samajh gayaa	Man sahmahj ga-yah
(fem.)	Mai samajh gayee	Man sahmahj ga-yeeh
I don't understand (masc.)	Mai nahi	Man na-heen sahmj- samajhaa huhah hoo
(fem.)	Mai nahi samajhti hu	Man na-heen sah-mahj-tee hoo
How much?	Kitnaa?	Kittnah?
Does anyone here speek English?	Koee angrezi bolta hai?	Ko-ee ahn-gray-zee bol-tah heh?
Sir, Mr.	Sahab, Shri, Ji*	Saw-haab, Shree, Jee
Madam, Mrs.	Shrimati, Ji*	Shree-mah-tee, Jee
Miss	Kumarii, Ji*	Koo-mah-ree, Jee

(*Put Sahab and Ji after the person's name. Put Shrimati, Shri, and Kumarii before the person's name.)

INDONESIA

Most of the world seems unaware of Indonesia's vast size. Indonesia is an archipelago over 3,200 miles long, with 13,677 islands and 155 million people — the fifth most populous country in the world. Most of Indonesia's population is crowded onto the island of Java.

Formerly the Dutch East Indies, ethnically diverse Indonesia has been an independent nation for only about four decades, accounting for much of its exuberance and nationalistic pride.

The increasingly touristy island of Bali is predominately Hindu, but most Indonesians are Muslim, and Islamic customs are followed in most parts of the country. Unlike other Muslim nations, however, Indonesia offers women active roles in society. You'll find women and men equal partners in business and the professions.

MEETING PEOPLE

- Visitors find the Indonesian people very friendly and approachable, although touchy about criticism of their country and its facilities, religion, or even the weather.

GREETINGS

- In Muslim areas (most of Indonesia), greet people of all social levels with *"Selamat"* (peace). Say it gently, without rushing into the conversation.

- "Hello" is often used to get someone's attention (for example, a waiter) or to confirm a telephone connection.

- When you make a formal introduction, use titles carefully (see Names and Titles).

- In less formal situations Western-style introductions are becoming increasingly common. Feel free to introduce yourself or ask for someone's name.

Names and titles. Most middle-class Indonesians have two names, but many lower-class people have only one. The well-to-do often have long names but choose to use a shortened name and an initial instead (Hendro M.).

- When you address people use only their first names, not their second (if they have a second name).

- A rural woman usually keeps her own name when she marries, but a middle-class, urban woman usually adopts her husband's.

- The Indonesian archipelago has many ethnic groups, each with its own honorific titles. In most cases you're safe using Mr., Mrs., and Miss.

- If a person has a prestigious title (such as Doctor or Professor), use it in conversation.

JAVA

- To introduce a man in a formal situation, start by saying *"Bapak"* (sir), followed by any academic title, then any noble title, then his given and family names, and finally his business or social position. To introduce a woman, use the same order but substitute *Ibu* (Madam) for *Bapak*.

- To address either a man or a woman, use just the first name preceded by an honorific. For men use the honorific *Bapak* in formal situations and *Mas* (gold or brother) in less formal situations (for example, address Hendro Martono informally as "Mas Hendro"). For women use the honorific *Ibu*. You may also use these honorifics in lieu of someone's name.

Correspondence. When addressing an Indonesian in a letter, never use his or her second name.

- When writing to Javanese, add the courtesy title *Bapak* for men and *Ibu* for women. Thus, if a man's name is Wage Mulyono, address him as *Bapak Wage.* A formal salutation would be, "To the most respected Bapak Wage:". To be less formal use "Dear Bapak Wage:".

CONVERSATION

- Good conversation subjects: Indonesia's beauty and culture, recreational interests, prices, local cuisine, and children.

- Subjects to avoid: Politics, the Indonesian annexation of East Timor, relations with foreign governments, Socialism, and religion. Indonesians tend to have very strong opinions on international politics and religion, so discussions might get heated.

- Indonesians enjoy talking about their families. They might also ask personal questions about you and your family. Even casual acquaintances will ask you personal questions, such as "Why aren't you married?" or "Does your wife work?" Ask them the same kinds of questions that they ask you.

- If an Indonesian asks you what form of birth control you use, don't be alarmed. In Indonesia birth control is an important issue that people discuss openly. If you don't want to answer truthfully, answer with a good-humored joke ("I send my husband away to Europe frequently"). Use the same tactic when someone asks how much your possessions cost — a perfectly acceptable question in Indonesia.

- If someone promises to do something "tomorrow" (*besok-besok*), don't take it literally. "Tomorrow" is a vague statement that means simply, "Yes, someday let's do that." If you really want to arrange something for tomorrow, agree upon a specific time.

- "Indo" is a derogatory term for people of mixed parentage. Don't use it as an abbreviation for "Indonesian."

- In Java don't ask questions about possessions and material wealth.

PHRASES TO KNOW

- Indonesian and Malaysian are basically the same language, but Indonesian is a bit simpler to learn and has some different vocabulary preferences. Pronouncing Indonesian is fairly easy, since it uses the Roman alphabet and phonetic spelling. The sounds are always the same and receive equal emphasis.

- A good phrase book for Indonesian is Margit Meinhold's *Indonesia Phrasebook* (Lonely Planet, Victoria, Australia, 1984, $2.95).

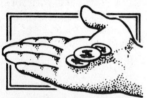

CURRENCY

- Indonesia's unit of currency is the *rupiah* (pronounced "rupee" and abbreviated "Rp"), which is divided into 100 *sen*. One U.S. dollar is worth about 1,592 *rupiah*s. Coins come in Rp 5, 10, 25, 50, and 100 denominations. Notes are available in Rp 100, 500, 1,000, 5,000, and 10,000.

- To change large amounts of currency, go to a bank (they give the best rates) but be prepared for a long wait. For small transactions see your hotel cashier. Avoid illegal, unregistered money changers. Rates get less favorable the farther you get from Jakarta.

- Traveler's checks bring a slightly higher exchange rate in hotels and banks (especially in Java), but many shops don't accept them.

- Whenever you change money, keep the receipt. You'll need all your receipts to convert any unused *rupiah*s when you leave the country.

- Indonesia has no black market for currency.

- Outside the cities, carry small bills with you. Rural shops (as well as some shops in the cities) can't make change for large bills.

ETIQUETTE

GENERAL MANNERS

- Indonesians rarely disagree in public, seldom say no (instead they say *"belum,"* not yet), and always have time for others.

- Indonesians hate to disappoint people, so they might give an untruthful answer that they think will please them. Don't force people to give a yes-or-no answer. Rather than asking "Is this the right way to town?" ask "Which way is the town?"

- Laughter is used to hide feelings of shock, embarrassment, and anger as well as to show amusement.

- Laughing at someone else's mistakes is very offensive. Don't laugh at something you find humorous if there's any chance that Indonesians will be embarrassed or think you are laughing at them.

- Indonesians' feelings are easily hurt. Don't mimic or parody anyone's behavior — even someone you know well. Satire is extremely risky.

- Indonesians express thanks with a smile or nod. They might feel uncomfortable if appreciative foreigners shower them with verbal thanks.

- If someone arrives late for an appointment, don't be upset. Indonesians never consider punctuality more important than personal relations. In fact, they don't consider punctuality very important at all — unless they're dealing with foreigners. They know that Westerners are fussy about punctuality and will think you're rude if you arrive late, even if they're late themselves.

- To get someone's attention quietly say, *"Sus"* (young lady), *"Mas"* (young man), or *"Pak"* (older man).

- Indonesians might approach you and ask to take your photograph; it's a way of honoring you.

- When you speak to someone or enter a home, remove your sunglasses.

- Eating in the street or

while you're walking is inappropriate.

JAVA

- In Java it's a matter of principle not to say what you mean. You can never be sure that yes really means yes.

- Most Javanese are Muslim, so observe traditional Muslim customs.

BALI

- Balinese often bathe outside in streams and open places. Respect their privacy and don't photograph them. Balinese women used to go topless and sometimes still do; don't photograph them, either.

- If you do take someone's picture, they might ask you for money and cause a scene if you refuse.

BODY LANGUAGE

- Kissing in public is not acceptable behavior for foreigners.

- Indonesians consider the left hand unclean because they use it for cleaning themselves after a bowel movement. Don't use your left hand to shake hands, touch anyone, point, eat food, or give or receive objects.

- When you're sitting down, try not to cross your legs. If you do, place one knee directly over the other.

In Bali when you sit keep both feet flat on the floor. Don't cross your legs; it's rude. Pointing your feet or exposing the soles to someone is an insult.

- Beckoning someone with a gesture is usually reserved for signaling children and *becak* (pedicab) drivers. If you do beckon someone, wave your fingers in a scooping motion with your palm facing down. Never beckon with one finger.

- Indonesians sometimes show approval with a pat on the shoulder.

- Touching someone's head is very disrespectful. The head is considered the home of the soul.

- Indonesians often express affection for children by pinching their cheeks and touching their arms. They often touch a blond or red-haired child's head out of curiosity. Don't, however, touch the heads of Indonesian children.

- When you're standing

talking to someone, don't put your hands on your hips. It signifies anger and is impolite.

- Extending your right thumb while making a fist with your other fingers means "please go first."

- Yawning should be avoided. If you must yawn, put your hand over your mouth.

- A male visitor to isolated rural areas should try not to let his jaw drop if he finds his penis being fondled by a rural Indonesian man while he's saying good-bye. It's only intended as a friendly parting gesture.

DRESS

- Indonesians dress very conservatively and are slow to accept new styles. Dress modestly in public.

- Shorts, tank tops, thongs, and revealing clothing are unacceptable. Jeans are all right for casual wear as long as they're not tight. Bikinis are acceptable at hotel pools and beaches.

MEN Wear pants and a white shirt and tie for business. Foreign businessmen often wear a jacket for a first meeting; otherwise, suit coats aren't worn except for formal occasions such as weddings or appointments with government officials (Indonesians rarely wear tuxedos). A long-sleeved batik shirt is acceptable for most formal occasions. For dinner in a home wear a shirt, slacks, and no tie.

- In Java wear a suit and tie to a first business meeting or any formal occasion.

WOMEN Wear a skirt and blouse (never sleeveless) or a dress for business or formal occasions, and avoid bright colors or extreme fashions. For most formal occasions an afternoon tea dress or evening dress is suitable. For a meal in a home, wear a blouse with short sleeves and a skirt or a dress.

- In Java wear a dress or a short-sleeved blouse and skirt for a business meeting. For all formal occasions wear a long dress or a long skirt with a sleeved blouse.

- In Java batik is the traditional style of clothing for both men and women, and Javanese will appreciate your wearing it.

TEMPLES AND MOSQUES

- If you visit a mosque or temple, don't wear shorts, sleeveless dresses, singlets, or revealing clothing.

- Before you enter any holy place, especially a mosque, remove your shoes.

- Menstruating women should not enter a temple or mosque.

- Inside a mosque, be very quiet, don't walk in front of people who are praying, and don't touch anything or anyone. Before you take any photographs, ask permission.

BALI

- At a Hindu temple remove your shoes before you enter unless other people are wearing theirs. You must wear a sash around your waist to enter; you may use a scarf if you have one, or buy a sash outside the temple.

- In a temple be careful not to put your head higher than the priest's (for example, don't climb on a wall to take his picture). Some of the seats are reserved for the gods, so

it's better not to sit down. In a room where people are kneeling in prayer, keep to the rear. Respect any instructions given by the temple custodians dressed in white.

PRIVATE HOMES

- Dropping in on a friend is considered flattering; nevertheless, it's best to call ahead or — since most people don't have phones — make arrangements ahead of time. Don't drop by someone's house before 4:00 P.M., when people take naps, or after 6:00 P.M., when many Muslims are at prayer.

- If you're invited to dinner, it's polite (although not expected) to bring flowers.

- If you bring a gift for your hosts, hand it to them or to the servant as you enter. Don't expect the recipient to open it in your presence.

- Before you enter, remove your sunglasses.

- If your hosts are not wearing footwear, it's polite (although not necessary) to remove your shoes before you enter the house. In any case, remove your shoes before you enter any carpeted rooms or feasting places.

- If your hosts keep you waiting when you arrive, consider it a compliment. They're changing into their nice clothes and making tea.

- Sit down when you're invited to, but rise when your host enters the room.

- Your host will almost always serve you a drink, but don't drink it until you're invited to.

- If you stay at a home, observe the following customs:

Don't offer to help clean up. Some middle-class families have servants who'll do your laundry and clean your room as well as serve meals, and an offer to help might offend. On the other hand, if your hosts don't have servants, your offer might be an embarrassing reminder.

Dress for breakfast. No one comes to the table in a robe.

Daily baths are customary, but be prepared for cold water in many homes.

If you visit another town during your stay with a family, bring back a gift for your hosts.

PERSONAL GIFTS

- Traditional Indonesians don't expect gifts, but welcome compliments and notes of appreciation. All Indonesians appreciate fruits, coffee, cosmetics, cigarettes, and imported sweets and other foods. Teenagers appreciate college T-shirts or notebooks with a university logo on the cover.

- If someone gives you a gift, receive it graciously; it's impolite to refuse anything. Don't open it in the presence of the person who gave it to you. (The only exception is if you're presented with a gift at a ceremony; on most such occasions you're expected to open the gift in front of the assembled group.)

TIPPING

- Tipping is not a tradition in Indonesia, but times are changing, and tourists are often expected to tip. Tipping is still rare in rural areas, however. In Bali or Lombok don't tip anyone but taxi drivers.

- Restaurants: Major restaurants often add a 10% service charge to the bill, but check the menu to make sure. If they don't add a service charge, tip 10%. Tipping is not necessary in small, family-operated restaurants.

- Hotels: Hotels add a 10% service charge, so tipping isn't necessary unless someone provides a special service.

- Taxis: Tipping is optional; if you want to tip, give Rp 100-200, especially if the driver helped with your luggage. In Bali, which has become very touristy, leave the driver the small change.

- Porters: Tip Rp 200-300 per bag.

- Barbers, bellhops, and bar attendants: Tip Rp 100-250 for good service.

- Washroom attendants: Tip Rp 100.

FOODS

MEALS

Breakfast (*makan pagi*): 7:00 to 8:00 A.M. A common breakfast is fruit, fried rice, oatmeal, and tea. *Nasi goreng* and *mee goreng* (see Specialties) are also favorite breakfast dishes.

Lunch (*makan siang*): Noon to 1:30 P.M. Typical fare is rice, *krupuk* (rice or shrimp crackers), beef or chicken in sauce, fish, *satay* (grilled meat on a skewer), and bean sprouts. A peanut sauce is served for dipping. Fruit is served as dessert. The usual beverages are iced tea and water.

Dinner (*makan malam*): 7:00 to 8:00 P.M. Dinner is lighter than lunch and often consists of leftovers from lunch.

WHERE TO EAT

- Most indoor restaurants close at 11:00 P.M.; many street vendors remain open until midnight.

- The word *"restoran"* on a sign usually indicates an expensive restaurant.

- In Java a restaurant is a *restorahsee.*

- Few restaurants post menus outside, and few have menus in English, so learn to recognize the names of your favorite dishes in Indonesian.

- If you're willing to take a risk, try the street vendors (*kaki lima*) who push their carts through the streets, tapping on glasses, bowls, or wooden gongs to announce their presence. You can try *cendol* (a concoction of pudding, shredded fruit, and sweet syrup), chicken porridge, *satay* (skewered, grilled meat), *bakso* (balls of pounded chicken, meat, or fish), or noodles. At night some carts sell *putu,* a confection of tapioca, steamed rice flour, melted brown sugar, and shredded coconut.

- At stationary stalls in the night markets you can find *martabak,* a meat and egg pancake not usually found elsewhere.

- If you want to eat from street vendors, do as the Indonesians do — bring your own dish. Otherwise you'll get a dish that has been in overused, soapy water all day.

- To minimize health risks at street stalls, stick to freshly cooked, well-done foods. Stay away from ice cream and other dairy products, which often are unpasteurized. Coconut milk is all right if it hasn't had water added.

- Snacks or meals of rice and condiments wrapped in banana leaves (or plastic) are called *bunkusan.* You can buy them on the street, in train stations, and elsewhere.

- Many workers take their lunches in a *rantang,* stacked containers held together by a long handle. *Rantang* vendors sell these meals door to door and on the streets.

- *Warung*s, small eateries that seat four to six people around each table, are found in every neighborhood. Some specialize in drinks, while others sell rice dishes and soups cooked in nearby homes. After you eat ask how much you owe and make sure the amount is correct before you pay. Count your change.

- At many eateries, especially *warung*s, the waiter will give you paper and a pencil for writing your own order. Either come prepared with the name of your favorite dish written on a slip of paper, or copy the name from the menu.

- Before you eat at a small restaurant or a street stall, look closely at the faces of the cooks and serving people. They eat the food there, and if their faces reflect ill health and the place isn't clean, walk on by.

- A *rumah makan* is a restaurant that offers complete meals and a wider selection. Most of the foods are precooked and then eaten at room temperature, but you can request that they be warmed up. Many of the items listed on the menu are not actually available; the available dishes are often displayed near the entrance. Ask what they have that's fresh: *"Sedia makanan apa?"*

- Indonesia has quite a few Chinese restaurants that are relatively clean, so you can try Chinese food for a change of pace.

- Indonesia also has many Western fast-food franchises where you can get a taste of home in clean surroundings. Chicken franchises are especially popular.

- You can also find Western foods from pizza to tacos at many of Jakarta's new pubs.

FOODS TO TRY

- Very few dishes can be considered "Indonesian," since the nation's cuisines tend to be localized. As you try various regional cuisines, keep in mind that the people are very proud of their foods and will be disappointed if you don't like them, so express your delight.

- Indonesian foods are quite spicy and often incorporate chili (*lombok*), coriander (*ketumbar*), garlic (*putih*), lemongrass (*serai*), and cloves (*cengkeh*).

- Most Indonesians are Muslims and consume no pork or liquor.

Specialties. Try *satay,* a very popular dish of grilled meat or chicken on skewers. The meat is usually marinated in soy sauce and oil and dipped in a spicy peanut sauce.

- In eastern Indonesia the staples of the diet are cassava, from which tapioca is made, and sago. Try *manioc,* made from cassava root.

- Sumatran food is really spicy. Padang (West Sumatra) cooking is very, very hot. Look for *sambal,* a hot dish of shrimp paste, lime juice, and chilies. To dilute its effect on your stomach lining, mix it with your rice and other food. If it's still too hot, sprinkle lemon juice and salt over it.

- Central Java's food is sweet and spicy; East

Java's is saltier and hotter. *Nasi liwet* (white rice and chicken in coconut cream), for example, is associated with Solo in Central Java, while *sayur asam* (sour vegetables) is a West Java dish.

- In Bali try pork and duck dishes, *kare* (curry), *babi guling* (spit-roasted pig), *mee goreng* (fried noodles and vegetables or meat), *mee kuah* (noodle soup), and *gado gado* (lightly cooked salad of potatoes, bean sprouts, and cabbage in peanut sauce). *Nasi goreng* (fried rice) or *mee goreng* (fried noodles) are fried in coconut oil with meat, eggs, cucumber, and tomato, and have shrimp paste, spices, and chilies added.

- Fresh fruits are widely available in Indonesia and are the most common dessert. Fruits to try are *jeruk* (a large orange-like fruit that tastes like a mixture between orange and grapefruit), mango, *salak* (a fruit with a lizard-like skin), *sawo* (a brown, potato-shaped fruit that tastes like a pear), pineapple, lichee, *blimbing* (a small, sour, yellow-green fruit), and jackfruit. The *durian* is a thorny green fruit with a musty yellow pulp; it's

popular throughout Indonesia but can cause ailments if you consume it with alcohol. There are fifteen varieties of bananas.

- At restaurants patronized by locals you can find black dog meat (popular in Minahasa), *gulai kambing* (goat curry), *gulai otak* (cow-brain curry), *jeroan goreng* (fried intestines, lungs, and kidneys), *sambal goreng saren* (dried, fried chicken blood), and *sop kaki kambing* (goat sinew, intestines, lungs, bladder, and penis blended in coconut cream).

- When served, bread is served as a dessert with butter and sugar on it.

Beverages. Ice water is difficult to find except in restaurants in international hotels. The Indonesians believe that cold water is bad for your health. So is unboiled water. Never drink water or eat ice unless you know the water was boiled.

- Tea is the usual drink with meals. It usually costs more with sugar, and even more with milk. Fresh milk is scarce and often unpasteurized.

- Try *bajigur,* a coconut-milk beverage sweetened with palm sugar.

You can find it at street stalls. Other drinks to try are *tuak* (palm wine) and *es pokat* (avocado juice).

- The Balinese love tea, warm beer, and coffee. They serve the coffee Turkish style. Try the local *air jeruk* (orange juice) and *markisa* (an alcoholic cordial made from passion fruit).

TABLE MANNERS

- Men and women often eat separately, either at home or in a restaurant.

- If a restaurant is crowded, ask people if you may sit at their table.

- Indonesian men usually respect the privacy of a woman dining alone, so feel free to explore on your own.

- To beckon a waiter or waitress, raise your hand. Don't whistle or beckon them with a single finger. Call them "Sir" or "Miss." To ask for the bill, pretend to be adding it up on your palm.

- Finishing a drink implies that you want a refill.

Utensils. Many Westernized Indonesians eat with a fork and a large spoon, but more traditional families eat with their hands. If you are eating with your hands,

never use your left hand — it's considered unclean.

- In Java the table setting includes finger bowls and napkins. Many Javanese eat with their fingers, using the finger bowls throughout the meal.

- If you're using utensils you'll be given a fork and spoon. Hold the fork in your left hand and the spoon in your right. Eat with the spoon, using the fork to push food onto it. Eating with your right hand is preferable, but if you're left-handed, you may reverse your utensils.

- To indicate that you're finished with the meal, place your fork, tines down, on your plate and lay the spoon down crossed over the fork. If you've been eating with your fingers, just move back from the table a little.

- Don't use toothpicks in public without covering your mouth.

Dining with Others. When you're dining as a guest, try to avoid making special requests for foods. Requests for meat dishes or beer, for example, might embarrass your host.

- In Java both sexes usually eat together. The male guest of honor sits next to the host, and the female guest of honor sits next to the hostess.

- If you're invited to a dinner at a home, the meal will usually begin with tea, coffee, or a cool drink served by the children or a servant (if the family has one). Rice cakes or bananas might be served with the drinks.

- Before you begin eating or drinking, wait until your host invites you to start, preferably two or three times. When you drink, leave a little in your glass.

- Vegetables, fish, and hot sauces are often served with the rice.

- During the meal, don't talk a lot. Indonesians like to concentrate on the food and save the talking for other times.

- In a home, don't ask for salt, pepper, soy sauce, or *sambal*. It would insult the cook by implying that the food is not spiced correctly.

- Hosts appreciate compliments, but jokes about the food are a serious breach of etiquette.

- When you finish eating leave a little food on your plate or your host will give you a refill.

- The person who invited the others or suggested the meal is expected to pay for everyone.

Banquets. Banquets often take the form of buffets. Before the meal begins, there's usually about a half hour of small talk.

- The guest of honor or ranking guest begins the buffet line. Servants or waiters will probably pass the food for seconds. Otherwise, diners serve themselves.

- Banquets and dinner parties usually end by 9:30 P.M. Coffee is sometimes served to signal the end of the evening. When you leave, excuse yourself by saying, *"Permisi"* (I beg your pardon).

- If you're a banquet guest, don't offer to pick up the tab.

- If you host a banquet, check on your guests' dietary restrictions before you order. Don't serve sweet potato (*ubi*), which is considered a "poor man's food." (Candied sweet potato, however, is sometimes served as a teatime snack.)

ACCOMMODATIONS

Hotels. Except in the very finest hotels, feel free to bargain for the room rate. Prices often show little relationship to quality, so look at the room before you register and use any complaint to bargain for a lower rate.

• Theft can be a problem. Before you leave your room, make sure that the windows and doors are locked. Keep your valuables with you or in the hotel lockbox. Always obtain a receipt for any valuables you leave with the hotel.

• For inexpensive (Rp 2,000-10,000) accommodations look for a *losmen,* a small hotel compound (often family run) with an outer wall and separate buildings around an inner garden. All of the rooms open onto the garden, so it's easy to meet other guests sitting on the veranda.

• If you stay in a *losmen,* you'll find that the wash-rooms usually have a large water tank (*mandi*), beside which you'll find a plastic bowl. Don't climb into the tank to take a bath. Instead, scoop the water out with the bowl and pour it over yourself, then soap down and rinse off. Leave the *mandi* clean for the next bather. Don't ask for hot water; there isn't any for bathing.

• To sample an Indonesian-style bed-and-breakfast, try a *wisma,* a small, family-run establishment featuring breakfast in bed (or at least brought to your room). Prices vary widely. The nicer *wismas* have a bath in each room.

• The local current is 220-volt, 50-cycle AC, so bring converters for your hair dryer, shaver, or other appliances.

Rest rooms. There are two types of rest rooms. One has a hole in the floor (*kamar kecil*), and the other (*kamar mandi*) is a cubicle with a drain in the floor. The *kamar mandi* is only for washing and urinating. Use the water in the tub or bucket to wash the floor after you use it.

• A men's room is a *laki-laki* or *pria,* and a women's room is a *perem-*

puan. You may also ask for the WC (pronounced "way-say"). Always carry toilet paper; rest rooms don't provide it.

TRANSPORTATION

PUBLIC TRANSPORTATION

- On public transportation systems all passengers are expected to give their seats to the elderly, and men are expected to offer their seats to women.

- If you're seated on a bus or train, offer to hold packages for people who are standing. If you're standing don't hesitate to hand your heavy items to seated passengers.

Buses. Local buses are very crowded and very difficult to use for foreigners who don't speak Indonesian. The tourist center can give you a route map.

- Buses have one ticket price no matter how far you travel. In Jakarta tickets cost Rp 100, payable as you enter. You can get on at either the front or the back; there's a conductor at both entrances. Pay the conductor as you get on and keep your ticket until you get off. Don't wait for the bus to come to a complete stop before you enter or exit; they keep rolling, no matter what.

Taxis. Taxis are always available. A houseboy or bellhop can call one for you, or you can hail one on the street. Most of the taxis are decrepit and have no air-conditioning.

- Major hotels have their own taxis. They're air-conditioned and have good drivers, but they're also more expensive than regular taxis. You can also hire them by the day.

- Only Jakarta's taxis have meters; elsewhere, you bargain for the fare before you get in. Expect to pay more during rush hours or when it's raining. In Jakarta the Bluebird and President cabs always seem to have meters that work. Taxi drivers don't carry much change, so always take some with you.

Trains. Trains are available only on the islands of Java and Sumatra. They're usually very crowded and have only one air-conditioned carriage, so book in advance.

- Train fares vary throughout the day. Try to travel on the most expensive (but much more comfortable) trains.

Other transportation. *Becaks* (pronounced "betchalk") are pedicablike vehicles that are as widely available as taxis.

- *Opelettes* are small, covered pickup trucks with side benches. They ply regular routes in the cities and are quite cheap. (In Sumatra *opelettes* are small buses that seat about 25 people.)

- *Bemos* are small, three- or four-wheeled covered vehicles that have a row of seats in the back for passengers. Fares are based on the number of zones you pass through. First ask the passengers the fare, then ask the driver. If you board an empty *bemo,* the driver might assume that you're chartering it.

DRIVING

- Driving in Indonesia is dangerous — roads are poor, drivers ignore regulations, and pedestrians walk into the streets without looking. Get a chauffeur-driven car rather than a self-drive rental car (which are scarce anyway). That way if you do have an accident, the driver will be liable, not you.

- If you do find a car to rent, you'll need an International Driver's License. Be ready for constant honking, especially in Jakarta. Keep the gas tank close to full; gas stations close early and often run out of fuel.

- Police might stop you (especially after midnight) not for a traffic violation, but rather to collect a few thousand *rupiah*s for "tea money."

- Driving is on the left, as in Britain.

- In an accident the driver behind is automatically at fault. Foreigners, however, are considered fair game for "instant insurance claims."

BUSINESS

BUSINESS HOURS

Business offices: 8:00 A.M. to 3:00 or 4:00 P.M. Monday through Thursday, 8:00 to 11:00 A.M. Friday, and 8:00 A.M. to 1:00 P.M. Saturday.

Banks: 8:00 or 9:00 A.M. to 2:00 P.M. Monday through Friday, and 8:00 or 9:00 A.M. to 11:00 A.M. Saturday. In Bali banks usually close for the day at noon.

Government offices: 8:30 A.M. to 3:00 or 4:00 P.M. Monday through Thursday, 8:30 to 11:00 A.M. Friday, and 8:30 A.M. to 12:30 or 1:00 P.M. Saturday. In Bali offices tend to close at 3:00 P.M. Monday through Thursday and stay open until 2:00 P.M. on Saturday. During the Islamic month of Ramadan, many offices keep shorter hours.

- Many businesses close for two or three hours in the middle of the day for lunch and a nap. Business and government offices close at midday on Friday for worship. Many businesses also close on Saturday and Sunday.

BUSINESS CUSTOMS

- The best time to visit Indonesia on business is September through June. Most Indonesian business people take their vacations in July and August.

- Arranging appointments before you travel is advisable. After you arrive, however, don't hesitate to contact a company executive to set up a meeting. Schedules aren't as rigid in Indonesia as they are in the West, and business people will make time if they want to see you. A letter of introduction from a mutual friend or a bank will help to open doors.

- Most Indonesian businessmen accept women as equals, so visiting businesswomen should experience no special difficulties in negotiating deals.

- Coming to agreement takes longer in Indonesia than it does in the West. Plan either one long visit or several shorter ones to complete your negotiations.

- Work hard to secure your counterpart's trust; it's essential for business interactions to begin. You'll need personal meetings to come to agreements.

- Contacting the right person in the organization is important, so try to have an intermediary (such as a government official) facilitate introductions and pre-screen contacts. Include the intermediary in your first official business call.

- Indonesians feel more comfortable in a hierarchical situation, so don't try to be "one of the guys." Bosses are father figures who are expected to be authoritarian.

- Lower-level employees and government officials are very conservative in processing work and making decisions; fear of losing their jobs makes them reluctant to take action. Showing anger with this slow progress, however, will only make the situation worse.

- Bribery is not uncommon in Indonesia. If you're trying to get some required paperwork done, don't be surprised to hear that the official you need to see is out or the office is out of the necessary forms. A "tip" seems to make both appear. Many people believe that corruption exists in both government and business; don't, however, mention the topic in conversation.

- The abbreviation "PT" means "limited liability." "CV" means "limited partnership."

Business etiquette. Exchange business cards when you're introduced. Cards in English are acceptable. Indonesians like to include on their cards the initials of any academic degrees they have. Some Westerners view this as pretentious, but you might want to have some made in this manner.

- When you make introductions or greet people, take your time. Haste is considered rude. Patience is important in all aspects of business.

- Indonesians value a quiet voice, an unassuming attitude, and willingness to seek a consensus. They think Westerners are too loud and assertive, so be modest and subdued.

- Indonesians also view Westerners as too quick to anger, too serious about themselves, and too committed to the idea that time is money. As you conduct business, don't fret over any "lost" time.

- Embarrassing someone in public is the worst possible insult, so handle any disagreement or criticism privately. Don't put anyone in the position of having to say no or admit an error. Try to have a trusted intermediary deliver any bad news; it will help the recipient save face.

- Indonesian government workers are accorded the respect that might be expected for an elder leader. Be very careful not to bruise civil servants' feelings or act as though an official is there to serve you.

- If you are opening an office or beginning a building project, be prepared for some Indonesians to want to sacrifice chickens, bulls, or goats and bury the heads at the site to bring good luck.

Appointments and meetings. Business meetings are formal and proper. Indonesians show respect to people conducting a meeting.

- Most agreements are made informally in preliminary meetings held before the formal, or-

chestrated business meeting. If the formal session does not result in agreement, renew the informal discussions.

- The best time to arrange a meeting is 10:00 A.M. Indonesians (especially the Balinese) prefer to do most of their work in the morning, when it's cooler. It's difficult to arrange Friday meetings with either government officials or business people.

- Indonesians are very flexible about punctuality but expect foreigners to be on time to meetings. Arriving a few minutes early shows respect — but be prepared to wait.

- In a meeting always defer, without any argument, to the most senior person present. The relationship between Indonesian supervisors and their employees resembles a father-son relationship (the boss is called *Bapak,* or father). Employees will drop anything to do as their boss asks, including canceling appointments they might have had with other people.

Business gifts and entertainment. Visiting business people are sometimes offered expensive gifts, but accepting them also means incurring an obligation. To avoid this situation don't admire a person's possessions or ask where to buy an expensive item. Your comments could by misinterpreted as hints.

• Indonesian business people love to entertain. They'll probably invite you to lunch, or possibly dinner, at a restaurant. Reciprocate with an equivalent meal before you leave the country.

• A Western man should not invite an Indonesian businessman's wife to the dinner unless his own wife will also be there.

• Western businesswomen should feel free to invite their Indonesian male counterparts and their wives to dinner, but should arrange payment ahead of time to avoid embarrassing their male guests.

TELEPHONES AND MAIL

Telephones. You'll find public phone booths along city streets, but they're often out of order. To use a phone, deposit Rp 50. The connection will automatically end after three minutes and a recording will tell you that your time is up.

• Shops and restaurants usually let you use their phones for local calls. Offer to pay for the call.

• To make long-distance or international calls, either go to the telephone office or book the calls from your hotel. You might have to yell into the phone to be heard.

• To communicate with your home office, you might want to use telex. Many overseas calls take a long time to connect, and hotel operators often botch incoming calls.

Mail. If you mail a parcel overseas, wait to see that the stamps are put on the package and canceled; otherwise, they're sometimes resold. Tourist hotels usually help wrap and mail packages.

LEGAL MATTERS

Customs and immigration. Visas are not required for tourist visits of up to two months, provided that your passport will be valid for at least six months. When you arrive you might need proof of onward passage. Don't overstay your visa or you might face a stiff fine when you depart.

• You may carry any amount of foreign currency into or out of Indonesia. It's illegal, however, to bring in or take out more than 50,000 Indonesian *rupiah*s.

• If customs officials raise their eyebrows at anything you want to bring into Indonesia, just act innocent and ignorant. Some officials merely want to exercise their power; if you get belligerent they'll be equally difficult in return. If all else fails, go to a higher-up.

• Because of the black market customs officials will probably note on your passport any cameras or electronic items you bring into the country. If you don't have them when you leave, you'll have to pay a steep import duty.

• Customs officials confiscate cassette tapes that they fear might contain propaganda or banned songs, so leave your cassettes at home.

Other Restrictions. Nude sunbathing is offensive and illegal in Indonesia.

SAFETY

Crime. Assault is very rare, but theft is all too common. Keep your valuables and passports either with you in a money belt or in a hotel lockbox.

• Walking alone at night is usually safe. Women should be more cautious in Muslim-dominated Java, where men are sometimes aggressive towards single women.

- Pickpockets are a problem on crowded buses and trains. Keep your wallet in your front pocket or your purse in your arms.

- Many transvestites (*banci*) masquerade as prostitutes and rob their unsuspecting customers. Although prostitution is officially discouraged, Surabaya has red-light districts. There's even a "prostitution village" in east Sumatra.

Health. You'll find running water only in large cities. Water must be boiled or otherwise treated for drinking. Don't drink beverages with ice in them unless you're certain the ice was made from boiled water.

- Before you eat any fruit, peel it. Don't eat too much fruit during December and January, when epidemics are more common.

- Medical facilities are fairly good in the major cities but are sparse in rural areas.

SHOPPING AND ENTERTAINMENT

Shopping. Shop hours are 8:30 A.M. to 4:00 P.M. Monday through Friday, and 8:30 A.M. to 12:30 P.M. Saturday.

- If you have an Indonesian buy your transportation tickets, food, or trinkets, you'll usually get a better price. As an alternative you can learn just enough Indonesian to make merchants think you already know the prices; then they won't overcharge you.

- In some large department stores, prices are fixed. In stores where bargaining is appropriate, the reasonable price is usually about one-half to two-thirds of the merchant's initial price.

- Bargain hard, but remember that the negotiating should be leisurely and friendly. Ask the merchant for prices; don't guess or take sticker prices at face value. Start by offering one-fourth to one-half of the quoted price. When merchants smile, your offer was too realistic; when they frown, the bargaining is nearing the end.

- You can get the best bargain if you're the first customer of the day. Merchants believe that making a sale to the first customer will mean good sales for the rest of the day.

- In Bali feel free to bargain for everything. Ask the merchant the price, offer half that amount, and start haggling.

- When you shop, take small change. People seldom use large bills unless they first ask whether change is available.

Entertainment. Much of Indonesia is Muslim; however, there are bars in hotels and a few on the streets. Local bars are not safe for women. Jakarta is full of massage parlors and "coffee" bars that don't serve coffee. Many of the young "women" you see in night spots are transvestites (*banci*).

- At a play or live theater, don't get alarmed if the audience shouts at the actors or throws money onto the stage. All theater seats are reserved,

and tickets for evening performances are best purchased early in the afternoon; however, foreign tourists are often shown to the best seats available.

- At parking lots, temples, and historical sites, guards sometimes try to make tourists pay a fee to enter. They'll usually drop the fee if you ask for a ticket with the price on it. Hide your camera; if they see it they might charge you Rp 100 to bring it in.

HOLIDAYS

Official holidays observed nationwide: New Year's Day (January 1), Idul Fitri (two days celebrating the end of Ramadan, August 2), Independence Day (August 17), Idul Adha (the Muslim Day of Sacrifice, October 8), and Christmas (December 25).

Unofficial holidays and festivals celebrated widely: Sekaten (January 11), Galungan (January 14), Grebeg Maulud (January 18), Kunigan (January), Chinese New Year (January/February), Wafat isa Aimasih (March/April), Sedang Sono Pilgrimage (May), Waicek (Buddha's birthday, May), Sarawati (May 30), Pagerwesi (June 3), Balimu (July 17), Galungan (August 13), Kuningan (August 23), North Sulawesi Anniversary (September 23), and Batara Turun Kabeh (December 23).

- The Muslim Ramadan lasts an entire month (the dates vary from year to year). During this time Muslims fast between sunrise and sunset. Don't eat, smoke, or drink in public during Ramadan.

- During Idul Adha, also a Muslim holiday, cattle are slaughtered and offered to the poor. Indonesians who can afford it make a pilgrimage to Mecca.

- Galungan is Bali's most important festival; it's so enjoyable, it's repeated in August. People celebrate the victory of good over evil with dancing and offerings.

- The Balinese New Year occurs every 210 days. It lasts for ten days, during which many temples hold public performances of Hindu dancing and plays.

KEY PHRASES

English	Indonesian	Pronunciation
English	*Indonesian*	*Pronunciation*
Good morning	Selamat pagi	S'lahmaht pahghee
Good afternoon	Selamat sore	S'lahmaht sawrreh
Good evening	Selamat malam	S'lahmaht mahlahm
Good night	"	"
Goodbye	Selamat tinggal	S'lahmaht teenggal
Please	Silakan	Seelakahn
Thank you	Terima kasih	T'rreema kasseehh
Excuse me	Minta maafkan	Minta ma'ahf-kahn
Don't mention it	Terima kasih kembali	T'rreema kasseehh k'm-bahlee
Yes	Ya	Yah
No	Tidak	Teedah'
I understand	Saya mengerti	Sahya m'ng-rr-tee
I don't understand	Saya tidak mengerti	Sahya teedah' m'ng-rr-tee
How much?	Berapa harganya?	Brr-ahpa hahrrga-nya?
Does anyone here speak English?	Apa kamu bicara bahasa inggris?	Ah-pah kah-moo bee-tjah-rah bah-hah-sah een-grees?
Sir, Mr.	Bapak	Bah-pahk
Madam, Mrs., Miss	Ibu	Ee-boo

PRONUNCIATION

A, i, o, and u are pronounced ah, ee, aw, and oo but are short.

e = neutral e as in "the"	s = ss (not z)
ai = ah-ee	ng = as in "singer"
au = ah-oo	
ua = oo-ah	ngg = as in "linger"

There's something about Japan that's hard to put your finger on — something that has allowed this nation of 120 million people to become one of the world's most modern countries while still retaining its age-old traditions. The juxtaposition of ancient and modern is enough to give outsiders (*gaijin*) cultural whiplash. Some observers claim that the apparent contradictions will catch up with Japan, with unforeseen results. Others point out that

Japan may be the most pragmatic culture on Earth — able to make sense out of demure teenagers who go to Tokyo's Yoyogi Park on Sundays dressed as 1950s American bobbysoxers, dance (without a hint of a smile) in the cordoned-off streets, and then change back into their muted pastels before heading home.

Japanese society exerts considerable pressure to conform. Once people enter the work force, they're expected to conform to an all-encompassing code of behavior that has given rise to a Japanese saying that the nail that sticks up above the board is the one that gets hammered down. Foreigners aren't expected to observe most of this unwritten code — after all foreigners aren't quite "human" (that is, Japanese) — but the *gaijin* who demonstrates at least awareness of the code will be respected. Japanese are very hard to get to know personally and sometimes seem ill-at-ease with foreigners.

Although the Japanese can be quite rude to strangers in public places (bumping in a queue or pushing an elevator's "close" button as someone rushes to get in), they are extremely polite to foreigners, business customers, and people they know. Don't make the mistake, however, of concluding that this courtesy means that you can move readily into the mainstream of Japanese life. Even long-term foreign residents of Japan complain that they are not truly accepted.

MEETING PEOPLE

GREETINGS

- The traditional Japanese greeting is bowing from the waist, a gesture (known as the *"ojigi"*) that expresses respect. Most Japanese, however, expect to shake hands with Westerners. Many Japanese also follow a bow with a handshake. Take your cue on which combination to use from the Japanese you're greeting.

- When you bow put your palms on your thighs and your heels together. Bow as low and for as long as the other person does, but not lower (that would signify humility).

- Every time you meet an acquaintance, whether on the street or indoors, bow. Be especially careful to bow to superiors. If you pass an acquaintance on the street or in a hallway, a short nod or dip of the head serves as an abbreviated bow.

- The Japanese do not appreciate arm-grabbing, kissing, back-patting, or any other physical contact during greetings. Handshakes are as far as they are willing to go. Many Japanese dislike even this Western gesture and will give you only a limp handshake.

- In general the Japanese do not like self-introductions. When you make an introduction, introduce the person of lower rank to the person of higher rank and always include each person's relationship to you or their title and company. By introducing two people you in effect take responsibility for their future relationship. If one does the other an injustice, you might be asked to correct the situation.

- When you are introduced say your name and express pleasure at the acquaintance.

Names and titles. In Japan the first of a person's two names is the family name; the second is the given name. When Japanese write in English, however, they transpose their names to conform with the Western tradition of placing the given name first and the family name last.

- When you address a Japanese person, male or female, always use the family name or title followed by the honorific suffix -*san*. If, for example, the English side of a man's business card says Akira Takasaka, address him as Takasaka-san. Never attach *san* to your own name; it would be honoring yourself. You may also address most Japanese Western-style (as Mr., Mrs., or Miss).

- Even Japanese who have known each other for years don't call each other by their given names (this is especially true of women). The only exceptions are young men, who sometimes use the given names of good friends in informal situations.

- When you speak to people of high position, use titles without family names (for example, *Shacho-san* for Mr. President or *Bucho-san* for Mr. General Manager).

Correspondence. To write business or formal letters the Japanese way, put the date in the top right corner and the address in the top left corner. Below the address write the full name of the addressee followed by *Sama* (for example, Takasaka-Akira-Sama).

• Japanese usually devote the first paragraph of a letter (except strictly commercial letters) to a comment about the season. This comment usually means more than meets the eye, so if you try it be careful to make simple, positive comments. (Better yet, just stick to writing Western-style letters.)

CONVERSATION

• Good conversation subjects: Your impressions of Japan and Japanese culture, baseball (popular in Japan), golf, food, and travel. Some of the most popular books in Japan are translations of foreign books about the Japanese people. The Japanese consider their culture unique and like to have this belief confirmed by foreigners.

• Subjects to avoid: Families (a personal matter), trade friction, World War II, prices of possessions, and politics. Most Japanese are not religious, so stay off this subject. Also avoid the subject of Japan's unfortunate minorities (the Koreans, the Ainu, and the *eta* or outcasts).

• Young people might approach you to practice their English. Always compliment them; don't take their efforts for granted. Because they're so interested in practicing, young adults are often the best people to approach when you need directions.

• Many Japanese understand written English much more easily than spoken English. If you have trouble communicating, write your question down.

PHRASES TO KNOW

• Japanese is spoken by almost 120 million people, but its use is largely restricted to the islands of Japan. The Japanese writing system is probably the most complicated in the world. It uses Chinese characters (which are pronounced differently in different contexts) supplemented by two different phonetic alphabets. One Japanese sentence might include three different forms of writing!

- Despite the difficulties try to learn a few phrases. It will endear you to the Japanese. Learning too much, however, might make them suspicious — after all, no one but the Japanese can speak Japanese.

CURRENCY

- The unit of currency is the *yen*. One U.S. dollar is worth about 150 *yen* (August 1987 rates). Coins are available in 1, 5, 10, 50, 100, and 500 *yen*. Notes are circulated in 500, 1,000, 5,000, and 10,000 *yen*.

- It's illegal to use any currency but *yen* in Japan. You can exchange foreign currencies only at Foreign Exchange Banks (including credit card offices) and large hotels. You can't exchange Korean and Taiwanese money at all.

- You'll usually get the best exchange rates at banks or American Express offices. Airport money changers give the poorest rates; hotel cashiers fall somewhere in between. Traveler's checks get a slightly better rate than cash, since there's less paperwork for the banks.

ETIQUETTE

- A foreigner would have to do something really unforgivable — like soaping up in the public bath or walking in shoes on a *tatami* (reed mat) floor — to rile the Japanese. (Japanese don't expect foreigners to be fully "civilized.") On the other hand, they'll be surprised and pleased if you observe their customs.

GENERAL MANNERS

- Punctuality is expected. Arrive on time for all social and business engagements.

- The Japanese value subtlety, so never speak in a

loud voice or be demonstrative.

- Frequent compliments make the Japanese uneasy — they don't like to be singled out from the group. Don't comment on someone's appearance. If someone pays you a compliment, politely deny it (above all don't say "thank you").

- When you walk on the street and on stairways, keep to the left. Some stairways and corridors in subway stations, however, are marked to keep you to the right.

- In Japanese gardens a round stone bound with straw rope in the shape of a cross signifies that the area beyond is off-limits.

- When you enter a hotel or other building, leave your wet umbrella in the umbrella rack. (Some racks require a coin deposit.)

- If you're invited to a Japanese wedding, be prepared to give a short speech incorporating advice for the couple. Stick to positive comments and avoid referring to breaks, destruction, or repetition.

- At either the high point or the end of a ceremony,

Japanese often raise both arms over their heads and shout *"Banzai!"* (literally, ten thousand years) three times. It's the equivalent of the Western "three cheers." Take your cue from the Japanese. Shouting at the wrong time can be extremely embarrassing.

- Eating or drinking on the street is considered crude. So is blowing your nose in front of someone.

- Older Japanese seldom send anniversary, get-well, or birthday cards (although these cards are growing in popularity among the young). They do send seasonal cards at midsummer and during New Year's, but they're often special cards. To get the right kind of card, consult a stationer or a Japanese friend.

BODY LANGUAGE

- Japanese prefer more personal space than North Americans do. Double the amount of space you'd put between yourself and another person in the West. Don't touch, pat, or even put a friendly arm around anyone, and don't kiss in public or show intimacy in any other way. (It's not unusual, however, to see

Japanese of the same sex strolling hand in hand.)

- Japanese smile or laugh not only when they're happy, but also when they're apologetic, embarrassed, sad, or angry. Smiles often mask intense feelings and don't necessarily mean the matter isn't being taken seriously.

- Yawning in public is impolite. If you can't resist, cover your mouth with one hand. (It used to be improper for Japanese women to show their teeth, so many older women also cover their mouths with their hands when they laugh.)

- Waving your hand back and forth in front of your face is a negative response ("I don't understand," "I don't know," or just "no"). When you receive a compliment it's polite to respond with this gesture.

- When a man (but not a woman) passes in front of someone or between two people, he should bow slightly with his right hand held stiffly in front of his face as though slicing the air (a gesture that looks somewhat like thumbing your nose).

- When you sit in a chair, sit erect with both feet on the floor. You may cross your legs either at the ankles or with one knee directly over the other. When women sit on the floor, they should sit with their legs bent under them, not cross-legged.

- To get the attention of service people, catch their eye, duck your head in a quick, shallow bow, and look at them expectantly. If they ignore you, you might need to make a full-fledged bow.

- Beckon someone by extending your right arm straight out, bending your wrist down, and waving your fingers with your palm facing down. Never use this gesture with older or senior people, and never beckon to anyone with your forefinger.

- Pointing at someone with your four fingers spread out and your thumb folded in is a very insulting gesture used to signify an *eta,* a person of Japan's outcast class.

- When Japanese acquaintances hold out a little finger in a hooked shape, they want you to join pinkies with them in a gesture signifying a promise.

- Japanese count on their fingers using only one hand. They fold their fingers, starting with the thumb, into the palm one by one and then reextend them, starting with the little finger.

DRESS

- The Japanese dress well, even for informal occasions. Don't dress too casually if you want to fit in. Adults, especially business people, rarely wear bright colors or flashy styles. Don't wear jeans (except designer jeans), shorts, or T-shirts outside of resorts.

- In the winter Japanese homes and inns are cold and drafty. Bring long underwear, thick socks, and sweaters to wear indoors.

- If you wear an overcoat, remove it and drape it over your arm before you enter a business meeting. Wait to put it back on until after you've left the office.

MEN For business meetings wear a dark suit and a tie. In better clubs and restaurants (especially in the evening), wear a jacket and tie; tuxedos are rarely worn. For a wedding wear a black formal suit with a black bow tie or a white or silver necktie. For a funeral wear a dark suit and black tie.

WOMEN For business wear a dark dress or suit. For an evening engagement at a good club or restaurant, wear a cocktail dress. (Traditional Japanese formal dinners call for sitting on the floor, so don't wear a tight skirt.) For a wedding wear any color dress except white, which is reserved for the bride. For a funeral wear a black dress without jewelry (pearls are ok).

NATIVE DRESS Japanese women often wear the traditional kimono on special occasions and during festivals. Brightly colored kimonos are reserved for the young. If you stay at a Japanese inn, you'll be provided with a cotton kimono (*yukata*) to wear to and from the bath and around the inn (see Hotels).

TEMPLES AND SHRINES

- Japan's two major religions are Shinto and Buddhism. A Shinto place of worship is a shrine; a Buddhist place of worship is a temple.

- Before you enter any building at a temple or shrine, always take off your shoes, hat, and scarf. Some temples provide plastic bags so you can carry your shoes around inside. Leave your wet umbrella in the umbrella holder (some require a coin deposit).

- Temples welcome visitors, but most temples charge an entrance fee.

- At Buddhist ceremonies visitors are expected to sit attentively on the *tatami* mats.

- Shinto shrines also welcome visitors; entrance is usually free. Shrines can be distinguished from temples by the high *torii* at the entrance. *Torii* are two large pillars supporting one or two cross beams. Don't drink from the water container near the *torii;* it's for washing and purifying the hands and mouth before entering the shrine. Don't enter the shrine's main building (*honden*).

- If you attend a Shinto ceremony at a shrine, either sit on the visitors' benches or stand. After the ceremony drop a donation in the wooden box near the exit.

PRIVATE HOMES

- Japanese people rarely entertain in or invite visitors into their homes. If you do receive such an invitation, consider it a great honor. The Tourist Information Centers arrange home visits for tourists; make the arrangements a couple of days in advance.

- Most Japanese homes and apartments are quite small by Western standards. If you visit one in the winter, take a sweater — most homes aren't well heated.

- When you visit a home, it's customary to bring a gift. Don't make it an expensive one; the Japanese feel obliged to reciprocate at the same level. Present the gift when you arrive. Good choices are appropriately wrapped foods, which you can purchase in department store sections that specialize in foods for gifts. Don't give flowers (some are associated with courtship and funerals) and don't give gifts in even numbers.

- If there is no doorbell, don't knock. Instead open the sliding door and say, *"Gomen kudasai."* When you're just inside the door, take off your shoes, hat, and scarf without turning your back on your host, and put on the slippers provided. After you remove your shoes, place them together pointing towards the outdoors. Inside the house take even the slippers off if you enter a room with *tatami* (straw mats).

- In homes with carpeted floors, follow the example of family members in walking on the carpet with or without shoes.

- It's not customary to give guests a tour of the house, so don't ask to look around. The kitchen is considered private, so don't peek into it or show an interest in it.

- Many Japanese homes have paper doors and walls that are easily soiled and perforated. Take care to avoid touching the paper.

- In homes without chairs people sit on the floor. Men sit cross-legged, not with their legs to one side. Women sit with their legs folded under them; when that position becomes unbearable, they may put their legs together tucked to one side.

- When you sit down in a room, it's polite to try to sit with your back to the door. Move to the place of honor (facing the doorway) only at the urging of your host. If you see a *tokonoma,* an alcove with a piece of art or decoration, don't sit in front of it unless the host insists; this position is reserved for honored guests. Don't set any object in a *tokonoma,* even for a moment.

- If you're seated on a *tatami* floor, move off the cushion and kneel directly on the mat whenever you're introduced to someone.

- If you see an item of decor that you like, don't compliment your hosts on it excessively, or they might feel obligated to give it to you as a gift.

- After a meal the serving of green tea signals that it's time to go. In any case don't stay after 10:00 P.M. (Japanese don't usually stay up very late).

- A few days after your visit, thank your hosts by letter or phone.

- If you're a house guest, don't offer to help with meals or cleaning up.

- If the home has a decorative garden, don't walk outside the designated path or off the stone pathway, and don't use the garden for recreation or sunbathing.

- If you stay overnight expect the bedding to consist of a *futon* mattress rolled out on the floor, with sheets and a hard pillow. Japanese homes are fairly small, and the *futon* saves space by permitting the family to use rooms for sleeping at night and for other activities during the day.

- If you stay with a family, remember that the hot bath (*furo*) is prepared for the whole family. Family members take turns soaking in the same tub of hot water. The family might bathe every night at a designated time. Ask what time you should bathe to fit into their schedule.

- As a guest you'll be invited to bathe first. For your own sake ask to go in later — the water starts out uncomfortably hot (about 110 degrees). Don't add cold water or drain the bath after you're done. To keep the water hot for the next person, replace the boards covering the tub.

- When you bathe be sure to soap, scrub, and rinse yourself outside the tub, then get in the tub to soak for a few minutes. The floors are designed to drain well, so feel free to slosh water around.

- Toilets in homes are seldom locked. Leave your slippers outside the door to let others know the toilet is occupied. You'll find a special set of slippers to use inside the toilet; just be sure not to wear them anywhere else.

PERSONAL GIFTS

- Western gifts that are especially popular in Japan include Native American art, local foods, Western belt buckles, and (for teenagers) T-shirts with overseas university logos.

- Japanese feel obligated to reciprocate in kind, so don't give expensive gifts. Don't give gifts in even numbers, especially in units of four (the Japanese word for four sounds the same as the word for death). Flowers are not a good choice, since some are associated with courtship and funerals, and neither are personal items such as shirts or ties.

- Wrapping gifts is a precise art in Japan, so have gifts wrapped locally. To make sure that the clerks use the right wrapping paper, be sure to tell them what the occasion is.

- Present and accept gifts with both hands and with a slight bow. Gifts are not opened in the presence of the person who gave them. (The delay shows that it's the thought, not the gift, that counts. It also permits the person who gave the gift to save face if it's not "worthy" of the recipient.)

- When someone gives you a gift, it's polite to refuse it once or twice before accepting it. And the next time you meet the person, be sure to mention the gift.

TIPPING

- Tipping isn't practiced as widely in Japan as it is in many other countries. When in doubt, don't tip.

- Hotels: Hotels usually add a 10-20% service charge to your bill, so extra tipping isn't necessary unless you receive a special service. Tip hotel porters about 200 *yen* per bag. If you stay at a *ryokan,* tip the maid about 5% of the bill.

- Restaurants: Most restaurants add a 10-20% service charge to the bill. Small, inexpensive restaurants often don't add a service charge.

- Taxis: Drivers don't expect tips, but leave the small change.

- Porters (airport): There's a set charge of 250-300 *yen* per bag.

- The Japanese usually wrap money or put it in an envelope before giving it to someone. This isn't necessary for most tipping, but it's polite for tipping a hotel maid or bellhop. Either put the tip (usually about 1,000 *yen*) in a regular envelope or buy one of the Japanese envelopes designed for this purpose. If you buy envelopes specially, you can find several varieties in department or stationery stores. Ask the salespeople which variety to use (receiving a tip in an envelope meant for sympathy gifts might shock a bellhop).

FOODS

MEALS

Breakfast (*asa-gohan*): 6:00 to 8:00 A.M. Expect fish, miso soup, dried seaweed, pickled vegetables, and rice. Hotels and fast-food restaurants serve Western breakfasts of eggs, juice, toast, and coffee.

Lunch (*o-hiru-gohan*): Noon to 1:00 P.M. Workers often eat a quick lunch in the company cafeteria or a nearby noodle shop, or eat a box lunch called a *bento*. Preferred quick foods are noodles (*soba*), mixed sandwiches (lunch meat and cucumber), curried rice, and thick *udon* noodles.

Dinner (*ban-gohan*): 6:00 to 8:00 P.M. People in large cities dine early, about 6:00 to 7:00 P.M. Family dinners often start rather late because the husband works long hours or goes drinking with colleagues before he commutes home. Rice and soup are staples eaten throughout the dinner.

- Make sure you go to lunch before noon. The concept of the staggered lunch hour hasn't caught on in Japan; all office workers seem to go to lunch precisely at noon.

WHERE TO EAT

- Japan has many different types of restaurants. An indispensable guide to Japanese food and res-taurants is *Eating Cheap in Japan,* by Kimiko Nagasawa and Camy Condon (Shufunotomo Company, Tokyo, 1984, $6.00). It not only describes the foods, it also provides photos and the Japanese name of each dish, so you can point them out to the waiter.

- Most small restaurants close at about 9:00 P.M.

- A *soba-ya* serves many kinds of noodle dishes but will probably be crowded at lunch time. You can try hundreds of varieties of noodles either at the *soba-ya* restaurants or at the small booths in most train stations. Noodles are very cheap (about 300 *yen*) and come in four basic types: *soba* (long, gray buckwheat noodles), *udon* (long, thick wheat-flour noodles), *somen* (thin, white noodles eaten cold), and *ra-men* (thin egg noodles). To eat noodles mix the condiments and a little soy sauce in your broth, then dip the noodles in the broth and slurp away.

- *Shokuji dokoro* are small restaurants that serve a limited number of the most popular traditional dishes.

- *Koryori-ya* are larger (but still small by Western standards) traditional restaurants that offer a wide variety of fish and vegetable dishes. They usually have a few semi-private *tatami*-mat rooms for small parties.

- *Sushi-ya* serve *sushi,* seasoned rice in rolls topped with slices of fish (usually raw). You can order either individual pieces or combination plates; prices are high if you order á la carte. *Sushi*-shop patrons are expected to drink some alcohol.

- A *shokudo* is a restaurant that offers a variety of foods such as curried rice, Chinese noodles, Japanese rice dishes, and desserts. You can see wax models of the available foods in the window display case. These places are favorites of college students.

- *Chuka ryori-ya* are inexpensive Chinese restaurants serving "Japanized" versions of Chinese dishes.

- *Kai-seki ryori-ya* are very expensive restaurants that feature the types of food served during the formal tea ceremony. These restaurants look like traditional Japanese inns and have very modest signs, mak-

ing them easy to overlook. You'll need reservations.

- *Okonimi-yaki* restaurants have grills where you can cook your own omelets. You'll be provided with a variety of ingredients to mix with the bowl of raw egg and spread on the griddle at your table.

- Many Japanese eateries have a short split curtain (*noren*) at the entrance. If the curtain is tucked inside, the restaurant is closed. The *noren* also identifies the type of restaurant (a red curtain signifies Chinese food, while a blue-and-white canvas curtain means a noodle or seafood restaurant).

- Look for reasonably priced restaurants in and around train stations. The basements and top floors of department stores also have dining halls and restaurants that won't break your budget. At some of these inexpensive eateries, you have to buy a ticket for each dish or drink before you order. If you see customers handing tickets to the waiter, look for a cashier or vending machine at the entrance where you can get your tickets.

- Coffee shops (*kissaten*) often offer Western set-meal breakfasts until 11:00 A.M. They're much cheaper than hotel breakfasts.

- You can buy box lunches (*bento*) both in stores specializing in them and in train stations. The *bento* itself is a flat, rectangular box made of wood, plastic, or lacquer. The contents vary, but rice is always the main ingredient. Other common ingredients are chicken, fish, sour plums, and pickles. Different regions specialize in unique types of *bento*.

- Many restaurants are on the second or third floors of office buildings. Fast-food restaurants often have ordering counters on the ground floor and tables on the second floor.

- The upper floors of department stores have a variety of eateries; they're usually open until 10:00 P.M. even if the store closes earlier. The only ones that are fast-food restaurants are the American-style ones.

- Japan's cities have many French, Korean, Chinese, and American (fast-food) restaurants. Pizza restaurants are popular with young people, but the cheese is milder than Westerners are accustomed to. At a pizzeria you'll be given a plastic tag with a number that will be called out when your pizza is ready. If you can't read Japanese numbers, sit near the pick-up counter and put your tag on the table where the employees can see it.

- Many restaurants close between lunch and 5:00 P.M. For a light meal during these hours, try coffee shops, which serve sandwiches, spaghetti, and other foods.

- At lunch set menus (*teishoku*) can save you a lot of money. At Japanese restaurants the set lunch usually includes a main dish, tea, rice, and soup (*miso shiru*). The drink will usually be served at the end of the meal.

- On restaurant bills over 2,500 *yen,* expect to pay a government tax. A service charge is sometimes added as well.

- For a quiet drink go to a neighborhood drinking establishment (*moni-ya*) with a red paper lantern at the doorway. These places offer small portions of food to go with your drink. You can sit and nurse a drink and snack for hours without being pressured to buy more.

- Beware of bars, cabarets, and other drinking establishments equipped with hostesses. These places are only for people on expense accounts. You might find yourself hit with an incredibly expensive tab at the end of the night. You might also be charged for the small snacks served with the drinks.

- Hotel bars charge high prices for drinks, but you don't risk the price-gouging of the hostess bars.

- The Japanese seldom drink alcoholic beverages during the day (although alcohol is sold throughout the day). You can purchase beer and even whiskey from alley vending machines anytime.

- Another good place to read, write letters, or discuss deals while slowly sipping a cup of coffee is a *kissaten* (coffee shop). These retreats also sell light snacks and desserts, and can be identified by the English word "coffee" displayed near the doorway. Most *kissaten* feature jukeboxes specializing in jazz, pop, or classical music.

- Look in the English-language newspapers for information on English-conversation coffee shops. English-speakers can get free coffee and meet Japanese who want to practice their English.

FOODS TO TRY

- The Japanese diet consists largely of rice, fresh vegetables, seafood, and fruits. Rice and Japanese tea are included in almost every meal, but many people also enjoy a Western-style breakfast or lunch, served with toast and coffee.

- Many restaurants have window displays with remarkably true-to-life wax replicas of their foods. Just point to what looks good. A rule of thumb is that if the food is in a bowl, it's Japanese in origin; if it comes on a dish, it's often of Western origin.

- Rice is the staple served with everything. (It's called *gohan,* which also means "meal.") Families and restaurants cook rice in electric cookers that keep it warm all day, ready for every meal.

- All meals include either clear soup or soup with a soybean base (*miso*), drunk from the lacquered wooden bowl in which it's served. Pickled vegetables also accompany every meal.

- Foods are usually served at a cooler temperature than Westerners prefer. If you like your food hot, ask for it that way. (Similarly, breakfast eggs are often cooked very lightly, so if you like them completely cooked, ask for them to be scrambled hard.)

- Desserts are not usually a part of Japanese meals, although fruit (especially oranges) is sometimes served at the end.

Specialties. For a meal with no surprises, try *tempura,* pieces of vegetables and fish dipped into batter and then deep-fried. Restaurants called *tempura-ya* specialize in this dish, but you can find it in most types of restaurants.

- *Sukiyaki* (chopped meat and vegetables) is another popular Japanese dish that most Westerners enjoy.

- Beef is very expensive in Japan. The famous Kobe beef is particularly expensive; the cows are fed special grains and massaged with beer to tenderize their flesh. You can get Kobe beef at *teppanyaki* steak houses, where you watch the chef cook your steak.

- *Yaki-tori* consists of small pieces of chicken or chicken livers grilled on bamboo skewers, then dipped in barbecue sauce. You're charged by the skewer.

- Westerners often confuse *sashimi* (slices of raw fish) with *sushi* (the sweet, vinegary rice that often accompanies the raw fish). *Sashimi* is often served as an early course in a Japanese meal, accompanied by *wasabi* (horseradish) and shredded *daikon* (white radish). When you eat *sushi* eat the rolled rice with chopsticks, but use your fingers to eat the raw fish (*sashimi*) after dipping it into the soy sauce. Don't dip the rice in the sauce. Between bites of *sushi* clear your palate with the slices of ginger in rice vinegar.

- Other specialties to try are *oden* (stewed vegetables and tofu), *katsudon* (pork cutlet with rice), *shabu-shabu* (beef, chicken, and vegetables cooked in boiling water at the table), and *skiyaki* (beef and vegetables cooked in soy sauce and sugar and served with a raw egg).

- For dessert try *mikan* (mandarin oranges), *nashi* (an apple-pear fruit), or *kaki* (persimmons). You might also want to try the rather dry cakes that are filled with sweet bean paste.

- In Chinese restaurants (*chuka ryori-ya*) try the *gyoza* — small fried dumplings with vegetables and either meat or seafood inside. Dip the dumplings in the soy sauce.

- *Fugu* (blowfish) is prepared only by licensed cooks. The liver and ovaries are poisonous, so the fish must be properly cleaned. (A few people have died from improperly prepared blowfish.) Some people enjoy both the flirtation with danger and the tingling sensation in the lips that the fish causes.

- Watch out for *natto,* a sticky, bitter-tasting glop of fermented beans. Japanese love to have unsuspecting *gaijin* try this dish to watch their reactions.

Beverages. Water won't be served with your meal unless you ask for it.

- Brown or green tea is served at the end of a meal. In a restaurant you'll often be given green tea (free of charge) before you even order. This green tea is different from the powdered green tea used in the traditional tea ceremony.

- Beer is always served chilled.

- The traditional alcoholic beverage is *sake,* a clear rice wine that is 16% alcohol by volume. *Sake* is served in a small clay vessel and drunk from thimble-sized cups. It is usually served warm and is quite easily assimilated into the bloodstream, so exercise caution. *Sake* is not considered to improve with age. There are three grades: the best quality (*tokkyu-shu*), the middle grade (*ikkyu-shu*), and the common grade (*nikyu-shu*).

- *Shoju,* a potent alcoholic drink made from sweet potatoes, rice, or *soba,* is gaining in both respectability and popularity.

- Japanese women do drink alcohol, so it's acceptable to offer them a drink.

TABLE MANNERS

- Eating while you're walking on the street is bad

manners. Snack foods are sold at street stands, but it's polite to stay at the stand until you finish eating.

- In most inexpensive restaurants you may seat yourself, but at more expensive places wait to be shown to a table.

- Blowing your nose in a restaurant will horrify the Japanese. Go to the rest room instead.

- Hotel restaurants often give you the bill to sign before the amount is filled in. Don't worry about signing it — cheating is unknown.

Utensils. Chopsticks are used to eat almost every solid food. Japanese chopsticks (*o-hashi*) are thinner and have more of a point than the thick, blunt-ended Chinese chopsticks. They are usually made of either slippery lacquered wood or ivory or bone. In all but the nicest restaurants, you'll be given plain pine chopsticks wrapped in paper and joined at the large end. Take the paper off and pull the sticks apart. Rubbing these rough sticks together gets rid of any splinters.

- Visitors who are not skilled with chopsticks can almost always get knives and forks. At least try to use chopsticks, however, and you'll earn the appreciation of your Japanese hosts. Keep both chopsticks in one hand and don't try to spear food with them (for more information on how to use chopsticks, see the Utensils sections of the Hong Kong or Taiwan chapters)

- Use your chopsticks to pull apart any pieces of food that are too large for one bite. If this proves impossible lift the food to your mouth with the chopsticks and bite off a piece.

- When you're not using your chopsticks, lay them parallel (not crossed) on your chopstick rest or lean them against your plate. Don't lay them flat on the table, and never stick them into your rice bowl — that's how an offering to the dead is made. When you finish your meal, place your chopsticks across your bowl or plate.

- Spoons are not provided for soups and broths. Just lift the bowl to your mouth and drink.

- Communal dishes are rare at Japanese restaurants but are common in Chinese restaurants and private homes. Don't use your chopsticks to take food from a communal dish unless you turn them around and use the ends you haven't placed in your mouth. Sometimes long serving chopsticks are provided.

- Pick up dishes on your left side with your right hand, and vice versa.

- Diners are often handed a damp hot or cold towel (*oshibori*) before the meal. Use it to wipe your hands and mouth before you eat, but don't scrub your neck or wash behind your ears. If the towel was delivered in a basket, put it back in the basket when you're done with it. Napkins, when available, are thin and non-absorbent.

- When you use a toothpick, cover your mouth with your free hand.

Dining with others. In a Japanese home or restaurant, the place of honor is in front of the *tokonoma,* an alcove decorated with a piece of art or flowers. If you are seated next to the doorway, this is a subtle sign that you should be the first to leave.

- Saying that you're hungry, either before or during a meal, is considered vulgar. Also refrain from taking large portions or eating quickly.

- Before you begin the meal, it's polite to say *"Itadakimasu"* (I will have some). Wait to eat until older or more senior people begin.

- All the dishes of a meal are served at the same time (usually in separate containers on a tray), not in a series of courses. Don't start eating until all the dishes have been placed on the table and the host has asked you to begin.

- If you have dietary restrictions inform your hosts early. It will embarrass them if you don't eat whatever they serve or order for you. Even if you find some of the dishes unusual or alarming, try to show outward (if not genuine) appreciation. Never ask suspiciously what the ingredients of a dish are.

- If your host extends a tray towards you, place your empty rice bowl on it to be refilled. Set the refilled bowl down on the table before you take any other food.

- Throughout the meal take a bite of rice or a slurp of soup between bites of the other dishes. Don't finish off one dish at a time; instead, alternate between dishes.

- For all but the most formal dinners, use your rice bowl as a resting place for bites of food before you put them in your mouth. Pick up the food with your chopsticks, put it in your rice bowl, and lift the bowl to chest level before you put the food in your mouth.

- Never pour anything over your rice (except for green tea at the end of the meal). Eat at least two bowls of rice during the meal; eating only one is impolite. When you finish your meal, make sure you eat every last rice grain in the bowl (leaving any rice indicates that you want a refill).

- When you eat noodles lean over the bowl, use your chopsticks to lift a few strands into your mouth, and then suck them in. Slurping and sighing are quite acceptable when you're eating noodles.

- When someone offers you tea or fruit, hesitate slightly before you accept.

- To toast say *"kan-pie"* "Drain the cup" while lifting your cup.

- Drinking *sake* (rice wine)

while you're eating rice is improper.

- Conversation during a meal should focus on the meal, its beauty, Japanese cuisine in general, and the seasonal aspects of the food. In general Japanese talk less during a meal than Westerners do.

- Before you eat the pickles served at the end of the meal, it's polite to rinse your chopsticks off in your tea cup.

- At the end of a meal, say *"Gochisosama"* ("It was an honorable meal") either to the person who treated you to the meal or to the waiter, who will then bring you your bill.

- When you drink, never pour your own. Lift your cup when your neighbor pours for you, then pour for your neighbor. Take a sip before you set your cup down. Your drinking companions might honor you by presenting you with their empty cups, then filling them for you to drink from. Don't refuse; instead, finish the cup and then fill it for your companion. To prevent refilling either keep your cup full or turn it over when it's empty. If you don't want to drink at all, put your hand over your cup when a drink is offered and say, "None for me today."

- It's polite to buy a complete round of drinks, but don't offer to split the cost with someone.

- The person who suggested the meal picks up the tab for everyone. Never offer to pay for only your portion.

- When you receive a meal or bar tab, don't examine it closely — especially if you're entertaining a guest. Tabs are invariably correct and, in the case of bars, non-negotiable.

Banquets and formal dinners. Many banquets take place at traditional Japanese restaurants with *tatami* floors. Don't wear shoes into these restaurants. And don't wear socks or nylons with holes in them.

- At a banquet *sake* is often served before the meal.

- For very formal dinners, follow these steps:

Remove the lid from the rice bowl with your left hand and place it to the left of the bowl.

Take the lid off the soup bowl with your right hand and place it to the right of the bowl.

Pick up the soup bowl with your left hand and take a sip, then put it back down.

Raise the rice bowl to chest level with your left hand and, using your chopsticks with your right hand, take a bite of rice.

Take a sip of soup, then use your chopsticks to remove and eat a piece of the solid food in the soup. (Make sure you sip your soup slowly, putting it back down each time, so that it lasts until the end of the meal.)

Next put the rice bowl back in your left hand and start sampling the side dishes one at a time. Save the pickles for last. Leave a mouthful of rice in the rice bowl to signal that you'd like a refill; an empty bowl indicates that you're finished.

Finish the meal with the last of the rice, followed by the pickles. If green tea arrives pour it into the rice bowl while you eat the pickles, and then drink the tea.

End the meal by saying, *"Gochisosama deshita"* ("That was a feast".)

ACCOMMODATIONS

Hotels. If you're planning a trip to Japan during late December, early January, or Golden Week (April 29 to May 5), make reservations two or three months ahead of time. These are holiday seasons during which many Japanese travel within the country.

- At large hotels check-in time is 1:00 P.M. If you arrive earlier you might have to wait for your room.

- To make sure your taxi driver understands which hotel to return you to, carry the hotel's card with the address written in Japanese. Have the hotel information desk write your destinations in Japanese, so you can show the note to taxi drivers or other people.

- Hotel rates vary little within each class and type of accommodation. Bargaining for a discount might be considered an insult.

- Hotel laundries automatically starch white shirts unless you request otherwise.

- Tourist hotels provide a small refrigerator in each room, so save on late-night meals by buying snacks at small nearby grocery stores.

- In Japanese-style hotels the bathroom is usually separate from the toilet, and has tiled floors with taps low on the wall. The bath itself, which is for soaking, is square and deep. Wash and rinse in the tiled area before you enter the bath. Never use soap in the bath water.

- Beware of any hotel sporting garish architecture, neon signs, separate entrances and exits, and pastel paint. It's probably one of Japan's ubiquitous "love hotels." These hotels charge by the hour and feature velvet and mirrors. After midnight budget travelers can get rooms for the night at a reasonable price (usually the cost for an hour).

- Staying at a traditional Japanese inn (*ryokan*) can be an expensive but unique experience. They're the perfect retreats, set in gardens with beautiful scenery.

Bring a phrase book; English-speaking service people are hard to find. Check with the JNTO (Japan National Tourism Organization) to find out which *ryokan*s welcome foreigners. Observe the following customs at a *ryokan:*

Check-out time is 10:00 or 11:00 A.M. Some *ryokan*s lock their doors at 10:00 P.M., so if you go out check to make sure you can get back in.

Ryokan prices include breakfast (soup, seaweed, fish, and pickles) and dinner. You can also get a Western breakfast if you order in advance. You'll get your meals in your room.

You'll be served green tea and cakes by the maid after you're shown to your room. She'll also have you sign the guest register. At expensive *ryokan*s you'll have a personal maid who will serve meals in your room, prepare the *futon* bedding, arrange the bath, and even help you undress for the bath.

Bedding consists of a thick quilt, sheets, and a hard pillow stuffed with grain husks. During the day the bedding is kept in a closet; at night the maid places it on the floor.

Theft is so uncommon in Japan that *ryokan* rooms have no locks on the doors. Asking for a lock would insult both the innkeeper and the other guests, so place any valuables in the innkeeper's care.

The innkeeper or maid will walk into your room at any time without knocking. If you're undressed they'll take no notice and you shouldn't either.

When you enter the *ryokan*'s communal bath, leave your clothes and bath towel in the baskets in the changing area. Remember to soap and rinse outside the tub. Never get any soap in the hot tub meant for soaking. Many people will soak in this water, so don't empty the tub when you finish.

- If you want fairly cheap accommodations, stay at a *minshuku,* the budget traveler's *ryokan. Minshuku* are found near train stations and often have Western-style exteriors. They have spartan facilities and decor and no maid service.

- Don't expect to take your meals in your room; instead go to the dining room, a great place to meet other guests. Eating and bathing are often restricted to certain times of the day. In winter the rooms are colder than American rooms, so plan your clothing accordingly.

- At any Japanese inn wear the slippers provided for walking around inside. Don't wear them, however, on the *tatami* (reed mats) or into the toilet. A special pair of slippers is usually provided at the toilet door to wear inside. Leave your "walk-about" slippers outside, and don't forget to leave the toilet slippers there when you leave.

- When you're relaxing in an inn or going to or from the bath, wear the kimono-like *yukata* supplied in every room. To wear the *yukata* properly, lap the left side over the right (lapping the right side over the left symbolizes death). Men should wear the sash low around their hips, with the knot on the right side. Women should wrap the sash high around their waists with the knot in the back. If you want to keep the *yukata* as a souvenir, buy one from the innkeeper — don't take the one in your room.

- Electric currents vary. Tourist hotels have two outlets, one for 110 volts and another for 220 volts, but the sockets usually accept only a two-prong plug. Otherwise the electric current is 100-volt, 50-cycle AC in eastern Japan and 100-volt, 60-cycle AC in western Japan.

Rest rooms. Many public and private rest rooms feature squat-type toilets consisting of ceramic pits in the floor. Plant one foot on each side of the pit facing the end that has a shield around the rim.

- Many public toilets are co-ed, especially in restaurants and coffee shops. Don't be surprised if people of the opposite sex join you. Just act as though you don't see them. Japanese usually knock on a toilet cubicle to see whether it's occupied; if you're in it, knock back.

- Toilets are usually in rooms separate from showers or baths. The English word "bathroom," as it's used in Japan, often refers to the room where you take a bath.

- Most public rest rooms don't provide toilet paper, so carry some with you. Kiosks in train and subway stations sell small packets of tissue paper, and some rest rooms now have vending machines that dispense them.

- If you visit a public bath (*sento*), remove your shoes at the entrance and put them in one of the lockers provided. Enter the appropriate room (men or women) and pay the attendant, who sits on a high box overlooking the changing area. When you enter the bathing area, use soap and wash — and rinse — at the water taps along the wall before you enter the hot bath. Never take soap or a soapy body into the bath; it's for soaking and relaxing only.

TRANSPORTATION

- Rush hours in cities last from 8:00 to 9:30 A.M. and from 5:00 to 6:30 P.M.

- Addresses don't follow a sequential order down the street as they do in the West. Many streets don't even have names. Addresses indicate in which district or ward a place is located.

- If you get lost ask the police for help and show them the address you're looking for. Among the functions of the police you'll see in the ubiquitous police boxes is to direct people to addresses in that neighborhood. Even taxi drivers need to rely on them to find addresses. Many police speak at least some English.

PUBLIC TRANSPORTATION

- Most Japanese are very good about forming and staying in queues while they're waiting for taxis, buses, and subways (although queues form for subways only during rush hours). When the subway doors open or it's your turn to go next, move swiftly. The only time people push is when a subway is crowded and the only way to exit is to push your way out the door.

Buses. Buses are difficult for foreigners to negotiate. They're subject to the same traffic jams that bog down taxis, and all the signs are in Japanese. If you see people board a local bus at the front, that means that the fee is set and you pay when you board. If people board at the rear, it means that the fee depends on the distance you travel and you pay when you get off. On the latter type take the numbered ticket from the machine inside the back door and, when you get off, pay the fare shown next to that number on the sign at the front door.

- Inter-city buses go almost anywhere, but they're usually slower and more expensive than trains. Bus stations are usually very close to train stations. Just get in line and tell the ticket seller your destination. Most people will help you find the right queue if you just say the name of your destination and look puzzled. Almost all the signs are only in Japanese.

Taxis. Taxis are expensive — about 1,000 *yen* for a short ride and about US$ 100 from Narita Airport to downtown Tokyo. To find a cab either go to a taxi stand or hail one by waving (don't whistle). Taxis with a red light in the lower left corner of the windshield can be flagged down on the street. A green light means the taxi is already taken.

- To get a ride late at night or during a rainstorm, you might have to hold up several fingers to show how much you're willing to multiply the metered fare. Taxi service from entertainment areas after 11:00 P.M. is especially scarce. It's difficult, for example, for tourists to get a late-night taxi out of the Ginza entertainment district; the drivers are looking for Japanese businessmen willing to pay extra for the long trip home. Drivers assume that tourists are staying in nearby hotels.

- Taxis have remote-control doors. The rear door on the left side is operated by remote control; let the driver open and close it for you.

Trains. For long-distance travel in Japan, the bullet trains (*Shinkansen*) are just as quick as traveling by air, if you consider the time it takes to travel to the airport and check in for your flight. There are two types of *Shinkansen:* a *Hikari* is a super-express with few stops, and a *Kodama* makes intermediate stops. Both types have buffet cars and telephones. The only non-smoking car is the No. 1 car; seats in this car aren't reserved, so non-smokers must dash for them. New double-decker cars with restaurants and private compartments are being added to the trains.

- If you plan to travel by train extensively, purchase the Japan National Railways (JNR) seven-, fourteen-, or twenty-one-day unlimited-travel railpass tickets. They're valid only on the JNR system. You must buy vouchers for them before you come to Japan; your travel agent should be able to get them for you.

- Train stations have many platforms, and many trains leaving simultaneously. Arrive early and double-check to make sure you're on the right platform for your train. Your ticket should note which car your seat is in. Car numbers are posted on the platform at the location where the car will stop.

- Pick up a copy of the condensed Railway Timetable from the Tourist Information Centers.

- Train stations have signs showing the names (usually romanized) of that stop as well as those just before and after it. You can tell when your stop is coming up by watching these signs.

Subways. In Tokyo and Osaka use the rapid subways to get around. You'll find coin-operated ticket machines in the stations. Keep your ticket; you must turn it in at your destination. Subway lines are color-coded, and English maps of the subway system are usually posted near the ticket machines.

- If you can't figure out the correct fare for your destination, just buy the cheapest ticket and then go to the fare adjustment window at your destination.

- The buttons under plastic covers on the ticket machines are for children's tickets. You must raise the cover to push the button.

- Like train stations, subway stations have signs showing the names of upcoming stops.

DRIVING

- Rental cars are available throughout Japan, but driving in the large cities is not recommended for foreigners — traffic is extremely congested, parking spaces are rare, and public transportation is very good. Some streets are so narrow that two cars can't pass each other. Pedestrians must walk in the street in the many narrow streets that have no sidewalks.

- If you do rent a car, you can use an International Driver's License.

- You can also arrange to rent a car and driver through your hotel. It will be expensive.

- Driving is on the left side, as in Britain. Be especially cautious when you enter a traffic circle (you must enter clockwise). In theory the principle of the right-of-way is like that in North America, but in practice it's quite different.

- The speed limit on expressways is 80 kilometers per hour; in most cities it's 30 km/hr.

BUSINESS

BUSINESS HOURS

Business offices: 9:00 A.M. to 5:00 or 6:00 P.M. Monday through Friday, with an hour break for lunch. Many offices are open until noon on Saturday, but Saturday appointments aren't appreciated.

Banks: 9:00 A.M. to 3:00 P.M. Monday through Friday, and 9:00 A.M. to noon Saturday. All banks close on the second Saturday of the month.

Government offices: Same as business offices, with no Saturday hours.

BUSINESS CUSTOMS

- Times of year to avoid when you're planning a business trip to Japan are mid-December to mid-January, Golden Week (April 29 to May 5), and July and August (when business people take their vacations).

- You'll need prior appointments for all business and government visits. Make arrangements by telex at least two weeks in advance or by mail at least six weeks in advance.

- Establishing a friendly relationship comes before getting down to business. It's not uncommon to have several initial meetings during which no business is discussed. Allow plenty of time for "courting" when you plan your negotiations.

- Negotiations begin with middle management. Avoid sending a top corporate officer for initial negotiations unless you know that a Japanese officer of about the same rank will be taking part. Stacking the deck with your corporate heavy-weights will cause embarrassment. Don't, however, underestimate the importance of middle managers in a Japanese company. Middlemanagers usually initiate the decision-making process, and their recommendations are usually followed.

- Negotiations will take longer than you expect. Decision-making is by consensus, and each manager who would be involved in a project must approve the written proposal (*ringisho*). Don't give in to your inclination to take charge and get things rolling. The decision might be slow in coming, but since everyone has approved the plan, you can count on swift and cooperative implementation.

- Because decisions are by consensus, Japanese negotiating teams include several members from various departments. A lone Western negotiator might feel overwhelmed by the sheer numbers on the other side of the table. For serious negotiations bring several decision-makers and technical people for your own team. Expect the negotiations to be detailed.

- You'll need an interpreter not only to assist in communications, but also to overhear comments made by the Japanese team. Your interpreter should also note how many times a topic is mentioned — a good indicator of priorities.

- When you make a presentation, use a low-key style and proceed step-by-step allowing the Japanese to ask questions throughout the presentation. Using pressure tactics won't work. Most Japanese read English much better than they understand spoken English, so provide written supporting materials.

- When you sign a major contract, the Japanese will expect a ceremony to seal the pact. Two senior executives and the negotiating party attend and give speeches. Gifts are exchanged and photographs are taken. A reception follows the ceremony. When everyone returns home the chief executive officers of the two companies exchange congratulatory letters.

Business etiquette. You'll need business cards

(*meishi*) with English on one side and Japanese on the other. Be sure they include your job title. Japanese want to know your rank in the company.

- When you're introduced bow and exchange name cards. Offer your card with both hands and with the Japanese side up. Take a few seconds to read your new acquaintance's card before you speak. Show that you're impressed with the other person's position in the company by inhaling audibly.

- Running out of business cards is inexcusable. Never offer one that you had in your back pocket or put someone else's card in a wallet that goes in your back pocket. Instead keep the cards in a coat pocket or card case. Don't write on the back of someone's card.

- To earn respect, be quiet and modest. The Japanese don't like to work with assertive, direct, loud "go-getters." They particularly resent any assumption that Western products are superior or are sought-after by the Japanese.

- Japanese respect age and seniority; in Japan the two go hand in hand.

They are wary of company representatives who seem too young by their standards to have decision-making authority. If two people are representing your company, let the older one speak for both, at least initially. A little gray hair will go a long way.

- Japan is a status-conscious society. Don't push informality with your counterparts (especially those of lower or higher rank). Instead be polite and formal and let the Japanese set the level of informality.

- Japanese business people are prone to long, silent pauses. These gaps in conversation are used to buy time, think about the next step, or unnerve Westerners who (misinterpreting the silence as rejection) give in on negotiating points. During these moments lift your head a bit and stare into the space above your counterpart's head as though you're contemplating.

- Saying no or flatly refusing a request is a mistake — it causes your counterpart to lose face. Instead say "It would be difficult" or "Let me think about it." The Japanese will interpret these as negative responses.

- Criticizing your competition, domestic or foreign, is considered rude.

Appointments and meetings. The best times to schedule business appointments are 10:00 A.M. to 2:00 P.M.

- Japanese are very conscious of time and expect people to be punctual for appointments. In Tokyo allow plenty of time to get from place to place — traffic is congested.

- If this is your firm's first meeting with a Japanese company, the Japanese will want to know about your company and how long you've been connected with it. To the Japanese, you *are* your company. This first meeting is even more important than in the West. It sets the tone for the future relationship.

- During initial "getting-to-know-you" meetings, don't bring up business. Talk about hobbies, golf, and your favorable impressions of Japan and ask for recommendations on what to see during your stay.

Business gifts and entertainment. For your first meeting with someone, bring a small gift such as fruit, cheese, or smoked meat from home. Special products made by your company are good gifts, but avoid anything boldly emblazoned with a logo. Try to give gifts in sets of three, five, or seven — never in fours (the word for four sounds like the word for death).

- If you buy gifts in Japan, get them at prestigious department stores, where they'll be wrapped properly in the store's distinctive paper. Gift-wrapping is such an exact art in Japan that it's best to have any items wrapped locally.

- When you receive a gift, it's polite to refuse it once or twice before you accept. The next time you meet, mention the gift.

- Japan has two gift-giving seasons during which businesses exchange greeting cards and gifts. *O-chugen,* the mid-summer gift season, takes place in mid-July in Tokyo and mid-August in some other regions. *O-seibo,* the year-end gift season, takes place during the first half of December. Good gifts for these occasions are fruit packages, specialty meats, whiskey, packaged cooking oils, and kelp. Ask a stationer to help choose the correct card to send.

- In business entertaining let the Japanese extend the first dinner invitation. Let the ranking Japanese person order your dinner for you. Before you leave Japan reciprocate the invitation — preferably in a Western-style restaurant where you know the customs. Look for fine Western restaurants in hotels.

- Business dinners almost never include spouses. Japanese men have little or no experience socializing with women, especially on an equal level.

- If you arrange a party or a banquet for business associates at an inn or restaurant, it's common to have a cash tip delivered in advance to ensure special service.

- After a business dinner be prepared for heavy drinking. Drinking is an integral part of establishing a business relationship in Japan. It's also the best occasion for letting others know how you really feel. Japanese often look almost hurt if a foreign guest at a meal does not join them in a beer. If you don't drink, about the only acceptable excuse you can use is that you

have a stomach disorder and are under a doctor's orders not to drink.

- Space your drinks. If you've had enough the only way to refuse more refills is to pretend to be very drunk (drunks are not expected to drink more).

- When you're out drinking, don't talk business. This is the time to relax and develop a relationship of trust. In Japan drinking is an accepted way to let off steam, and little disapproval is shown toward drunks. Getting drunk together is a demonstration of camaraderie.

- The Japanese might take you to a *karaoke*, an "empty-orchestra" bar where patrons sing to taped music. Be prepared to sing. If someone hands you the microphone, it's impolite not to sing to one of the well-known American songs they have taped.

- If your Japanese hosts take you to a party featuring *geisha*, don't make the unforgivable blunder of thinking that these women are prostitutes. Their jobs are to help guests relax and to perform classical music and dance. Being treated to a *geisha*-accompanied party is an honor. They're very expensive.

- If you arrange for one of Japan's half-million bar hostesses to accompany you after hours or on her day off, don't commit the faux pas of bringing her to a business-related social event.

- Business breakfasts are unknown.

TELEPHONES AND MAIL

Telephones. Look for public phones in subway stations, hotel lobbies, coffee shops, and on the street. There are five colors and types. Red, pink, and blue phones are usually limited to local calling and accept only a few (six to ten) 10-*yen* coins at a time. Green and yellow phones, which also accept 100-*yen* coins, are used for inter-city as well as local calls. The charges depend on time and distance. To find a quiet place for a call, look for pay phones in banks and building lobbies.

- To make a local call, deposit a 10-*yen* coin and wait for a buzz. You'll have three minutes. If you need more time, insert more coins before your time is up or you'll be cut off. If you deposit too many coins, the excess will be returned. To avoid interruptions it's best to insert several coins at the beginning of your call.

- When you make long-distance calls from the yellow or green phones, you can insert several 100-*yen* coins at a time, but you won't get change for the unused portion of a coin.

- The green phones also accept magnetic telephone cards. Look nearby for vending machines (with English instructions) that issue these magnetic "credit" cards in various denominations. (Nearby shops often sell them as well.) You can use a 1,000-*yen* card any number of times until your calls total 1,000 *yen*.

- Most public phones have a button near the base that you can press to make free emergency calls. Dial "110" for the police.

- When you answer the

phone, say *"moshi-moshi,"* the usual telephone greeting. If you answer at an office, say *"Hai* (your name) *dess"* (*hai* means "yes," and *dess* means "is"). During the conversation say *"hai"* periodically, or else the other person will start saying *"moshi-moshi"* over and over again, thinking the connection has been broken. To sign off say *"Shitsure shimasu"* (pronounced "She-tsoo ray she-mahs").

- Phone numbers have nine or ten digits. The first three or four (the ones in brackets) are area codes. Use them only if you're outside that area.

- If you need travel assistance outside Tokyo or Kyoto, dial "106" and tell the operator you're calling collect for the Tourist Information Center (TIC).

Mail. Most post offices are open from 9:00 A.M. to 7:00 P.M. Monday through Friday, and 9:00 A.M. to 3:00 P.M. Saturday. The largest post offices are also open on Sunday morning.

- Mailboxes are red. You'll find them on street corners. In Tokyo the slot on the right of the box is for inter-city mail only;

the left slot is for all other mail.

- To mail packages overseas go to a large post office. Many small post offices don't provide this service.

- You can buy stamps at shops and kiosks displaying the postal symbol (a capital "T" with a bar over the top).

LEGAL MATTERS

Customs and immigration. U.S. citizens require visas for stays of up to 60 days; you can extend them twice. You can also get 15-day transit visas, four-year, multiple-entry tourist visas, and commercial visas for up to 180 days. Canadian citizens don't need visas.

- Foreign tourists must carry their passports with them at all times. If you ask for directions at a police box, you might be asked to show your passport.

- If you purchase an item at a duty-free shop, be sure the "Record of Purchase of Commodities Tax Exempt for Export" form is attached to your passport. Give it to the customs official when you leave the country. Many stores omit the tax on items such as cameras, pearls, and electronic goods to foreigners who show their passports.

- Guns, drugs, and pornographic materials cannot be brought into Japan.

Other restrictions. Most cities have no restrictions on hours for selling alcohol. The drinking age is twenty, but anyone can buy bottled beer and whiskey from the vending machines found everywhere.

- The penalties for drug possession are severe.

SAFETY

Crime. Japan has very little crime, even in the largest cities. In fact its crime rate is one of the lowest in the world — only one-fifth that of the U.S. Don't be afraid to travel or walk alone.

- Hitchhiking is uncommon

in Japan, but is understood and safe (even for women). It's not permitted on expressways.

Health. Drinking water is safe throughout Japan.

- If you get sick you'll find hospitals and clinics in every town. Medical service is excellent.

- Toiletries and medicines are readily available. Antibiotics are available without prescription.

SHOPPING AND ENTERTAINMENT

Shopping. Department stores are open from 10:00 A.M. to 6:00 P.M. Monday through Sunday, although they all close one day a week (usually Wednesday or Thursday). Small shops and large urban shopping areas stay open longer, often until 8:00 P.M., and don't close for lunch.

- Most large stores have an information desk at the entrance with English directories. Look for major department stores near subway and train stations.

- Cashiers seldom count change back to the customer. Instead they just do their calculations and then hand you your change in a plastic dish. You can depend on them to be accurate.

- Foreign tourists don't have to pay the value-added tax on items such as cameras, pearls, and electronic goods that they're going to take out of Japan. Just show your passport to the salespeople and fill out the forms they give you. You must give a copy of the form to customs officials when you depart.

- Paying in cash will get you the best bargains. Japan is still a cash-based society, and paying by check is uncommon. Many smaller shops don't accept traveler's checks or credit cards.

- Credit card receipts are written entirely in Japanese (Chinese) characters, or *kanji*. Write down the shop and the item on the receipt, so you won't forget which receipt goes with which purchase.

- Sales aren't as common as they are in the West, since the social status of a product is related to how much you paid for it.

July and December are the annual sale periods; except during these months deep discounting is rare for most items. Large stores also hold an annual sales fair to sell everything that didn't sell at the other sales. These fairs usually take place outdoors and are advertised in the papers.

Entertainment. Most of Tokyo's bars have standing room only after 10:00 P.M., so arrive early. Even at the least expensive bars, an evening's drinking (including a side dish or two) will cost 5,000 *yen*.

- Some bars turn foreigners or "non-members" away. They've seen too many foreigners get outraged when presented with extremely expensive, non-negotiable bills. Some of these night spots charge inflated prices because they cater to businessmen on very generous expense accounts. If you get turned away, be thankful that you've been spared a crippling tab.

- Most bars with a "private-club" appearance are patronized primarily by men on expense accounts and feature hostesses for whom you're expected to buy drinks. These places charge whatever a client looks like he can afford — often up to ten times what you'd expect to pay. Arguing over the amount will get you nowhere.

• Some drinking establishments have barkers outside who try to lure passersby inside. These are **Pinku Sarons** (Pink Salons), where customers pay for the amount of time they spend inside drinking and grabbing hostesses. The basic fee is 3,000 *yen* per half hour. Prices escalate with the activities you request. Pinku Sarons and Turkish baths (*torukoburo*) are clustered around train stations.

HOLIDAYS

Official holidays: New Year's (January 1-3), Adult's Day (January 15), National Foundation Day (February 11), Vernal Equinox Day (late March), Emperor's Birthday (April 29), Constitution Memorial Day (May 3), Children's Day (May 5), Respect-for-the-Aged Day (September 15), Autumnal Equinox Day (late September), Health and Sports Day (October 10), Culture Day (November 3), Labor Thanksgiving Day (November 23), New Year Holiday (December 28 and the following days).

• If a holiday falls on a Sunday, it's observed on Monday.

• On New Year's Eve be sure to eat *soba,* the buckwheat noodles that on this day are called *"Toshikoshi soba"* (seeing out the old year noodles). These long, thin noodles symbolize longevity.

• New Year's Day is the biggest celebration of the year. Houses are decorated with bamboo, pine boughs, and plum tree branches to symbolize longevity and energy for the new year. Temples and shrines are crowded with people making the obligatory *hatsumode,* or first visit of the year. On the second and third days of the new year, people make short visits to friends, relatives, and employers. Women wear their best *kimonos* and serve *o-mochi,* ceremonial rice cakes that everyone should eat. If you visit a Japanese home during these first days of the year, bring money in envelopes for the children. If you bring your children along, expect them (as well as yourself) to be offered *toso,* a special liquor made from vegetable extract, *sake,* and herbs.

- Just before New Year's, the Japanese exchange gifts and settle all debts. Look in department stores for the traditional packaged gift sets of foods, cooking oils, towels, and other items. If someone gave you a gift in the past, give them a gift of approximately equal value (a more expensive gift will embarrass them and lead to an escalated "gift war").

- On Adult's Day you can see young women wearing colorful new kimonos in parks and hotel gardens, being subjected to family photographers. This day celebrates the coming of age of anyone who has turned twenty that year.

- The Emperor's Birthday starts off the "Golden Week" of holidays (May 1, 3, 5). Many businesses close during this week.

- The Sanno Festival, although not an official holiday, is Tokyo's largest festival. It takes place every other year at the Hie Shrine on June 10-16. Near the shrine, in the Chiyoda area of Tokyo, you can see processions of palanquins (covered litters carried on poles) on June 15th.

- The Bon Festival, which features multitudes of lanterns to honor the souls of the dead, takes place throughout Japan on July 13-15. Folk dances to comfort the souls of the dead are performed in *yukata,* or cotton kimonos. Look for folk dancing in town squares or on the grounds of shrines.

- During the spring months, various cities host a number of festivals for fertility, such as Komaki-shi (May 15) and Jamochi-machi (June 15). These unusual festivals celebrate the sex organs and fertility. Don't be shocked to see large wooden phalluses parading around in the streets, or plays featuring simulated sex acts. These festivals have become big draws for foreign tourists.

- May Day (May 1) is observed by manufacturers, who close for the day. Service organizations remain open.

PRONUNCIATION

Vowels a, e, i, o, and u are pronounced as ah, eh, ee, aw, oo. Vowels with a bar over them should be pronounced the same but about twice as long.

The u at the end of a word is usually sounded very lightly if at all. Stress should be even for all syllables. Doubled consonants are doubled in speech; konnichi as kawn-neechi.

g = ng as in "singer"
ng = same as "g" above, but held longer
aw = "oe" as in "doe"

KEY PHRASES

English	Japanese	Pronunciation
Good morning	Ohayo gozaimasu	O-highyoh gaw-zighmahss
Good afternoon	Konnichi wa	Kawn-neechi-wah
Good evening	Komban wa	Kawm-bahn-wah
Good night	Oyasumi nasai	O-yah-soomi nah-sigh
Goodbye	Sayonara	Sighyo-nahrra
Please	Dozo	Dowzow
Thank you	Arigato	Ahrree-gah-tow
Excuse me	Gomen nasai	Gaw-mehn na-sigh
Don't mention it	Do itashimashite	Dow i-tahshee-mahshteh
Yes	Hai	High
No	Iie	Ee-eh
I understand	Wakarimasu	Wah-kahrree-mahss
I don't understand	Wakarimasen	Wah-kahrree-mahss-ehn
How much?	Ikura desu ka?	Eekoo-rra desska?
Does anyone here speak English?	Eigo-o hanasu hito imasuka?	Eh-ee-go-o hah-nah-sue hee-toe ee-mahs-kah?
Sir, Mr.	San (follows surname)	san
Madam, Mrs.	"	"
Miss	"	"

MALAYSIA
SINGAPORE

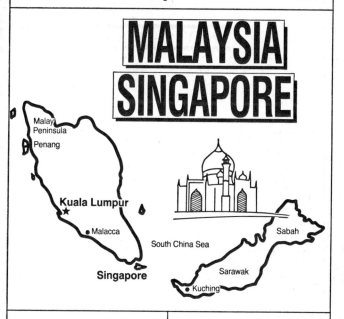

Malaysia and Singapore are multicultural societies composed of ethnic Malays, Chinese, and Indians. Both nations are former British colonies. For a short time after independence, the island of Singapore was part of Malaysia but in 1965 it broke away, led by its first and still only president, Lee Kuan Yew.

Singapore is very much the reflection of hard-working Prime Minister Lee: He doesn't smoke, so the government discourages smoking; he doesn't like long hair, so customs refuses entry to "hippie-types"; and he loves order and cleanliness, so the government slaps heavy fines on litterers, expectorators, and jaywalkers. Many of Singapore's historical relics have vanished under high-rises, and both visitors and residents complain that the republic has become too sterile. Still, tourists come away raving about the island's beauty, bargains, and people. The residents are predominately Chinese (76%), with some Malays (15%) and Indians and Pakistanis (7%).

In Malaysia only 54% of

the people are indigenous Malays (*bumiputras,* sons of the soil). The rest are of Chinese (35%) and Indian (10%) ancestry. In general the Malays control the government, and the Chinese control the economy. Although ethnically diverse, Malaysia is primarily a Muslim nation and most of its people follow Islamic customs in public. Remember that "Malaysian" is a political term referring to all citizens of the nation of Malaysia; the term "Malay" refers to a member of the Malay ethnic group.

MEETING PEOPLE

GREETINGS

(MALAY) Whenever you greet, leave, or pass people (especially the elderly), bow slightly to be polite.

- Malay men greet each other with a handshake. Devout Muslim women and elderly people seldom shake hands; they sometimes offer verbal greetings to men. Malays often shake hands with Western men and women, understanding that Westerners are unaware of Malaysian rules pertaining to handshakes. The most polite way for a Western woman to greet a Malay man is to nod her head and smile.

- To impress Malays with your understanding of their customs, greet them with the respectful *salam* gesture. Offer both hands to the other person and lightly touch the other person's outstretched hands. Then bring your hands to your breast as if to say, "I greet you from my heart." (Friends often make this gesture with only one hand.)

- A common greeting, especially in rural areas, is "Where are you going?" This is only a greeting, not a request for an answer, so the polite reply is "Just for a walk."

- When you introduce someone mention the older or more important person first. Mention a woman before a man.

- At a party the host might introduce you either to everyone or just to the people around you. In either case be sure to greet each person individually.

(INDIAN) Indians of the same sex usually shake hands in greeting. When introduced to an Indian man, a Western woman should either nod her head and smile or offer the *namaste* gesture, placing her palms together under her chin and making a slight bow (see Greetings in India chapter). A Western man should make the same gesture when greeting an Indian woman.

(SINGAPORE) Men and women of Singapore usually greet each other with a handshake. It's best for a man to wait for a woman to extend her hand.

- If you attend a party, you'll be introduced to everyone — but very quickly. You don't need to shake hands as you're whisked by.

Names and titles. (MALAY) Malays don't have surnames. They trace descent through their fathers and add the father's name onto the end of their own given name. A Malay man named Ali bin Isa, for example, might be the son of Isa bin Osman. Ali is his individual name, *bin* means "son of," and Isa is his father's name. A Westerner should address him as Mr. Ali or, in Malay, *Encik Ali.* (The Minangkabau people of Malaysia trace descent through their mothers rather than their fathers.)

- Malay women follow the same custom but use *binti* (daughter of) rather than *bin.* You should address a married woman named Zaitun binti Osman as Mrs. Zaitun or, in Malay, *Puan Zaitun.* Women who marry do not necessarily take their husbands' names; however, some do drop their fathers' names and replace them with their husbands'.

(CHINESE) Chinese names have three parts — the family name followed by a two-part given name. Always address a Chinese person as Mr., Mrs., or Miss followed by the family name. Address a man named Lee Kuan Yo, for example, as Mr. Lee.

(INDIAN) Most Indians of Singapore and Malaysia don't have surnames; instead, they place their father's initial before their own name. If a man's name card says that he's T. Manickavasagam, you can deduce that his name is Manickavasagam and his father's name began with a "T" (perhaps Thiruselvam). Address him as Mr. Manickavasagam.

- An Indian woman usually drops her father's initials when she marries and uses her husband's name (Mrs. Manickavasagam).

Correspondence. English is widely used as the language of commerce, and English salutations are the most common ("Dear Mr. Wang,").

(MALAY) If you prefer to use a Malay salutation (use it only for ethnic Malays), the usual titles of address are *Encik* for men, *Puan* for married women, and *Cik* for unmarried women. There are variations, however (for royalty, for example, or people who have completed a pilgrimage to Mecca), so choose carefully.

- Remember to address Malays by their given names preceeded by Mr., Mrs., Miss. Address Ismail Abdullah as Mr. Ismail.

- The Malay phrase for "Yours sincerely" is *Yang benar.*

(CHINESE, INDIAN) See the Correspondence sections of the China, Taiwan, and India chapters.

CONVERSATION

(MALAYSIA) Good conversation subjects: Your host's business or social achievements, places of mutual interest, football (soccer), Malaysian cultural history, and regional cuisines. Malaysians do not like to hear comparisons between their standard of living and that of the West.

- Subjects to avoid: Strife between Malaysia's ethnic groups, domestic or world politics, Israel (Malaysia is a Muslim country), and religion. Off-color jokes are risky because of Islamic fundamentalist influence in some areas (especially the east coast of the Malay peninsula).

- People might ask you what seem like very personal questions ("How much money do you make?" "What is your religion?"). They're just showing interest; ask the same questions of them. No one is obliged to give an honest answer.

(SINGAPORE) Good conversation subjects: Local cuisines and restaurants, favorite travel destinations, and your host's business success.

- Subjects to avoid: Discussions of a personal nature, local politics (or lack thereof), racial friction, spouses, and religion.

PHRASES TO KNOW

- English is widely understood and often used for communication between people of different ethnic groups. Malaysian (called "Bahasa Malaysian") is the same language as Indonesian except for some different vocabulary preferences. Malaysians use the Roman alphabet and phonetic spelling, so pronunciation is fairly easy. Sounds are always made the same way, and there are no accented syllables.

- A good phrase book for Bahasa Malaysian is the *Malay Phrase Book* written by Jh Ismail Ahmad and Andrew Leonki (Times Books International, Singapore, 1986).

CURRENCY

(MALAYSIA) The unit of currency is the *ringgit,* or Malaysian dollar (M$), which is divided into 100 cents (*sen*). One U.S. dollar is worth about 2.5 *ringgit* (August 1987 rates). Coins are available in 1, 5, 10, 20, and 50 cents and one *ringgit.* Notes are issued in M$ 1, 5, 10, 50, 100, and 1,000.

- Authorized money changers usually offer a better exchange rate than those of banks or hotels, but they often refuse to change traveler's checks.

(SINGAPORE) The unit of currency is the Singapore dollar (S$), which is divided into 100 cents. One U.S. dollar equals about 2.1 Singapore dollars (August 1987 rates). Coins are minted in 1, 5, 10, 20, and 50 cents and S$ 1 and 10. Notes are available in S$ 1, 5, 10, 20, 50, 100, 500, 1,000, and 10,000.

- Exchange rates vary

from bank to bank. Some banks add a service charge for foreign exchange transactions. Look for authorized money changers near Change Alley and Raffles Quay; they usually offer a better rate than those at banks.

• In both countries shops that cater to tourists accept credit cards and traveler's checks. Other shops, especially in rural areas, accept only cash.

ETIQUETTE

GENERAL MANNERS

• Compliments are appreciated but are usually denied out of modesty.

• Elderly people are accorded great respect. Invite them to take your seat on a bus, hold doors open for them, and don't smoke in front of them unless they invite you to do so.

• If someone laughs or smiles at what seems like an inappropriate moment, don't be surprised

or angry. A smile is used to cover embarrassment or shock as well as to show happiness.

• If people are sleeping or resting on the floor, never step over them, no matter how much of a hurry you're in.

• In Singapore if you receive a printed invitation to a dinner or social affair, be sure to respond in writing.

BODY LANGUAGE

• Public displays of affection are frowned upon. When you greet people, don't hug or kiss them. Avoid touching anyone of the opposite sex.

• The head is considered the home of the soul and should not suffer the indignity of being touched. Don't touch anyone's head, especially a child's.

• When you sit keep your feet flat on the floor, if possible. It's rude to expose the sole of your foot or shoe to anyone. If you do cross your legs, put one knee directly over the other. Don't cross your legs in the presence of elderly people.

• The feet are the lowest part of the body and are considered too dirty to be used for touching objects. Don't use them to move chairs, doors, or anything else.

- When you're standing talking to someone, putting your hands on your hips signifies anger.

- Hitting your fist into your other cupped hand is an obscene gesture.

- Beckon someone by extending your hand, palm down, and fluttering your fingers. Never gesture with one finger.

- Among Malays and Indians never use your left hand to eat, touch people, handle merchandise, or pass objects. It's considered unclean.

- When you yawn cover your mouth with your hand.

DRESS

- Malaysia and Singapore straddle the equator and are hot and humid most of the year. Clothing made of synthetic fibers will be quite uncomfortable. Instead, wear natural fabrics that breathe, such as cotton.

- The Malay peninsula has two monsoon seasons: June to September in the southwest, and October to March in the north-

east. Bring an umbrella.

MEN For business meetings wear a white shirt, tie, and slacks. Except for meetings with government officials, jackets aren't required because of the heat. Feel free to wear one, however, until you see that your counterparts are not. Jeans are fine for casual wear.

- If you're invited to a meal in a home, don't wear a suit — no one else will. If you're dining in a fine restaurant, inquire about the dress ahead of time; some restaurants require a jacket and tie.

WOMEN For business wear a sleeved blouse and skirt or a pantsuit. For casual wear your best bet is a skirt or slacks. Chinese women sometimes wear shorts, but Indian and Malay women don't. You're better off avoiding shorts, short skirts, or any other revealing clothing, especially in Malaysia. And don't go braless.

NATIVE DRESS Native batik shirts are acceptable garb for men even at elegant restaurants. Western men and women may feel free to wear local batik shirts and dresses; it will create a good impression.

- In Malaysia yellow is reserved for royalty (there

are quite a few members of the Malaysian royal family), so avoid wearing yellow clothing for formal events or when you visit the palace.

TEMPLES AND MOSQUES

- Before you enter most religious buildings, remove your shoes.

- When you enter a Chinese temple, remove your hat; you seldom need to remove your shoes. Enter through the right door and exit through the left, and don't step on any threshold. Dress and behavior in Chinese temples is more informal than in Hindu temples.

- In Hindu temples refrain from touching statues or paintings and from smoking. Women who are menstruating should not enter. (See India chapter for more information.)

- When you visit mosques observe the following customs:

Before you enter, get permission. Try to get a Muslim acquaintance to accompany you. The National Mosque and the Jame Mosque in Kuala Lumpur are two of the few mosques that are open to all visitors, including women.

Put on the robe supplied at the mosque entrance, and put your shoes in the racks provided. Women will be provided with head coverings to wear inside.

Women should be careful not to touch a man anywhere on the mosque grounds, or he'll have to redo a washing ritual.

Inside a mosque be careful not to walk in front of people who are praying, walk or stand on a prayer rug, or smoke.

Mosques don't contain pictures or other images of humans. They're forbidden by Islamic law.

PRIVATE HOMES

- Before you enter a home, remove your shoes. The hosts might politely insist that you keep them on, but if you can see that the family is not wearing shoes inside, take your own off.

- Usually hosts serve their guests tea or coffee. If you prefer ice water (usually safe in cities), a polite request won't offend your host.

(MALAY) Malays drop

in on each other unannounced. Just don't drop in on Muslim families between 6:00 and 7:30 P.M., the Muslim hours of evening prayer.

- When guests arrive the host usually offers them drinks. Receive your drink with both hands, your left hand lightly supporting your right.

- In some Malay homes you'll sit on chairs, but in others you'll sit on mats on the floor. When sitting on the floor, men should sit cross-legged and women should tuck their feet to the left.

- If you see a Muslim family's Koran (holy book), don't touch it. Be careful not to stand or sit on a prayer rug.

- If you stay in a Malay home, ask permission to leave the house before you go out.

- If you plan to stay for several days, bring gifts for the family but present them at the end of your stay, not the beginning.

- Daily baths are the norm, but expect cold water.

(INDIAN) Many Indians remove their shoes before they enter their homes; watch what the family members do. Even if shoes are worn in the house, never wear them in the kitchen or prayer room.

- Guests are usually entertained in the family room. Don't enter the kitchen (it's considered private), request a tour of the house, or take a tour on your own.

- Before you smoke, ask permission. If no one else is smoking, try to refrain. It's impolite to smoke in front of elderly people.

- If you stay in a home, say "I'll go and come back" when you leave the house. When someone else goes out, say "Go and come back." Never say just "Goodbye."

- If you're a house guest, bring a gift for the family, such as crafts from your home region or boxed sweets. Women will appreciate fabric for making the traditional dresses called *saris*. Try not to give money as a gift; if you do, never give an even amount.

(CHINESE) Some Chinese don't wear shoes in the house. Before you enter check to see what the household custom is.

- As in Indian homes it's impolite to take a tour or peek into the kitchen.

(SINGAPORE) Friends

and associates often drop in on one another unannounced, but if you don't know a family well, phone ahead. In any case don't visit just before meal time; the family will feel they have to invite you to stay.

- Before you enter look to see whether family members are wearing shoes inside. If they aren't, remove yours.

- If you visit for dinner, offer to help clean up after the meal. Your offer will usually be refused.

- If you make a phone call, always offer to pay.

- If you're staying for a few days, your hosts will expect you to bathe or shower every day, but be sure to ask permission each time.

PERSONAL GIFTS

- If someone gives you a gift, reciprocate with either a gift of about equal value or a dinner invitation.

- Use your right ("clean") hand to give someone a gift.

- Gifts are never opened when they are received or in the presence of the person who gave them.

(MALAY) Don't wrap a gift in white paper; white is associated with funerals. Most Malays (and some Indians) are Muslim, so don't give liquor, knives, pork, or images of dogs. Instead, stick with packaged fruit or sweets, perfumes, toys (but not toy dogs), or crafts from your home region.

(CHINESE) Good gifts are sweets, fruits, cakes in reusable tins, and crafts from your home region. Men appreciate Scotch or brandy. A gift consisting of a pair of items is the best choice; odd numbers signify unhappiness or separation. Don't give clocks, knives, scissors, handkerchiefs, straw sandals, or flowers. all of which have superstitions attached to them.

- Avoid white, black, or blue wrapping paper (these colors are associated with funerals). Have gifts wrapped locally to avoid a faux pas with symbolism. Paper with storks on it, for example, signifies a woman's death.

(INDIAN) Don't use black or white wrapping paper; instead, use green, red, or yellow. If your Indian acquaintance is of the Sikh religion, don't choose cigarettes, cigars, or ashtrays as gifts (smoking is forbidden among Sikhs). Liquor is also a risky choice.

TIPPING

(MALAYSIA) Restaurants: A 5-10% service charge is usually added to the bill except in small restaurants, which are often family run. Tipping is not the rule, but a small tip for unusually good service is appropriate.

- Hotels: A 5-10% service charge is added to hotel bills, but reward smiling service with a small tip (about 50 *sen*).

- Taxis: Tipping isn't customary, but many people let the driver keep small change (20 to 50 *sen*).

- Porters: Tip 1 *ringgit* per bag.

- Gas station attendants: Round the cost up to the nearest *ringgit.*

- Washroom attendants and other small services: Tip 50 *sen*.

(SINGAPORE) The government actively discourages tipping and prohibits it at the airport, in rest rooms, and in hotels and restaurants that add a 10% service charge.

- Restaurants: All restaurants except small, family-run eateries add a 10% service charge to your bill. No additional tip is necessary.

- Hotels: Offer bellhops up to a S$ 2 for extra services, but don't be surprised if they refuse.

- Taxis: Don't leave anything except the small change. Additional fees for extra people and luggage are posted inside the cab.

FOODS

MEALS

Breakfast (*makan pagi*): 7:00 to 8:00 A.M. *Nasi lemak,* rice cooked in coconut milk with fish, is a popular Malay breakfast. Other popular dishes are *curry ikan* (fish curry) and *katchandral* (corn dip). Indians often eat *roti* (pancake-like bread) dipped in one or two side dishes of puréed vegetables or yogurt. Chinese often have *yu-tiao* (fried bread sticks) and warm soy milk.

Lunch (*makan siang*): Noon to 1:30 P.M. Typical

main dishes are rice and a meat or fish curry. Side dishes usually include salted eggs, hot chili paste, and vegetables such as cabbage, spinach, and cucumbers. Dessert is seldom served; when it is it's usually fruit (mango, pineapple, or papaya). Tea accompanies the meal.

Dinner (*makan malam*): 7:00 to 9:00 P.M. Dinner is much the same as lunch.

WHERE TO EAT

- Singapore and Malaysia (especially the heavily Chinese areas) are bursting with sidewalk walk-in restaurants. It's hard not to find a good one.

- Except at finer restaurants in Singapore, you'll rarely find menus posted outside restaurants. Most moderate and lower-end eateries have menus posted on the wall. You might have to ask for an English menu.

- If you don't see a price posted for the dish you want, be sure to find out the price before you order.

- In Malaysia women who want to eat alone can usually find privacy and safety in hotel restaurants and bars.

- Hotels are also the best places for pastry shops, which are usually in the basement or on the ground floor.

- Local coffeehouses also serve pastries and desserts as well as soft drinks, coffee, or tea.

- The stalls that line some streets after dark are sources of foods you can't always find in restaurants. In Singapore they're licensed and inspected by the government and are usually safe. In Malaysia they're generally sanitary as well as incredibly inexpensive.

- Vegetarians can find Brahmin vegetarian restaurants in the Serangoon Road area of Singapore, and Buddhist Chinese restaurants in both Singapore and Kuala Lumpur. These eateries provide an inexpensive alternative for anyone. Be sure to try the vegetarian *satay* in Kuala Lumpur.

FOODS TO TRY

- Many Malays are Muslims and do not consume pork, shellfish, or liquor (at least, not in public). In general Malay food is spicy and rich. Rice is the staple, and coconut is used in many dishes. The most popular meats are seafood, chicken, and beef.

- Most Indians are Hindu and do not eat beef; many others are strict vegetarians. Indian food is well cooked (salads and uncooked vegetables are rare), and its outstanding characteristic is the complex and generous use of spices.

Specialties. (MALAY) Don't miss *satay,* bits of marinated beef, mutton, or chicken grilled on skewers. These "kebabs" are dipped in a spicy sauce and then in a peanut sauce when you eat them.

- Other main dishes are *otak otak* (white filet of fish on a banana leaf), *laksa asam* (noodles with meat and spices), *rendang* (meat prepared with spices and coconut milk and served with vegetables), *tahugoreng* (fried cubes of soybean curd and sprouts in peanut dressing), and *nasi biriyani* (fried rice with chicken).

- Soups of interest are *laksa,* a hot soup made with fish stock and noodles, and *soto,* a chicken soup with bean sprouts, rice, celery, and onion.

(INDIAN) Try the hot salad (*rojak*) made from shrimp paste, cuttlefish, hot chilies, and *balachan* (a type of curry).

- Other dishes to try are mutton *mysore* (bits of dry-fried lamb), *murtabak* (a flour pancake filled with fried green peas, minced meat, and eggs), and *sop kambing* (a spicy lamb soup). Don't miss *nasi biriyani,* a mixture of saffron, rosewater, and rice steamed in milk and meat stock.

(CHINESE) Regional Chinese cuisines that are widely available are Cantonese, Sichuan, Mandarin (Peking), Hakka, Teochew, and Hainan (see Specialties in China and Hong Kong chapters).

- Malaysia and Singapore both feature *nonya* cuisine, a unique hybrid of Chinese and Malay cooking. *Nonya* cuisine is hard to find outside of homes, but you might be in luck at a few restaurants or food stalls. Try *sambal,* a spicy prawn stew served with either rice or *nasi lemak,* rice cooked in coconut milk. And don't miss *mee siam,* thin rice noodles fried with vegetables, covered with peanut gravy, and served with a hard-boiled egg.

Beverages. In rural areas don't use ice or drink water unless you know the water's been boiled.

- The Chinese don't serve ice water because they believe that cold drinks are a shock to the body. They do, however, put ice in their beer.

- Tea is often served with condensed milk already added. If you don't want milk, ask for *teh-o*.

- Fruit juices (orange, papaya, and others) are widely available, usually packaged in small boxes. Puncture the box with the sharpened straw that's attached.

- Locally brewed Tiger Beer and Anchor Beer are widely acclaimed.

TABLE MANNERS

- If a restaurant is crowded ask someone if you can share their table; at medium-class restaurants, the waiter will ask for you. If you do sit with other people, you aren't expected to talk with them. They'll probably act as though you're not there.

- To get a waiter's attention, simply raise your hand. If necessary, wave it around. Never whistle, hiss, or shout, or gesture with one finger.

- Clearing your throat or blowing your nose at the table is intolerable to other diners. Go to the rest room instead.

- Many outdoor markets have food stalls and tables where you can sit to eat dishes purchased from several stalls. Take care not to mix the cutlery from a Muslim stall with that from a Chinese stall. Muslims don't want to use cutlery that has touched pork, a common ingredient in Chinese cooking.

Utensils. Malays and Indians eat both with their hands and with spoons. Follow the lead of your fellow diners. Remember, however, never to use your left (unclean) hand.

- If you're given a spoon and fork, hold the spoon in your right hand and the fork in your left. Use the fork to push food onto the spoon, then eat from the spoon. The food is cut into bite-sized bits, so you won't need a knife. When you finish put the fork and spoon down on your plate.

- The Chinese eat with chopsticks and porcelain spoons, using the spoons for the liquid part of soup and the chopsticks for everything else. (For information on how to use chopsticks, see the Utensils section under Hong Kong or Taiwan.)

- Indian food is sometimes served on a banana leaf. To indicate that you are finished, fold the leaf in two, with the fold toward you.

- At a lunch or dinner, you'll usually find four to six serving dishes in the middle of the table. You'll be given your own plate of rice. Use the serving spoon in each communal dish to put food on your plate, then mix the food with the rice.

- When you eat *satay* (grilled meat on skewers), use the skewers to spear and eat the rice cakes and garnishes.

- In a Malay home you'll be given a towel and a small bowl of water. Don't drink the water; use it to wash your hands.

- When you use a toothpick, cover your mouth with your free hand.

Dining with others. If you are invited out to dinner, don't expect to have drinks and appetizers before dinner. Let the host order all the dishes.

- If you invite others to a dinner, try to have an even number of people at the table to ensure good fortune.

- If someone offers you a drink, accept it with both hands, your left hand supporting your right and your right hand grasping the glass. Offer drinks the same way.

(MALAY) If you're invited to a Malay home for dinner, be on time. There are no appetizers or drinks beforehand, and the dinner is usually ready on time.

- If you're the guest of honor, expect to be seated either to the host's right or at the head of the table. In traditional homes the women will eat after the men are finished.

- If you have any dietary restrictions, tell your host discreetly before the meal. It's impolite to refuse any offers of food or drink. Even if you can't stand something, take at least a little bite. To refuse more helpings place your hand above your plate and say, "No, thank you."

(CHINESE) The Chinese throughout Southeast Asia follow similar eating customs. For more complete coverage of Chinese table manners, see the chapters on Hong Kong or Taiwan.

- The hosts usually sit opposite each other at a round table. The guests of honor sit facing the room entrance, to the left of the hosts.

- Before the meal starts the host usually offers a toast with wine. Raise your glass with both hands, the right hand holding the glass and the left hand supporting the right, and take at least a sip.

- Most Chinese just spit bones or seeds onto the tablecloth or the floor. Don't put them back on your plate or in your rice bowl.

- If you're given steamed filled buns (*baozi*), eat them with your chopsticks. Pick one up, dip it in soy sauce, and bite off a piece.

- Before you begin eating wait until your host invites you to start and begins eating.

- A Chinese host usually apologizes for the "miserable" meal you're receiving. Reply that the meal is more than adequate — it's wonderful.

(INDIANS) For more detail on Indian table manners, see the India chapter.

- Before and after a meal, always make a point of going to the washroom to clean up.

- When you serve yourself from a communal dish, don't let the serving spoon touch your plate (anything that touches someone's plate is tainted). For the same reason don't offer your leftover food to anyone, not even your spouse or children.

- Wait to begin eating until your host has begun and invited you to do the same.

- Indian women rarely drink, so don't offer them alcoholic beverages.

- After the meal expect to stay for about an hour for conversation.

Banquets. The Chinese love to offer banquets, especially in honor of visitors and business people. Always reciprocate with an equal feast before you depart. (For more information see the Banquet sections under China, Hong Kong, and Taiwan.)

ACCOMMODATIONS

Hotels. Before you register always ask whether a seasonal discount is available. Discounts are common during the monsoon season (November through April). Singapore has a glut of international hotels, so many offer discounts to attract customers.

(MALAYSIA) For very inexpensive (but often run-down) accommodations, look for Chinese hotels near train and bus stations. Many have rooms available for 10-20 *ringgit.* These hotels are spartan — just the essential furniture, with no complimentary toothbrushes or shower caps. Bathrooms (showers and squat-type toilets) are communal. A "single" has one double bed, and a "double" has two. You pay by the room, not by the number of people, so to save money pack several people into your room.

- Youth hostels are cleaner and even less expensive than the Chinese hotels, but are usually on the outskirts of town. Check your mattress for small bedmates before you lie down.

- Hotel restaurants automatically add a 10% government tax and a 10% service charge to the bill.

- Some hotels will not serve bacon or sausage for breakfast. Islamic beliefs forbid eating pork, so many Muslims refuse to either prepare pork or eat where it is prepared.

(SINGAPORE) You'll find inexpensive Chinese hotels scattered throughout Singapore. They're a good bargain except during the Chinese New Year, when rates go up.

- International tourist hotels are clustered around the Orchard Road and Padang areas.

Rest rooms. You'll find squat-type toilets (a cubicle with a hole in the floor) in small shops, rural homes, and inexpensive restaurants. In nicer homes these holes are modern ceramic flush toilets, but still of the squat type.

- Most rest rooms have a bucket of water or a tap next to the toilet. Malays and Indians use the water and their left hands to clean themselves after a bowel movement. You might want to carry toilet paper with you; it's seldom supplied.

TRANSPORTATION

PUBLIC TRANSPORTATION

- Malaysia prohibits smoking on most public transportation systems, including taxis.

Buses. It's polite to give your seat to an elderly person, male or female, before you give it to a younger woman.

(MALAYSIA) You can catch local buses at the many bus stands. Fares are based on distance, so tell the conductor your destination, then pay. On some buses you can't get change.

- Malaysians don't queue for buses. When you catch a local bus, or an inter-city bus without reserved seats, rush for the seats with everyone else. Secure your purse or packages before the door opens.

- Minibuses ply set routes in the larger cities and charge a standard fee (about fifty cents) from any terminal along their route.

- Inter-city buses are fast and scary. Look for bus stations near train stations and ferry terminals. Most seats are reserved, so check your ticket and get in the right seat. In some small towns the bus station is just a counter in a shop where buses make brief stops to pick up passengers. Either look for a bench on the sidewalk or ask locals where the bus stop is.

(SINGAPORE) The buses are very convenient and not too crowded. Signs are in English and bus stops are clearly marked. Buy a Minibus Guide in a bookstore. The route numbers and destinations of buses are posted at most bus stops. Tourists can get a special unlimited-travel ticket at hotel desks. No change is given on buses.

Trains. The railway system is extensive, and one route will take you from Singapore through peninsular Malaysia and on to

Bangkok, Thailand. Trains have first (air-conditioned), second, and third classes. You can book in advance through travel agents or at the train station. First- and second-class tickets can be purchased thirty days in advance.

- First- and second-class cars have numbered seats, and passengers must sit according to their ticket numbers. Avoid third class (seating is on a first-come, first-served basis, and is often very crowded).

- Sleeping berths are available on the trains and are especially helpful for the long trip through Malaysia. The first-class compartments hold two people and provide privacy. Second-class berths have only curtains for privacy.

- All trains have buffet cars. You can buy Malaysian food and drinks either at the buffet car or from attendants who go through all the cars selling snacks and drinks.

Taxis. (MALAYSIA) Taxis (*teksi*) are painted yellow on the top and black on the body and have registration numbers beginning with "H." Air-conditioned taxis (look for the rolled-up windows) cost an extra 20% or so. Taxis will wait for passengers by request, but charge a fee for each eight minutes. They also add a 50% surcharge for service between midnight and 6:00 A.M.

- In Kuala Lumpur taxis are metered and most drivers speak a little English. Outside the capital you must bargain the fare before you get in.

- A taxi coupon system designed to prevent overcharging is used for airport-to-city transportation. When you arrive check at either the airport information office or the coupon stand outside. The coupon booth will calculate your fare in advance. Don't give the coupon to the taxi driver until you reach your destination.

(SINGAPORE) Look for taxis at hotels and taxi stands. They're easy to catch except during rush hours or on the outskirts of the island. All taxis have meters, but be sure the flag drops when you get in. Almost all the drivers speak English and are honest.

Other transportation. In some Malaysian towns, especially around Penang, you can still find trishaws. The minute you get off the ferry in Penang, you'll be surrounded by trishaw drivers. Bargain the fare; never accept the quoted price.

DRIVING

(MALAYSIA) Renting either a self-drive car or a car and driver is quite easy, but be sure you get the fee in writing before you set out. Most of the roads are in good condition, but watch out for motorcycles. Driving in the cities can be frightening and dangerous.

- If you do drive yourself, you should know that staged "accidents" sometimes occur in which motorists are robbed and beaten.

- Traffic moves on the left side of the road, and steering wheels are on the right.

- Passengers in the front seat must wear safety belts.

- Parking is illegal along any street that has a continuous white line down the center.

- Along the major highways expect frequent toll gates. Tolls range from 50 *sen* to 1 *ringgit*.

- If you have car trouble, stay with your vehicle until a jeep from one of the many towing services arrives. Towing within a city costs about 50 *ringgit*.

(SINGAPORE) Singapore is so small, and public transportation is so convenient, you probably won't need to rent a car. If you do want to have your own transportation or plan to drive into Malaysia, bring an International Driver's License.

- Driving is on the left, as in Britain.

- Front-seat passengers must wear safety belts.

BUSINESS

BUSINESS HOURS

Business offices: (MALAYSIA) 8:00 A.M. to 5:00 P.M. Monday through Friday.

(SINGAPORE) 9:00 A.M. to 1:00 P.M. and 2:00 to 5:00 P.M. Monday through Friday, and 9:00 A.M. to 1:00 P.M. Saturday.

Banks: (MALAYSIA) 10:00 A.M. to 3:00 P.M. Monday through Friday, and 10:00 to 11:00 A.M. Saturday. In some states (primarily on the East coast) banks are open on Sunday and closed on Friday.

(SINGAPORE) 10:00 A.M. to 3:00 P.M. Monday through Friday, and 9:30 to 11:30 A.M. Saturday.

Government offices: (MALAYSIA) 8:30 A.M. to 4:45 P.M. Monday through Friday (with time off for prayer on Friday from noon to 2:30 P.M.), and 8:30 A.M. to 1:00 P.M. Saturday.

(SINGAPORE) 9:00 A.M. to 5:00 P.M. Monday through Friday, and 9:00 A.M. to noon Saturday.

- In Malaysia, Islamic influence on the East coast of the Malay peninsula and in other heavily Muslim states means that many offices and businesses close on Thursday afternoon and Friday, but open on Saturday and Sunday.

- A five-and-a-half-day work week is common, although some businesses operate six or seven days a week.

BUSINESS CUSTOMS

- The best time to visit on business is between March and July. Most

business people vacation from November through February. Avoid the Muslim Ramadan month in Malaysia; it varies from year to year, so check with a Malaysian consulate for current information. Also avoid the Chinese New Year (January or February).

- Before you leave home arrange appointments by telex a month ahead of time. If you're communicating by mail, start two months before your trip. Business people in Malaysia and Singapore travel frequently and are often out of the office.

- Business people tend to be cautious until they know something about both you and your company. A letter of introduction from a mutual acquaintance or a bank will help you establish relationships and get appointments. Without one your request for a meeting might not even be answered.

- When you choose a negotiating team for Singapore, it's more important that negotiators have a broad knowledge of company operations than that they be corporate officers.

- Negotiating business agreements requires

patience. Decision-making is slow, and your counterparts will want to get to know you before you begin. Plan on making follow-up trips.

- After you've agreed on a price, don't be surprised if your counterpart attempts to renegotiate — a common practice designed to gain concessions.

- Malaysia uses a quota system to ensure that ethnic Malays have a voice in the economy, which is largely dominated by ethnic Chinese. Every board of directors must have a *bumiputra,* or Malay.

Business etiquette. Exchange business cards after you're introduced. Most people in the business community speak English, so you don't need to have them printed in Malay, Chinese, or Indian. In Singapore some government officials do not have business cards.

- If a counterpart loses face because of your criticism or correction, you'll never be forgiven. Avoid embarrassing someone at all costs.

- Singapore is a cosmopolitan city, but it's still customary to consult a geomancer or *fengshui* man before opening a new office or building. He'll check to make sure that doors, windows, and furniture are arranged correctly and that all the other arrangements are suitable. If you do not consult a geomancer, local residents will blame any lack of success in the new office on your oversight.

Appointments and meetings. Westerners are expected to be on time, so be punctual and, if you're going to be late, phone.

In Malaysia punctuality is not as important as it is in the West. Appointments often start late because people are considered more important than schedules. In Singapore, you can usually get to appointments on time. The business center is compact, and getting to a meeting usually doesn't take very long.

- First meetings usually take place in conference rooms; subsequent meetings might take place in restaurants or coffee shops.

- In a meeting don't smoke unless you're invited to do so.

In Malaysia it's impolite to

MALAYSIA

209

smoke around members of
the royal family, many of
whom are in business or
attend meetings.

In Singapore the government is on an anti-smoking
campaign, so don't smoke
around government employees.

Business gifts and entertainment. (MALAYSIA)
Good choices for business
gifts are pens, engagement diaries, books for
business cards, and other
items with your company
logo on them. Don't give
liquor.

(SINGAPORE) Be careful
not to give any gift that
could be construed as a
bribe — the country is virtually corruption-free.
Government officials accept small tokens, but
don't try to give a gift to a
civil servant or any other
government employee.
Some companies are government-owned, and the
same rules apply to them.

• At the first meeting try
to avoid exchanging gifts,
but have one ready in
your briefcase in case
you receive one. Good
gifts are pens, executive
toys, leather or metal
holders for name cards,
and Scotch or brandy (except for Muslims).

• In either country if you
receive an invitation to
lunch or dinner, try to accept. It's very important
to establish a friendly relationship with your
counterpart in a nonbusiness context. The
first invitation to a meal is
usually issued after your
second meeting.

• If a dinner is social, and
business will not be discussed, invite spouses.
Most lunches are very
business-oriented, so
bringing a spouse is not
appropriate.

• Before you leave either
country, be sure to reciprocate any dinners or
banquets. Don't throw a
more expensive dinner
than your hosts did — it
would embarrass them.
Be sure to invite everyone present at your
host's dinner. Ask your
guests about their food
preferences (Muslims,
Hindus, and Buddhists
have different dietary restrictions).

TELEPHONES AND MAIL

Telephones. You'll find public phones in hotels, restaurants, and transportation centers, and on the street.

• To make long-distance or international calls, call from your hotel room — provided that the hotel's surcharge isn't too high. If the surcharge is high, call from the post office or telecommunications office. Most international-class hotels have direct dialing. Connections from the cities are quite good and easy to make.

(MALAYSIA) When you arrive at Kuala Lumpur's Subang Airport, use the free phones to make local calls. Phone directories are available in both English and Malay.

• At any public phone deposit 10 *sen,* then dial. Local calls have no time limit.

(SINGAPORE) Deposit 10 cents and dial. Your connection will cut off automatically after three minutes, and you'll have to redial.

• Local phone calls are free, so most shops and restaurants will let you use their phone if a pay phone isn't available.

Mail. (MALAYSIA) Mailboxes are painted red and can be found along the streets.

Post offices are open from 8:00 A.M. to 6:00 P.M. Monday through Friday and from 8:00 A.M. to noon Saturday.

(SINGAPORE) Post offices are open from 8:00 A.M. to 6:00 P.M. Monday through Friday and from 9:00 A.M. to 1:00 P.M. Saturday.

Packages entering or leaving the country are often x-rayed, so don't mail undeveloped film.

LEGAL MATTERS

Customs and immigration. In either country customs will confiscate pornographic materials and will want to screen any videotapes you're bringing into the country.

(MALAYSIA) You won't need a visa for stays of less than three months, but your passport must be valid for the next six months or you'll be denied entry.

- It's illegal to bring more than 10,000 *ringgit* into the country or to take more than 5,000 *ringgit* out. Declare your foreign currency when you arrive to avoid problems when you depart.

(SINGAPORE) If you're a man with very long hair, you might not be able to enter the country. At best, you'll be closely scrutinized.

Other restrictions. (MALAYSIA) The penalty for illegal drugs in Malaysia is death. Even recently, foreigners convicted of possessing or trafficking in drugs have been put to death.

(SINGAPORE) Singapore also takes drug offenses very seriously.

- Littering is punishable by large, on-the-spot fines. Spitting is considered littering. There are also heavy fines for smoking where No Smoking signs are posted.

- Jaywalking is illegal and is

fined both readily and heavily. Use only designated crosswalks.

SAFETY

Crime. Never try to bribe anyone. Both governments strictly enforce anticorruption laws.

- Beware of pickpockets on crowded buses.

(MALAYSIA) Beware of transvestites, especially in the area of Kuala Lumpur north of Jalan Tunku Abdul Rahman. These female impersonators and pickpockets prey on inebriated victims.

- Women traveling alone should be cautious in the heavily Muslim East Coast area, where men tend to harass single women.

(SINGAPORE) Singapore has a low crime rate, and tourists are rarely victims.

Health. (MALAYSIA) Drinking water is usually safe in the cities. In rural areas avoid unboiled water and ice. Stay away from dairy products, and don't eat fruit without peeling it.

- Government hospitals charge according to your ability to pay. Private hospitals are available but are usually more expensive.

- Medicines and health-care products are readily available in the cities.

(SINGAPORE) The water is generally safe.

- Hygiene is very good in Singapore. Exercise the normal precautions at street vendors.

- Health-care products and medicines are widely available.

SHOPPING AND ENTERTAINMENT

Shopping. In Malaysia shops are open from 9:00 or 10:00 A.M. to 7:00 P.M. every day.

- In Singapore shops are open from 10:00 A.M. to 7:00 P.M. Monday through Saturday. Many small shops stay open until 10:00 P.M. and are also open on Sunday.

- Before you buy a big-ticket item, check prices in at least three shops. Know the price of the item back home, and compare local prices by visiting department stores.

- Bargaining is expected for most items except in department and fixed-price stores. Bargain good-humoredly. If your offer is accepted, you're obliged to buy.

- If you buy any electronic item, obtain an international warranty. Make this requirement clear before you begin to bargain. Also make certain that you can use the item with your country's voltage and current.

Entertainment. In Malaysia Islamic influence discourages overt frivolity. Kuala Lumpur has barely enough bars to sustain a pub crawl. Most of them are in hotels.

- In Singapore night-time entertainment centers on the Orchard Road tourist hotels, which feature discos and bars on their premises. For a change of pace, try a Chinese nightclub. They come and go, so to locate one check with your hotel.

HOLIDAYS

Malaysian holidays:
New Year's Day (January 1), Birth of Prophet Mohammed (January), Federal Territory Day (celebrated only in Kuala Lumpur, February 1), Labor Day (May 1), Hari Hol (in Pahang only, May 7), Kadazan Harvest Festival (in Sabah only, May), and the Birthday of Dymn Seri Paduka Bainda Yang Dipertuan Agong, when people of all religions offer thanksgiving prayers (June 3).

- The celebrations of Prophet Mohammed's birthday feature processions and chanting of holy verses. A huge rally also takes place in Kuala Lumpur's Merdeka Stadium.

- Muslims celebrate Hari Raya Puasa in the tenth month of the Islamic calendar at the end of Ramadan, a month of fasting. After morning prayers at the mosque, Muslims put on new clothes and go out to patch up any quarrels they have with others. A common greeting at this time is, "Forgive me if I have done you any wrong."

- Hindus celebrate Deeppavali (Festival of Lights) in November to commemorate the victory of Rama over the demon king. Look for firewalking demonstrations at temples, and expect Hindu friends to invite you to their homes.

Singapore holidays:
New Year's Day (January 1), Chinese New Year (January/February), Chingay Procession (February), Good Friday (April), Hari Raya Puasa, (June 30, celebrates the end of Muslim Ramadan), National Day (August 9), Hari Raya Haji (October), Deepavali (October/November), and Christmas (December 25).

- The Chinese New Year is the most important holiday, and businesses close for a week. Fireworks are banned in Singapore, so most of the celebrations consist of special street markets, games, performances of singing and dancing, and parades of youths banging gongs. Families usually stay home to feast and wear new clothes to visit friends. Elders usually give children gifts of money (crisp new bills in even amounts) wrapped in red envelopes. Wearing black during this week is bad luck; the colors of good fortune are orange, gold, and red.

- The Dragon Boat Festival takes place in June and is one of Singapore's most colorful celebrations. Dragon-boat races highlight the festival, and people feast on *chang,* glutinous-rice dumplings.

- During the Muslim Ramadan (thirty days of fasting between sunrise and sunset), the stalls behind Sultan Mosque sell colorful cakes in the evening, and Singapore's Arab Street is lively after sundown.

KEY PHRASES

ENGLISH	MALAYSIAN	PRONUNCIATION
Good morning	Selamat pagi	S'lahmaht pahghee
Good afternoon	Selamat tengah hari	S'lahmaht teng-gah ha-ree
Good evening	Selamat malam	S'lahmaht mahlahm
Good night	"	"
Goodbye	Selamat tinggal	S'lahmaht teenggal
Please	Minta	Minta
Thank you	Terima kasih	T'rreema kasseehh
Excuse me	Minta maafkan	Minta ma'ahf-kahn
Don't mention it	Terima kasih kembali	T'rreema kasseehh k'm-bahlee
Yes	Ya	Yah
No	Tidak	Teedah'
I understand	Saya mengerti	Sahya m'ng-rr-tee
I don't understand	Saya tidak mengerti	Sahya teedah' m'ng-rr-tee
How much?	Berapa harganya?	Brr-ahpa hahrrga-nya?
Does anyone here speak English?	Bolehkah kamu beibalasa inggris?	Bo-leh-kah ka-moo bei-ba-la-sa en-gres?
Sir, Mr.	Encik	In-seek
Madam, Mrs.	Puan	Poo-ahn
Miss	Cik	Seek

PRONUNCIATION

A, i, o, and u are pronounced ah, ee, aw, and oo but are short.

e = neutral e as in "the"	s = ss (not z)
ai = ah-ee	ng = as in "singer"
au = ah-oo	ngg = as in "linger"
ua = oo-ah	

NEW ZEALAND

Auckland

North Island

★ **Wellington**

Christchurch

South Island

Dunedin

Given the country's scenic beauty, the most surprising thing about New Zealand is that so few people live there — only a little over three million. The original inhabitants were the Polynesian Maori (pronounced "Mau-ree," not "Mayori"); 300,000 Maori live in New Zealand today.

Virtually everyone else is of British descent.

When you're packing for your trip, don't forget that New Zealand is in the Southern hemisphere. Winter runs from June to August, and summer runs from December to February.

MEETING PEOPLE

- New Zealanders (or as they call themselves, "Kiwis") tend to be more reserved and formal than Australians but are very friendly and polite.

GREETINGS

- When you first meet someone, be polite and formal until you can sense a more informal feeling. Typical formal greetings are "How do you do?" or, after you've been introduced, "I'm very pleased to meet you."

- Use "hello" for informal greetings (some New Zealanders say "Gidday").

- New Zealanders greet each other with a handshake. In formal situations men should wait for a woman to offer her hand.

Names and titles. In formal situations use titles (Mr., Mrs., Miss, Dr.). The New Zealand social climate is becoming more casual, but it's still best to use first names only after you're invited to do so.

Correspondence. Formal or business letters are written in the English style, with a comma following the salutation ("Dear Mr. Rothchild,").

CONVERSATION

- Good conversation subjects: Sports (rugby, cricket), the weather, international politics, and New Zealand's beauty. New Zealanders love to talk about politics and are often opinionated. They'll let you know what they think. To hold up your end of the conversation, bone up on current affairs.

- Subjects to avoid: Very personal questions, domestic politics, and religion. If you end up talking about the nuclear arms issue, be prepared for some strong opinions — it's a hot political topic in New Zealand.

- Don't confuse New Zealand subjects with those of Australia. There's some rivalry between the two nations, so New Zealanders bristle when visitors lump them in with Australians.

- When you make observations about New Zealand, choose your words carefully. New Zealanders are quite sensitive about criticism from outsiders.

PHRASES TO KNOW

- English is the primary language of New Zealand. Even so, many words will be unfamiliar to English-speakers from other countries (or have unfamiliar meanings). Quite a few Maori words have also found their way into New Zealand English. It's difficult to understand the nuances of using "New Zealandisms" correctly, so stick with your own version of English.

CURRENCY

- The unit of currency is the New Zealand dollar (NZ$), which is divided into 100 cents. (New Zealand switched from the British system of pounds in 1966.) One U.S. dollar is worth about 1.7 New Zealand dollars. Coins are issued in 1, 2, 5, 10, 20, and 50 cents. Notes come in denominations of NZ$ 1, 2, 5, 10, 20, and 50.

- Many banks require a day's notice to convert New Zealand dollars into foreign currency, so check with the bank well before you leave the country.

- Credit cards are widely accepted.

- If you use traveler's checks, you'll get the best exchange rate at banks. (Hotels and stores offer rates very much in their own favor.)

ETIQUETTE

GENERAL MANNERS

- In general New Zealanders are friendly but reserved. They might wait for you to approach them, but once you do they respond warmly.

- Keep your voice low. New Zealanders speak fairly quietly and consider loud speech rude and irritating.

- If you see a friend on the street, you may wave from a distance.

- If people excuse themselves to "spend a penny," don't tag along. They're heading for the rest room.

- Chewing gum or using a toothpick in public is impolite.

- Before you photograph anyone, ask permission — especially if you want to photograph Maoris (many object).

BODY LANGUAGE

- If you can't suppress a yawn, cover your mouth.

- In case you win your rugby match, note that the "V" for "Victory" sign (first and second fingers held up and apart) is obscene.

DRESS

- When you choose your wardrobe, remember that the seasons are reversed from those in the Northern hemisphere. Even for the summer (December-February) take windbreakers — the evenings tend to be cool.

- New Zealand is relatively

formal, even at sport. If you play tennis wear white tennis clothes. For golf women should wear skirts, not shorts.

- Some of the finest restaurants require men to wear a jacket and tie and women to be dressed well.

MEN For business appointments wear a conservative suit and tie (but don't be surprised to see some businessmen wearing shorts, a shirt, a tie, and knee socks to work). For formal functions wear a suit and tie (it doesn't have to be as conservative as the day suit). If you're invited to a home for dinner, ask how formal it will be. Many men wear a jacket and tie to such affairs, but open-necked shirts are becoming increasingly common.

WOMEN For business appointments wear a dress, a blouse and skirt, or a pantsuit. For dinner in a home, wear a skirt or dress.

PRIVATE HOMES

- New Zealanders love to entertain at home, so don't be surprised if you receive a dinner invitation. If you receive an invitation to "supper," it means a late-evening snack (usually small sandwiches and tea), so eat before you go.

- If you know a family well, feel free to drop in unannounced. The best time is around 3:00 or 4:00 P.M., when tea is served.

- If you visit a home, you may bring flowers or a gift, but it's not expected. It's polite to bring a gift if you're invited for dinner. Good choices are chocolates or packaged sweets for the hostess and whiskey or imported beer for the host.

- After dinner offer to help clean up and do dishes. Your offer will probably be refused.

- If you make any long-distance phone calls, offer to pay for them. There's no charge for local calls.

- To avoid embarrassment don't praise an item of decor excessively. You might receive it as a gift.

- If you stay with a family, find out whether hot water has to be heated every time someone takes a bath.

PERSONAL GIFTS

- A good gift for teenagers is a T-shirt with a foreign university logo. Adults appreciate wines, handicrafts from your home region, and packaged foods from overseas.

TIPPING

- Restaurants and hotels: Tipping is not customary unless the same person provides good service several times. Even then some service people might refuse a tip. Hotel and restaurant bills don't include service charges because their employees don't rely on tips for their income. In very touristy areas tipping is becoming increasingly common.

- Taxis: Tip drivers only if they help with a great deal of luggage.

- Porters: Tip 25 cents per bag.

FOODS

MEALS

Breakfast: 7:30 to 8:30 A.M. Cooked breakfasts are hearty; typical fare is cereal or fried eggs, grilled tomatoes, and bacon. In the winter New Zealanders like porridge with cream. Sandwiches made of Vegemite (a salty spread made from yeast extract) and toast are often provided.

Lunch: Noon to 1:00 P.M. Lunch is usually a light meal of salads, sandwiches, or a hot pie. Toast is usually served, but cold and with the crust removed.

Dinner: 6:00 to 8:00 P.M. This is the main meal of the day and is often called "tea." A typical dinner has a meat such as lamb, a vegetable dish, potatoes, and a dessert such as pudding or fruit pie. A light supper is sometimes served in the late evening.

WHERE TO EAT

- You can find good breakfasts at bed-and-breakfast guesthouses.

- For brunch try one of the many tearooms, which serve hot pies, meat-filled rolls, baked beans, and sausages.

- A typical restaurant dinner includes an appetizer, soup, main dish, dessert, and beverage. An "entree" is an appetizer, not a main course;

entrees tend to be pricy. Most restaurants stop serving dinner between 8:00 and 10:00 P.M.

- Restaurants that have a sign outside saying "licensed restaurant" can serve alcohol with your meal at any hour. If the sign says "BYO," the restaurant can't provide liquor, but you can bring your own wine and they'll serve it (for an uncorking fee). These unlicensed restaurants are cheaper.

- Licensed restaurants or hotel bars can serve you a drink with a meal at anytime. They can serve drinks with no meal only between 11:00 A.M. and 10:00 P.M. weekdays (11:00 P.M. Saturday). They are closed on Sunday.

- Pubs are good places to eat almost any time of the day, although they close on Sunday. They serve cold sandwiches or hot plates of fish or lamb. You can find inexpensive lunches at the pubs known as "bistros."

- Fish-and-chips shops are everywhere. Many serve shark but call it "lemon fish" or "flake." If you want catsup with your chips (french fries), ask for "tomato sauce." You can get catsup in

New Zealand, but it's quite different from the American version.

- For a snack and something to drink, pop into a coffee shop or tea shop, where you can choose meat pies, salads, fish, and sandwiches from display cases. They also serve sweets, buns, coffee, and tea as well as complete lunches.

- For a quick bite look for pie carts set up outdoors, usually in the town square. They serve bacon-and-egg pies, steak-and-kidney pies, sausages, and potatoes.

- If you want a meal "to go," ask for a "take-away."

FOODS TO TRY

- New Zealand is moving toward a cuisine of its own, but most foods are still quite British in flavor. Mutton, lamb, beef, fish, pork, and venison from deer farms are very popular. New Zealanders consume more meat per capita than any other people in the world.

Specialties. Lamb is very popular in all its varieties. Try lamb spare ribs or "hoggett," an older lamb with more flavor.

- Meat pies are very popular. You can find them in restaurants, pubs, and take-out shops. Minced meat and beef and kidney are favorites.

- Try New Zealand's fresh seafoods — whitebait (young smelt), snapper, or sea trout. "John Dory" is a general term for any fish with a large dorsal fin.

- For a snack or at teatime, try scones and "piklets," cold pancakes served with jam or whipped cream.

- For dessert try the many puddings, Pavlova (a large baked meringue with whipped cream and fruit), or the fruitcake-like Dundee cake.

- Availability of specific fruits and vegetables depends on the season more than it does in North America, but a variety is available year-round. Try aubergines (eggplants) or courgettes (tiny zucchinis). Globe artichokes, asparagus, and avocadoes are quite popular and inexpensive.

- Fruits and vegetables unique to New Zealand are *kumara* (a waxy sweet potato), *tamarillo* ("tree tomato," a yellow or red fruit eaten either raw or cooked), *babaco* (a papaya-like fruit that tastes like a banana), and *feijoa* (a round fruit with a unique taste). Although not unique to New Zealand, kiwi fruit is the "national" fruit. It's often served mixed with strawberries.

- When you order hamburgers or sandwiches, they'll automatically have red beets (called "beetroot") on them. If you don't like beets, be sure to say "No beetroot, please" when you order.

Beverages. If you want ice water at a restaurant, you'll have to ask for it. It isn't usually served with meals.

- Tea with milk and sugar is served at every meal. For most people it replaces coffee. Morning and afternoon tea breaks are common. New Zealand ranks third in the world in per-capita tea consumption.

- A "cuppa" is a cup of coffee or tea. A "fizzy" is a carbonated drink.

- New Zealanders drink a lot of chilled beer, and it has regained respectability as a mealtime drink. Note, however, that some New Zealand beers have twice the alcohol content of American beers. Domestic wines and gin-and-tonic are also popular drinks. Beer and wine are served throughout the meal.

- Try New Zealand's light, fruity white wines. Although the country does produce red wines, locals prefer white wines by a margin of six to one.

- If you're drinking beer with four or five people, you can save money by ordering a "jug of draft," which holds five eight-ounce glasses of beer.

- If you don't wish to drink alcohol, order a fruit cordial (concentrated fruit syrup in water) or "Lemon and Paeroa," a lemon-flavored mineral water.

TABLE MANNERS

- Pay the wine steward separately for drinks; they're not usually added to the meal bill.

Utensils. New Zealanders eat continental style, holding the fork in the left hand and the knife in the right.

- Use your fork to eat the small, shallow pies called "tarts." You may eat tea cakes with your fingers (watch how your companions are eating them).

• Napkins are called "ser-viettes" in New Zealand.

Dining with others. If you're invited to dinner, be punctual. The meal will be ready at the specified time. Cocktails and appetizers are not usually served.

• Communal dishes are uncommon. Usually food is delivered in individual bowls or arranged on your plate.

• Don't talk too much during the meal. New Zealanders save most of the conversation for after the meal.

• Before you smoke at the table, ask permission. Some people smoke between courses as well as after the meal.

• A drink is often served after rather than during the meal, but you may request it during the meal if you prefer.

• Coffee and tea are served after the meal, and people talk for about an hour before they leave.

ACCOMMODATIONS

Hotels. New Zealand families usually vacation at Christmas and into January, so if you're planning to visit at this time, book accommodations well in advance. You'll also have to pay the highest seasonal rates.

• The off season is May through September. Always ask whether a discount is available during this season.

• Check-in time is usually 2:00 P.M.; check-out time is usually 10:00 A.M.

• People might ask you what "pub" you're staying in. The word "pub" often means "hotel" — a situation that arose when regulations started requiring public houses to have rooms for rent in addition to their more profitable bars.

• Few hotels and guesthouses add a service charge to your bill, but some add a small "linen charge" to cover laundering costs if you're only staying one night.

- Washcloths are seldom provided, except in the international chains.

- Many hotels provide a complimentary bottle of milk in each room.

- For inexpensive accommodations with a friendly atmosphere, try a motel flat. Each room in these owner-operated places has a lounge, a fully equipped kitchen, a bath, and a bedroom with linens. Few provide maids, so guests are expected to clean up after meals and before they leave.

- You can find bed-and-breakfast accommodations in many areas; they feature a shared bath and a good breakfast. Some include dinner with the room, and some serve meals only to guests, so ask for details before you book.

- If you're traveling by car, try a farm holiday. Some farm families open their homes to tourists who want to see what dairy, cattle, sheep, or high-country farming is all about. The daily cost usually covers a bed, dinner, and breakfast. Check with the tourist office for locations and booking arrangements.

Rest rooms. Rest rooms are all of the modern type. A "bathroom" is a room with a bath and basin, usually separate from the toilet. The toilet is often called a "cloakroom."

TRANSPORTATION

PUBLIC TRANSPORTATION

Buses. You can find maps of local bus routes at kiosks at the city bus centers. Most local bus authorities offer unlimited travel passes good for one day. You can buy them from the bus driver.

- Long-distance buses are very comfortable but make many stops for rest room visits (called "wee-tea stops") and package deliveries. Reserve seats in advance, especially during the summer (December through February).

- On buses men should give their seats to women who are standing. Children are required by bus company regulations to stand and allow adults to be seated if there aren't enough seats. If they don't they must pay full fare.

Taxis. Taxis don't cruise for hire; instead, they operate from stands. They are on call twenty-four hours a day, and in some cities you can hail them on the street. If you phone for a taxi, you'll pay a small surcharge.

• Taxis in some cities have meters, but in some small towns they operate on a flat-fee basis. Don't try to bargain the fare. Taxi fares usually have additional charges for night and weekend trips and extra luggage. Find out the rate before you set out.

Trains. Trains are ideal for traveling around the country. They have no separate classes, but some have sleeper cars and dining cars. Book in advance either through travel agents (even those overseas) or at train stations.

• If you plan to do a great deal of train travel, buy a Travelpass (also good for the inter-island ferry), which permits you to travel for about half the usual fare. Some versions of the Travelpass (especially for travel dur-

ing December and January) must be purchased overseas before you arrive. Check with your travel agent.

• The "Silver Fern" train between Auckland and Wellington has a hostess to serve refreshments and a guide to point out the sights.

Other transportation. To travel between islands (there are two main islands), use the inter-island steamers. They're sometimes sold out, especially in December and January, so book in advance. They have no separate classes but do have bars and cafeterias.

DRIVING

• If you're over 20 years old, self-drive car rental is easy (but expensive). Just bring your driver's license or, preferably, an International Driver's License. All rental agencies offer comprehensive insurance coverage; third-party personal insurance is compulsory. The law prohibits anyone not mentioned in the rental agreement from driving the car.

• Driving is on the left, as in Britain, so cars are right-hand drive.

- Wearing seat belts is compulsory.

- Maximum speed limits are 100 kilometers per hour on highways and 50 km/hr in cities. A sign that says "L.S.Z." (Limited Speed Zone) means the speed limit is 100 km/hr unless safety conditions dictate a lower speed. you'll usually see L.S.Z. signs on the edges of towns or cities.

- Always yield to traffic approaching from the right.

- Drunk driving is severely punished, and breathalyzer and blood tests are compulsory. If you're intoxicated it's illegal even to sit in a parked car with keys in your possession.

- New Zealand's cities have one of the highest traffic-to-population ratios in the world, so driving — although well-regulated — can be congested. Parking spaces are hard to find in the cities.

- Ask what kind of gas the car uses. More and more cars are being fitted for condensed natural gas or liquid petroleum.

BUSINESS

BUSINESS HOURS

Business offices: 8:00 or 9:00 A.M. to 4:30 or 5:00 P.M. Monday through Friday.

Banks: 9:00 or 10:00 A.M. to 4:00 P.M. Monday through Friday.

Government offices: Same as business offices.

BUSINESS CUSTOMS

- The best times to come to New Zealand on business are from February through May and during October and November. December and January are full of holidays; vacationing business people and tourists fill the hotels. Most workers in New Zealand are entitled to three or four weeks of vacation every year.

- Arrange meetings by telex or phone about three weeks before you come to New Zealand.

- The pace of business is

slightly slower than in North America but faster than in Australia. The New Zealand business atmosphere is also more formal than that of Australia.

Business etiquette. When you're dealing with New Zealand business people, don't ask your counterparts about hierarchies or rank, especially in a group setting. New Zealanders have a passion for equality and don't react well to drawing distinctions between people.

• To be able to converse intelligently with New Zealand businessmen, learn a little about rugby and cricket. They'll be impressed if you know something about their favorite sports.

Appointments and meetings. Punctuality is very important, so always be on time for meetings or even a few minutes early.

• Your first meeting will probably take place in the private office of the person you're meeting. As the meeting starts you'll probably be served tea or coffee.

• Subsequent meetings might be held over lunch at a hotel restaurant.

Business gifts and entertainment. Business people don't usually exchange gifts at a first visit or business meeting.

• Overseas visitors are usually invited out to dinner by their New Zealand hosts. The invitation usually includes spouses, and no one discusses business. Lunches are for business.

TELEPHONES AND MAIL

Telephones. Public telephone booths (call boxes) are found on many streets. Also look for the red phones in restaurants, hotels, and shopping centers.

• To make a local call from a pay phone, deposit ten cents and dial. If there's no answer push the return button labeled "B." If there is an answer, push button "A." Local calls have no time limit.

• Telephone dials have the numbers in reverse order — the "1" is where the "0" would be on a North American phone.

- A ring is a *Burr-Burr-Pause-Burr-Burr* signal. A busy signal is a *Buzz-Pause-Buzz.*

- Dial 111 for emergency assistance.

- Overseas and long-distance calls are easy to make from hotels and post offices. Most hotels require you to place long-distance and international calls through the switchboard operator. International direct-dialing is available at other phones.

Mail. Post offices are open weekdays from 9:00 A.M. to 4:00 P.M.

LEGAL MATTERS

Customs and immigration. Canadians and Commonwealth citizens require only temporary entry authority, obtained when they arrive, to stay up to six months. U.S. citizens can obtain temporary permits for stays of up to thirty days when they arrive. Before you travel

check current regulations with your travel agent.

- You may bring any amount of domestic or foreign currency into or out of the country.

Other restrictions. People under twenty years old may not enter pubs. (Some pubs don't welcome women, either.) The minimum drinking age in licensed restaurants is eighteen.

SAFETY

Crime. The crime rate is lower than in most Western countries. Women traveling alone or hitchhiking should be careful.

Health. Water throughout the country is safe to drink.

- Medications, toiletries, and medical care are readily available.

- New Zealand sunshine can be very brilliant; you can get sunburned even in low temperatures. Take along a good sunscreen lotion.

SHOPPING AND ENTERTAINMENT

Shopping. Shop hours are 8:30 or 9:00 A.M. to 5:00 or 5:30 P.M. Monday through Friday, and until mid-afternoon on Saturday. Shops stay open until 9:00 P.M. at least one night a week, but the day varies from city to city. Most tourist shops and attractions are open seven days a week.

• Prices in tourist areas are always fixed; bargaining is virtually unknown. For unusual buys look for sheepskin products, Maori woodcarvings (especially in the East Cape area), and jade (called "greenstone").

Entertainment. Nighttime entertainment is generally limited to drinking in pubs, eating, and going to theaters and musical events. Many restaurants and pubs feature live entertainment or large-screen movies. Both Wellington and Auckland have free tourist papers that list arts and entertainment events.

HOLIDAYS

Holidays: New Year's Day (January 1), Waitangi Day (February 6), Good Friday and Easter Monday (April), Memorial or ANZAC Day (April 25), Queen's Birthday (first Monday in June), Labor Day (fourth Monday in October), Christmas (December 25), Boxing Day (December 26).

• Each province has an Anniversary Day to commemorate its founding. If the holiday is on a Saturday or Sunday, the following Monday is also a holiday. The dates are as follows: Auckland (January 29), Canterbury (December 16), Hawke's Bay and Marlborough (November 1), Nelson (February 1), Northland (January 29), Otago and Southland (March 23), Taranaki (March 31), Wellington (January 22), and Westland (December 1).

• Nearly everything (including most restaurants and attractions) closes down on holidays. Plan accordingly.

KEY PHRASES

North American English	New Zealand English
New Zealander	Kiwi
Male friend	Mate
Good man	Dag
Funny person (sense of humor)	Hard case
Body shop	Panel beaters
Buy someone a beer	Shout
Car accident	Prang
Drug store	Chemist
Food	Tucker or kai
French fries	Chips
Sweater	Jumper
Toilet	Cloakroom
Two weeks	Fortnight (common)
Truck	Lorry
Umbrella	Brolly
It'll be OK	She'll be right

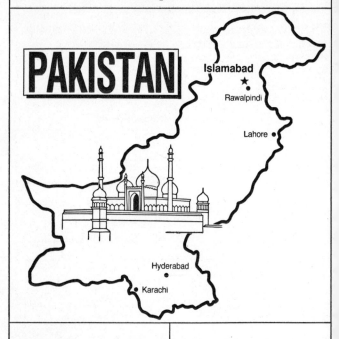

Most outsiders hurry through Pakistan. Business people conduct their business and leave. Tourists, the few that there are, scurry on to India. Even in the heyday of the overland Asian journeys, travelers rushed through Pakistan from Afghanistan to India as though it were a transit lounge. It's a mistake, however, to miss the stunningly beautiful mountains of northern Pakistan, the Moghul masterpiece of the city of Lahore, or the ancient city of Hyderabad.

The nation of Pakistan was born when British India was partitioned in 1947. In seven weeks Sir Cyril Radcliffe drew a line separating Muslim Pakistan from Hindu India — a difficult task, since in some areas the two groups were equally distributed. The result was a disaster, the partition resulting in mass migration, violence, and many thousands of deaths.

Pakistan is home to a number of ethnic groups that differ in both physique and culture. Several languages are spoken, Urdu being the major local languages.

Virtually all the ethnic groups, however, share the Islamic religion and the same customs followed by Muslim people in other nations. In recent years Islamic fundamentalism has been on the rise, and the government has incorporated traditional Islamic law into the legal code. The Islamic code of conduct can be quite stifling, especially for women. Some women are still killed by their families if they're found talking with male strangers.

Visitors find the Pakistanis, despite their restrictions, more outgoing and friendly than their Indian neighbors.

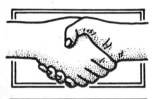

MEETING PEOPLE

GREETINGS

- The most common greeting among men is a handshake, although close friends sometimes embrace. Most women don't shake hands. Foreign men should shake hands with men but not with women (unless a woman offers her hand first). A Western woman should feel free to initiate a handshake with a Pakistani man.

- Even if a Pakistani woman shakes hands with a man, the man should not touch her arm or touch her in any other way. In Pakistan members of the opposite sex don't touch each other in public.

- Pakistanis of the same sex embrace when they haven't seen each other in a long time.

- A Pakistani host greets a guest with *"A-Salam-Alaikum."* The guest should reply, *"Alaikum-A-Salam."*

- Most Pakistanis you will meet in formal situations understand English greetings.

- At a party your host will introduce you to all the guests.

Names and titles. Pakistani names have up to four basic parts (a personal name, a patronymic, a caste name, and an honorific):

The personal name might be either one word (Omar) or something more elaborate (Mohammad Zia-ul-Haq).

The patronymic, the father's name, is sometimes

used as part of a person's full name. The caste or tribal name is often part of a person's full legal name.

People qualified to use honorifics often use them in addition to or in place of the caste name. There are many honorifics and religious titles, for example, *Hafiz* (one who has memorized the Koran) and *Haji* (a layman who has made the pilgrimage to Mecca).

- To address a Pakistani with a title, you may use the caste or religious title followed by the word *sahab* (*Haji sahab*).

- Foreign visitors are not expected to comprehend the complicated use of titles, so for most situations use Mr., Mrs., Miss, and Dr. (for physicians).

Correspondence. Business and formal communications with foreigners are usually in English. A typical English salutation ("Dear Mr. Zia,") is acceptable.

CONVERSATION

- Good conversation subjects: Pakistan's beauty, culture, and crafts, and sightseeing tips.

- Subjects to avoid: Domestic politics, the Islamic religion, relations with India, the topic of Israel. Pakistani men might seem to talk a lot about sex, but Westerners should steer clear of the subject (many Islamic fundamentalists don't appreciate the topic).

- Pakistanis often ask very personal questions ("How much do you make?" "Why don't you have children?"). Women might be grilled on why they are traveling alone. If you don't want to answer these questions seriously, give a light answer and start asking questions of your own.

- If you speak about Mohammed, the founder of Islam, call him "The Prophet" or "The Prophet Mohammed." Don't refer to him only by name. And don't refer to Muslims as "Mohammedans"; their religion is "Islam."

PHRASES TO KNOW

Urdu is the official language of Pakistan; English and Bengali are also widely used. Urdu is almost identical to Hindi, one of the official languages of India. The main difference between Urdu and Hindi is that Urdu is written in

Arabic script, while Hindi is written in the Sanskrit alphabet. Urdu also contains a number of words derived from Arabic.

CURRENCY

• The unit of currency is the Pakistani *rupee,* abbreviated "Rs" (plural) or "Re" (singular), which is divided into 100 *paisas.* One U.S. dollar is worth about 16.8 *rupee*s (August 1987 rates). Coins come in denominations of 1, 5, 10, 25, 50, and 100 *paisas.* Notes are in 1, 5, 10, 50, and 100-*rupee*s.

The *rupee* used to be divided into 16 *annas,* a term you might still hear occasionally, especially in markets.

• When you enter the country, hide most of your easily-exchanged hard currency. Customs officials and police occasionally use threats to obtain a bribe or "tax" visitors. This is not a problem at the international airport.

• When you receive change count it carefully and refuse tattered bills (you might have trouble using them elsewhere).

• International credit cards are accepted in tourist hotels and restaurants. Some shops don't accept traveler's checks.

ETIQUETTE

GENERAL MANNERS

• Pakistani Muslims are very religious and take time for prayer — wherever they are — five times a day. Don't interrupt someone at prayer.

• When you eat or hand objects to others, use your right hand. The left hand is considered unclean.

• Pakistani women are closely protected and must be very conservative in dress and behavior. A few observe the custom of *purdah,* being seen only by their husbands and close family. Photographing a Pakistani woman is risky.

• Men take priority in Pakistan. Visiting women

must be assertive in shops, banks, and offices, or men will be helped first and get the best selections. Pakistani women are sheltered from situations that require self-reliance.

- Pakistani men are often quite forward towards Western women. Intentional bumping in crowds is not uncommon; women should either avoid crowds or wear a lot of clothing. Women should be careful not to give men the slightest encouragement, even unintentionally. A smile, a wink, or a touch on the arm might be misinterpreted as an invitation for more.

- Most parties and dinners are segregated by sex, with the men and women in separate rooms. Men should not talk to a Pakistani woman for very long. Her husband might resent it.

- If you have a dinner or party, don't serve liquor, pork, or shellfish to your Muslim guests. Islam forbids their consumption.

- Before you photograph anyone, ask permission.

BODY LANGUAGE

- Staring is common in Pakistani culture. Don't consider it rude or threatening.

- When you sit on the floor, tuck your feet under you. It's not polite to either point your foot at someone or expose the soles of your feet or shoes.

- A clenched fist is an obscene gesture.

DRESS

- Pakistani dress always covers the wearer's legs. Shorts, skimpy dresses, and other types of revealing clothing are considered in poor taste.

- Bring lightweight clothing for the hot, dry season (May-June) and the monsoon season (July-August).

MEN For business wear a suit and tie during the cooler months (October through March) and for meeting with government officials anytime of year. For other business meetings during the summer months, wear either a white shirt, tie, and dress pants or a safari suit. For formal receptions and social affairs, wear a dark suit (no one wears tuxedos).

For casual wear jeans (but not T-shirts) are fine.

WOMEN For all occasions dress conservatively and avoid exposing your upper arms or your legs (it's considered immoral and could be dangerous). Pakistani men aren't accustomed to seeing women expose much of their bodies. Never wear a bikini except at hotel swimming pools or hotel beaches.

- For business wear dressy pantsuits or long dresses. Never wear a knee-length skirt. For formal occasions wear a long dress. For casual occasions jeans (but not T-shirts) are acceptable. If your jeans are tight, wear your shirt outside them rather than tucked in.

NATIVE DRESS The traditional apparel is the *shalwar-kameez,* which includes trousers, a tunic, and a stole. The style, color, and jewelry all vary.

- Most Pakistani businessmen in the past wore Western wear, but a recent government edict requires that all government employees wear traditional dress. This traditional attire is rapidly replacing Western attire throughout the country.

- Western women may wear the Pakistani woman's traditional pants and blouse (*shalwar* and *kameez*), but not for business.

MOSQUES

- When you visit mosques and holy places, remove your shoes. Both men and women should wear clothing that completely covers their arms and legs.

- Women are not welcome at Friday prayers at mosques.

- When you enter a mosque, avoid walking in front of people at prayer, talking loudly, touching anyone or any object, or smoking.

- Before you take any photographs, be sure to ask permission. There are restrictions and taboos.

PRIVATE HOMES

- Calling ahead is polite, but many people drop in on friends unannounced. The best time for visiting is on Friday (the Muslim day of rest) around 5:00 to 6:00 P.M. Leave by 7:00 P.M. unless you're invited for dinner. Avoid visiting around 2:00 to 3:00 P.M., when many people take naps.

- When you're invited to dinner, you're not expected to bring a gift, but if you do it won't be refused. Flowers, fruits, or sweets are appropriate. Don't give liquor unless you're sure your host drinks.

- You'll find servants in most middle- and upper-class homes. Volunteering to help clean up is unnecessary and inappropriate.

- If you make a telephone call, offer to pay. Your host has to pay for all calls, even the frequent connections to wrong numbers.

- Because Pakistan is so hot, people who can afford it bathe often — up to several times a day. If you stay in an upper-class home, you might find a bath with each bedroom. (Be prepared, however, for repeated water shortages.)

PERSONAL GIFTS

- When you choose gifts, don't select liquor or cigarettes.

- Good choices for gifts are packaged foods (no pork) or folk crafts from your home country, and overseas college sweatshirts.

TIPPING

- Hotels: Tourist hotels add a 10% service charge to the bill, but room porters still expect a small tip.

- Restaurants: A 10% tip is expected, but first check to see whether a service charge was added to the tab.

- Taxis: Tip 10% of the fare.

- Train and airport porters: Tip 5-10 *rupees* no matter how much luggage you have.

- Homes: At a home where the dinner was catered by servants, discreetly tip each servant about 25 *rupees* when you leave.

FOODS

MEALS

Breakfast (*nasta*): 7:30 to 8:30 A.M. Omelets, fruit,

bread, tea, and milk are typical.

Lunch (*dopahar kaa khaanaa*): Noon to 2:00 P.M. Usual fare is a curry dish with rice, fruit, bread, and tea.

Afternoon tea: 4:00 P.M. Tea is served with milk and sugar (which are often added before the tea is boiled). Fruit salad, *samosas* (deep-fried pastry with meat or vegetables inside), *pakoras* (fried chickpea balls), and *cholas* (chickpeas, green chilies, and spices) accompany the tea.

Dinner (*saam kaa khaanaa*): 8:00 to 9:00 P.M. The main meal of the day, dinner often features *kebabs* of grilled meat on a stick, curry (made with chicken, fish, or beef), fruit, rice, and *roti* bread.

WHERE TO EAT

- Many restaurants close between meals, so try to eat during normal meal hours (see above). Train station restaurants stay open throughout the day.

- If a restaurant turns you away, it might be because some restaurants serve only Muslims.

- During Ramzan (Ramadan) month restaurants close from dawn to dusk, so stock up on snacks. Aircraft and trains might have food available, but buses don't.

- Women dining alone in restaurants can expect to be approached by men, especially at night. Hotel restaurants are the best bet for dining in peace.

- The more expensive restaurants levy a 7½% tax on food and beverages.

- Most cities have Chinese restaurants.

- Western meals are best in the international hotels. Many restaurants, especially those in train stations, serve bland English food.

- For inexpensive meals (but risky from a sanitation standpoint), try the restaurants clustered around train stations.

- Before you buy sweets or any other food in open-air places, check to make sure that flies are kept away from the food.

- Vegetarian restaurants are rare. To avoid meat ask for *dahl* (lentil purée), *nan* (flatbread baked in an earthenware oven), and a vegetable curry. The word for vegetables is *sabziiya*.

FOODS TO TRY

- Most visitors like Pakistan's highly spiced, Moghul-style cuisine. It's not as hot as India's, but still makes good use of curry. You can also find Indian, Middle Eastern, and Afghani foods.

- The mainstay of the diet is *chappati* or *roti,* an unleavened bread usually accompanied by *dahl* (lentils), which is scooped up with the bread. Beef, lamb, chicken, and fish are also common. Yogurts are a favorite.

- Pakistan is a Muslim country, so pork is not served.

- Alcohol is also restricted. It is served only in the most Westernized homes and cannot be consumed in public. Only foreigners can buy it in hotels (and even then only for consumption in their rooms, not in public). Resident foreigners can obtain special liquor-buying permits.

- Wednesday and Thursday (in Karachi, Tuesday and Wednesday) are usually meatless days, when you can obtain only fish or chicken.

- Desserts are not served except on special occasions. Fruit is served often — but peel it before you eat it.

Specialties. Try *sheikh kebab* (minced, grilled meat on a skewer), *sajji* (roast leg of lamb), *tikka* (chicken, mutton, or beef spiced and barbecued), or *pulou* (chicken or lamb mixed with rice and spices).

- For desserts or snacks try mangoes, pomegranates, *kulfi* (similar to ice cream), and the many kinds of small pastries on display in restaurants.

Beverages. To be safe drink water only in international hotels. At least make certain that it's been boiled, or bring some purifying tablets from home.

- Tea is the most popular beverage. Coffee is available but is usually instant.

- Soft drinks are available everywhere and are often drunk with meals. Ask for soda by brand name (Pepsi, Coke); "soda" is club soda.

- Other popular drinks are *nimbu pani* (a fresh lime drink), *lassi* (iced yogurt), and *shabaz chai* (green tea flavored with jasmine or cardamom).

TABLE MANNERS

- During the month-long holiday of Ramzan (Ramadan), Muslims do not eat or drink between sunrise and sunset. Non-Muslims need not fast but are expected to refrain from eating in front of Muslims.

- Restaurants are often small and crowded. Even so, don't sit down at a table with strangers.

Utensils. Pakistanis eat many traditional foods with their hands. Be sure to use only your right hand to eat or pass someone a dish. The left hand is considered unclean.

- Cutlery (a fork and spoon) is often available for Westerners. Hold the spoon in your right hand and the fork in your left. Push the food onto the spoon with the fork.

- Communal dishes are placed in the middle of the table. Use the spoon supplied with each dish to transfer food to your own plate.

- To signal that you've finished eating, set down your cutlery in the center of your plate. If utensils weren't used, signal by either pulling back from the table or going to wash your hands.

Dining with others. Men often eat before women and children do, especially at formal occasions such as weddings.

- Men are often invited to dinner without their wives. Even if wives are invited, men sometimes come alone.

- Hosts repeatedly urge guests to have more helpings. Eat small helpings so you can accept a number of them. When you've had enough politely refuse another helping.

- It's customary to socialize before a meal and leave soon after the meal is finished.

- The person who suggests a meal is obliged to pay for everyone. Never offer to "go Dutch" and pay only for your share.

ACCOMMODATIONS

Hotels. You'll find international-standard hotels

only in the major cities (Karachi, Lahore, Peshawar, and Islamabad). Make reservations well ahead of time; rooms in first-class hotels are limited.

Karachi hotel rates are subject to a 7½% government tax and a bed tax of 50 *rupees* per person.

- Outside of the cities look for the clean, reasonable motels and rest houses run by the Pakistan Tourism Development Corporation. Check with the PTDC for locations.

- For very inexpensive accommodations in small towns, look for *muzzaffar khanas* (local inns) around train or bus stations. Don't be surprised, however, if some of them don't accept foreigners. These inns have dormitory-style accommodations with rope beds (*charpoi*).

- Theft is a problem, so never leave money or valuables in your hotel room (especially in Lahore).

Rest rooms. Look for rest rooms in hotels, restaurants, and train stations. Carry tissue with you; most public toilets don't supply it.

- Bathing facilities often consist of cubicles with buckets of water and dippers. Wash by pouring the water over yourself. Most people bathe with cool water, so the water in the bucket won't be heated unless you request it.

For a cool, refreshing wash in the summer, look for *hammams* next to barber shops. They're bathing centers where for a modest fee you can wash in a small cubicle. Towels are available.

TRANSPORTATION

PUBLIC TRANSPORTATION

Buses. Buses are incredibly crowded and unsafe. If you want to ride one for the adventure, note that women board at the front of the bus and men board at the rear. Occasionally there is a partition separating the sexes. If there isn't women can expect to have men pinch and rub against them.

Bus fares depend on the

distance you travel. Hand your fare to the conductor.

- Minibuses are a little more expensive than the regular buses but are both faster and more comfortable.

Taxis. You can either find taxis in front of hotels or hail them on the streets. Most have meters, but make sure the meter is used or else bargain the fare before you get in. Inquire at your hotel what a fare should cost.

- Taxis are not recommended for women traveling alone.

- At the airport beware of taxi touts who overcharge tourists unfamiliar with the country. (They have even been known to pay hotel shuttle-bus drivers to "disappear" when an international flight arrives.) Look for licensed black-and-yellow taxis at the terminal; since their meters always seem to be broken, bargain for the fare. The twenty-minute drive from airport to Karachi should be about 100 *rupee*s.

Trains. Like buses, trains are extremely crowded — you have to fight for seats in unreserved cars. There are three train classes: Air-conditioned first-class

(sleepers and seats); regular first-class (sleepers and seats); and second-class (seats only).

- To get first-class seats and sleepers, make reservations several days ahead. Station porters will "reserve" seats for you if you give them a "tip." Express and mail trains usually have a dining car attached. You must rent linen for overnight travel in advance.

- Visitors can get up to a 25% discount by obtaining a Tourist Certificate from the tourist offices. Show this document to the railway superintendent when you buy your tickets.

- Most major train stations have free shower rooms for passengers.

Other transportation. Three-wheeled motorcycles with two-passenger sidecars serve as taxis in many places. Bargain for the fare in advance (it should be about half the taxi fare).

- For domestic air travel PIA (Pakistan International Airlines) operates daily flights between Karachi, Rawalpindi, and Lahore.

DRIVING

- It's inadvisable to drive yourself in Pakistan. The roads are clogged with vehicles, people, and animals, drivers ignore all traffic regulations and signs, and reliable maps are scarce. Instead, check with your hotel to rent a car and driver at reasonable rates.

- Driving is on the left, as in Britain, but both right- and left-hand-drive vehicles are used.

- Many trucks and animal-drawn carts don't have taillights, so try to avoid driving at night.

- Bribes (tips) to police officers at the scenes of minor accidents are common. Fines, however, cannot be paid on the spot.

BUSINESS

BUSINESS HOURS

Business offices: 9:00 A.M. to 4:00 or 5:00 P.M. Sunday through Thursday (Friday is the Muslim holy day). Some offices close early on Thursdays; some are open on Saturday. Many businesses open and close earlier during the summer.

Banks: 9:00 A.M. to 1:00 P.M. Saturday through Wednesday, and 9:00 to 10:30 A.M. Thursday.

Government offices: 7:30 A.M. to 2:30 P.M. Saturday through Thursday.

BUSINESS CUSTOMS

- The best time for business visits is from October to April. Pakistani business people vacation during the summer monsoon season (July-August).

- Arrange appointments well ahead of time, especially if you are coming from overseas. If you use the mail, start asking for an appointment two months early. Telex or cable is more reliable; start making arrangements about a month before you wish to meet.

- Many corporations are government-owned, at least in part, so learn the structure of the government.

- Western businesswomen often experience considerable difficulty doing business in Pakistan because of Pakistani attitudes towards women. Often they're not taken seriously.

- A translator is not necessary. English is the language of commerce in Pakistan and is spoken widely.

Business etiquette. Business cards are widely used. You can have them printed inexpensively in Pakistan (you don't need to have them printed in Urdu).

- Most Pakistanis like to establish warm relationships and personal rapport with guests, and might be offended if you're standoffish. Pakistani business people, on the other hand, tend to be formal and restrained until they get to know you.

- Visitors are often treated to coffee or tea and some other refreshment, and might be invited to a meal. Declining this hospitality is impolite.

Appointments and meetings. The best time to schedule appointments is around 10:00 or 11:00 A.M. If the meeting goes well, you might be invited to lunch.

- Western business people are expected to be punctual, but don't be surprised if your counterparts aren't punctual themselves. Time just isn't as important in Pakistan as it is in the West.

Business gifts and entertainment. Gifts aren't required for your first visit, but have one ready to present if your hosts give one to you.

- Appropriate business gifts are electronic gadgets, watches, pens, and packaged fruits.

- Pakistani businessmen usually entertain guests at their clubs. It's unusual for a first-time acquaintance to be invited to a home.

If you are invited to a home, consider it an honor. If you don't see the wife at home, don't ask about her. She might be in *purdah* (not associating with men outside the family).

If you invite a male counterpart to dinner, ask whether his wife would like to come (if she is not in *purdah*).

Men always pay for a woman's meal. The only way for a businesswoman to avoid this is to entertain at her hotel's restaurant and make prior arrangements with the restaurant staff.

TELEPHONES AND MAIL

Telephones. Public pay phones don't exist, so go into a shop, restaurant, or hotel and ask to use their phone. Offer to pay; there's a charge for each call. You might have to shout into the phone to be heard.

• To make long-distance or international calls, call from either your hotel or the post office or telegraph office. Booking calls is a haphazard process, and connections often take a long time. To save up to 50%, have someone at home call you at your hotel.

Mail. Most hotels will accept mail to be posted. Many will also package parcels.

• Register or insure any important letters or packages.

LEGAL MATTERS

Customs and immigration. Visas are required. You must obtain a visa (valid for three months) before you arrive. (American citizens can no longer obtain visas at the airport.)

• You'll need an International Health Certificate showing that you've been immunized against cholera and smallpox.

• Bringing liquor into the country is illegal. So is exporting antiques.

Other restrictions. All of Pakistan's laws must now be based on Islamic principles; the legal code is now being rewritten to conform to them.

• It's illegal to consume, sell, or distribute alcoholic beverages.

• Keep Pakistani laws in mind at all times and don't break any of them. Many people — from street merchants to hotel managers — are police stooges who specialize in setting foreigners up and receive a commission on the "fine" extracted. Take special care in Lahore, where drugs reportedly have been planted in rooms at inexpensive hotels.

SAFETY

Crime. If someone offers you tea or a smoke in your hotel room, don't accept — there's a chance you might be drugged and robbed. (This problem seems to be most prevalent in Lahore.)

Health. Unless you see water being boiled, assume it hasn't been boiled and don't drink it. You can also purify water with iodine tablets, which you can obtain in the West.

- Except in international hotels sanitation is often inadequate, so avoid dairy products.

- Any prepared food that is served hot should be safe to eat. Have meat prepared "well done" and avoid raw vegetables and mayonnaise.

- Medical services are lim-ited, but when you can find them, they're usually very good. All doctors speak English, and medicines are sometimes free. Although urban areas have fully equipped hospitals, they are usually understaffed. Outside of the cities medical care is scarce — the ratio of doctors to patients is about 1 to 6,000.

- Before you go to Pakistan, ask your doctor for anti-malaria medicine.

- Prescription drugs, sanitary napkins, and some medicines might be hard to find, so bring them with you.

SHOPPING AND ENTERTAINMENT

Shopping. Shop hours are 9:00 A.M. to 6:00 P.M. Saturday through Thursday.

- Prices are fixed in grocery stores, shoe stores, and fruit and vegetable markets. Elsewhere, bargain hard. Good humor in bargaining is essential.

- Few tourists visit Pakistan, so you can still find bargains. Good buys are brass, onyx, leather goods, carpets, worked gold and silver, leather goods, and copper and brass vessels. Karachi is where you'll usually find the best bargains.

Entertainment. The only evening frivolity in Pakistan is the movies. There are no nightclubs, bars, or massage parlors. One Karachi hotel has a disco, but it's open only on Thursday.

HOLIDAYS

- Pakistani holidays are related to either independence or Muslim religious observances.

Secular holidays: Pakistan Day (March 23), May Day (May 1), Independence Day (August 14), Defense of Pakistan Day (September 6), Death of Quaid-e-Azam (September 11), Birthday of Quaid-e-Azam (December 25).

- Pakistan Day celebrates the 1940 decision to work for a Muslim nation separate from India.

- Quaid-e-Azam (the honorific name of Mohammed Ali Jinnah) headed the Muslim movement that led to Pakistan's separation from India and creation of the nation in 1947. He is revered, so refer to him with respect.

- Bank holidays, during which other businesses remain open, are July 1 and December 31.

Religious holidays: Muslim holidays vary from year to year as determined by the Muslim calendar, which is ten days shorter than ours. The major holidays are Eid-ul-Asha (Feast of the Sacrifice), Ramzan, Eid-e-Milad-un-Nabi (birthday of Prophet Mohammed), and Eid-ul-Fitr (Feast of the Breaking of the Fast).

- Ramzan (the Urdu pronunciation of Ramadan) is the most important religious holiday and lasts thirty days. Muslims refrain from eating or drinking between sunrise and sunset during this time. It is an inconvenient time to visit Pakistan — most businesses close in the afternoons, and it's inadvisable to eat or drink in public between sunrise and sunset. Check with the Pakistani consulate or tourist office to find out the specific dates.

At the end of Ramzan, send Muslim friends *Eid* cards to be polite. You can find them in hotel stationery shops.

KEY PHRASES

English	Urdu	Pronunciation
Good morning	Namaste (Salam)	Na-mahssteh (Sa-lahm)
Good afternoon	"	"
Good evening	"	"
Good night	(Khuda haafiz)	(Khooda hahfiz)
Goodbye	"	"
Please	Mehrbaanii	Mah-hehr-bahnee
Thank you	Sukria	Shookree-a
Excuse me	Maaf kiijiye	Mahf keejyeh
Don't mention it	Koii baat nahi	Koee bahtt na-heen
Yes	Jii ha	Jee hahn
No	Jii nahi	Jee na-heen
I understand	Mai samajh gayaa	Man sahmahj ga-yah
I don't understand	Mai nahi samajhaa	Man na-heen sahmj-hah
How much?	Kitnaa?	Kittnah?
Does anyone here speak English?	Koee angrezi bolta hai?	Ko-ee ahn-gray-zee-bol-tah heh?
Sir, Mr.	Sahab	Saw-haab
Mrs., Madam	Begam	Bea-gham
Miss	Sahab	Saw-haab

PRONUNCIATION

Double consonants should be pronounced double. Stress is relatively even.

a = "u" as in "cut"

e = eh

i = "i" as in "bit"

o = oh

u = "oo" as in "look"

ai = "a" as in "bat"

t = th

d = th

n = ng if before k, g, or h

Luzon

PHILIPPINES

Quezon City
★ Manila

Leyte

Sulu Sea

Mindanao

The first things that visitors to this nation of 7,000 islands notice — especially if they're arriving from the reserved cultures of Northeast Asia — are the smiles. Filipinos are very outgoing, and smiles are everywhere. You'll find it easy (sometimes too easy, as in the case of touts) to meet people from all walks of life.

The Philippines is the third-largest English-speaking country in the world, and you'll find it easy to get around and communicate. Malay origin, four centuries of Spanish rule, and several decades of American influence have combined to make the Filipinos a unique people. More Westernized than any other Asian people, they welcome foreigners and treat them as equals. A word of caution, however: Don't be fooled into thinking you're back home. Beneath the Western veneer lie major cultural differences.

MEETING PEOPLE

GREETINGS

- In the cities use common English greetings — English is widely used.

- Among both men and women, a handshake is the everyday greeting for acquaintances and friends (a limp handshake is the norm). Western men should wait for a Filipino woman to extend her hand first. Women who are close friends often hug and kiss when they haven't seen each other for a while.

- When you greet a family,

greet the eldest members first. Filipinos take the right hand of an elder and touch it to their foreheads to show respect, but foreigners are not expected to do this.

- At a social function you'll be introduced to all the guests. Shake each person's hand.

Names and titles. In both male and female names, the given name comes first, followed by the initial of the mother's surname and then the father's surname. Most Filipino families acquired Spanish names during the four centuries of Spanish occupation.

- Address elders and superiors either as "sir" or "ma'am," or else by their title (Mr., Mrs., Miss, Dr., etc.) and name. These Western terms of address are customary even among rural people.

- When you speak with engineers, architects, and other professionals, use their professional titles. (It's customary to call lawyers "attorneys" even if they're not practicing law.)

- Many Filipino women retain their maiden names when they marry, adding their husbands' family names after a hyphen

(Mrs. Maria Santos-Cruz). If a woman writes "vda" between her maiden name and her husband's family name, it means she is a widow.

Correspondence. English is widely used. A standard American salutation is acceptable.

- To use the native Tagalog salutation, write *"Kagalang-Galang* (title) (name):" (for example, Kagalang-Galang Direktora Mrs. Lucena:).

- Formal business letters end with "At your service, thank you (your name)."

CONVERSATION

- Good conversation subjects: Education, professions, families, children, and Filipino culture and cuisine.

- Subjects to avoid: Domestic political strife, religion, and recent Philippines history. Don't joke about the Catholic Church, political figures (including the Marcos family), or a person's family.

- One of the first questions you'll be asked is "Where do you come from?" Answer with the name of your hometown. Filipinos are hometown-oriented and won't feel comfortable with an answer such as "Canada."

- Even new acquaintances will ask you very personal questions ("How much money do you make?" "Are you a Catholic?"). Don't be offended; these are normal questions indicating interest. Ask the same questions in return.

PHRASES TO KNOW

- Tagalog (Filipino) is the most widely spoken of the hundred or so native languages and is understood by about half the population. Tagalog is written in the Roman alphabet.

- English is widely spoken and will get you almost as far as Tagalog. Both Tagalog and English are the official languages. A few people still speak Spanish.

CURRENCY

- The unit of currency is the *peso,* which is divided into 100 *centavos.* One U.S. dollar is worth about 20 *pesos.* Coins are minted in 1, 5, 10, 25, and 50 *centavos* and in 1, 2, and 5 *pesos.* Notes are available in 2, 5, 10, 20, 50, and 100 *pesos.*

- There's no restriction on how much foreign currency you can import, but you can't take out more than you brought in. It's illegal to import or export more than 500 Philippine *pesos.*

- You can exchange currency at banks, hotels, and authorized money changers, including some restaurants, tourist shops, and travel agencies. Always get a Central Bank receipt; you'll need it for purchases in duty-free shops.

- To get the best exchange rate, ask local residents. In Manila you can find good rates at some of the department stores (even shoe stores).

- There is an active black market for U.S. currency. Official and unofficial money changers abound, especially in Manila's Ermita district. If you deal with unauthorized money changers, you run the risk of getting counterfeit *pesos.*

- Traveler's checks might not be accepted off the tourist trail.

ETIQUETTE

GENERAL MANNERS

- When you speak, speak softly. Harsh, loud speech signifies anger. Filipinos would not want passersby to hear your loud voice and think you're criticizing them.

- Maintaining your composure is very important. A public display of anger will lower people's opinion of you.

- Filipinos are subtle in their speech and often feel that Westerners can't take a hint that the answer is "no."

- Filipinos are very sensitive about personal and family honor. Don't criticize or tease anyone (especially in public) and don't denigrate the country.

- Bringing shame to individuals also reflects on their families. Avoid inflicting shame on anyone at all costs. The belief that failure brings shame causes Filipinos to view innovation, change, and competition as gambles.

- Filipinos often use laughter to relieve tension or cover embarrassment. Don't be angry if someone laughs or giggles at another's misfortune or a sad moment.

- Age is respected, so always defer to the elderly by greeting them first, offering them seats, inquiring after their health, and refraining from smoking in their presence. Never overtly disagree with an elderly person.

- Filipinos can easily detect insincerity, and it can ruin a relationship. Making relationships run smoothly is more important than expressing personal views. Frank, outspoken behavior is considered rude and uncultured.

- Accepting a favor obligates a person to repay with a greater favor (never with money). This obligation is strictly binding for Filipinos, but not for foreigners.

- If you invite Filipinos to dinner or a party, they probably won't take your invitation seriously unless you call to remind them or have a friend assure them that you're serious. Filipinos often extend offers and invitations in passing, as polite thoughts. The answer is often "yes," but neither side takes the offer seriously.

RSVP invitations might go unanswered, but people might show up anyway. For an invitation to appear sincere, it must be reiterated.

- Punctuality at social affairs is impolite (it gives the impression of being overeager). Don't be surprised if Filipinos arrive late for dinner or a party.

- Drinking too much is considered greedy, so don't get drunk at parties or dinners. Being rude — whether you're drunk or sober — is taboo.

- If you snack on a train, in an office, or anywhere else, offer to share with others nearby. It's rude to eat in front of other people without offering them some.

- Filipino women rarely drink or smoke in public, so don't offer them liquor or cigarettes.

- Before you take someone's picture (especially an elderly person), it's polite to ask permission. Few people object.

BODY LANGUAGE

- Filipinos often greet each other by raising their eyebrows in recognition. This gesture can also mean "yes" or "I understand" or indicate recognition or surprise.

- People of the same sex often hold hands simply as a gesture of friendship.

- Prolonged direct eye contact is rude. In tense situations avoid eye contact; it might be interpreted as a challenge and result in violence.

- To attract the attention of people standing nearby, lightly touch on their elbow — a polite version of the Western tap on the shoulder.

- To point out a direction politely, either shift your eyes in that direction or point with pouted lips.

- Beckon someone with your arm outstretched (palm down) by wiggling your fingers up and down. Never crook one finger to summon someone. It's insulting.

- Standing with your hands on your hips signifies anger. Other people might consider it a challenge.

DRESS

- The rainy season lasts from June to October.

- People seldom wear coats, except in Baguio City from November to February.

- Filipinos dress well for most occasions; you should do the same.

MEN For business wear a jacket and tie. If you're invited to dine at someone's home, wear a suit. Some fine restaurants require jackets at dinner, but you may wear the native *barong* instead (see below). Don't wear shorts on the street.

WOMEN For business, or if you dine at someone's home, wear a dress or a blouse and skirt with stockings. Slacks or jeans are fine for casual wear, but don't wear shorts in public. Don't wear sleeveless dresses on Sunday or bright colors to church.

NATIVE DRESS The national costume for men is an elaborately embroidered, long-sleeved shirt (*barong tagalog* or just *barong*) that hangs out over the pants. For women it is a full-length dress (*balintawak*) with a scooped neckline and butterfly sleeves. Both costumes are worn for formal occasions. Short-sleeved *barongs* are worn for informal occasions. *Barongs* are transparent, so if you wear one wear a T-shirt under it.

- For business Filipino men wear a less elaborate white or pastel *barong* with dress slacks, and women wear Western dress.

- In rural areas women wear wraparound skirts that reach almost to their ankles.

PRIVATE HOMES

- Even new Filipino acquaintances will often invite you home for dinner or to stay overnight. Don't accept unless they repeat the offer at least three times.

- Before you visit someone, phone ahead or make arrangements in advance. If you do drop by, don't come just before a meal, or the family will feel they must invite you to stay.

- If you're invited for a dinner party, arrive fifteen or thirty minutes late.

- When you greet the family, greet the eldest members first and make sure you talk with them during your visit.

- You're not expected to bring a gift, but fruits or sweets are appreciated. Your hosts won't open the gift in your presence.

- You'll probably be entertained in the living room. Don't take an unguided tour of the house or peer into the kitchen or bedrooms. Before you go into the bathroom, ask permission.

- Your hosts will probably offer you a soft drink and cookies. Refusing is impolite.

- As a guest, be tactful and solicitous. Filipinos appreciated genuine concern, expressed openly and compassionately. They do not like insincerity.

- Don't use the word "hostess" to refer to

your female host. Instead, refer to her by title and surname.

- Your male host might answer questions that you direct to the women of the house (this is customary behavior for fathers and husbands).

- The best way to compliment your hosts on a meal is to eat heartily.

- If you stay with a family, observe the following customs:

They'll probably want to act as your tour guides. Refusing their offer might hurt their feelings.

If you stay for several days with a family that has servants, discreetly tip each servant about 50 *pesos.* Servants will do your laundry during your stay.

Most middle- and lower-class homes don't have hot running water. People will think it odd if you don't bathe daily (most people bathe more than once a day to beat the heat), but expect to either take cold showers or have water heated on the stove.

If you visit another town or tourist spot during your stay with a family, bring the children a small gift from the place you visited.

PERSONAL GIFTS

- If people give you a gift, don't open it in their presence. Instead, thank them and set it aside until they leave. (Filipinos are embarrassed to have the relative value of their gift displayed for others to see.) The next time you see them, express your thanks.

TIPPING

- If you don't have *pesos* for a tip, people will accept a U.S. dollar gratefully.

- Hotels: Most hotel bills include a 10-15% service charge; additional tipping is optional. Tip bellhops and porters 2 to 5 *pesos,* depending on how much baggage you have. Don't tip doormen.

- Restaurants: Leave 10% if a service charge hasn't been added to your bill.

- Porters: Tip 2 *pesos* per bag except at the airport, where the set rate is 5 *pesos* per bag.

- Taxis: Don't tip unless the driver has done a special service or the trip has taken over an hour.

- Barbers and beauticians: Leave 2 *pesos.*

- Washroom attendants: Leave 2 *pesos*.
- If a young man or boy finds a parking place for you or "watches" your car while you're gone, tip 1 *peso*.

FOODS

MEALS

Breakfast (*almusal*): 7:00 to 8:00 A.M. Fish and rice are very popular, as are fruits, eggs, sourdough bread, and *ensaimada* (sweet buns). The usual beverages are tea, coffee, and hot chocolate.

Lunch (*tanghalian*): Noon to 1:00 P.M. A typical lunch is noodle soup, a pork dish such as *adobo* (pork marinated in vinegar, garlic, and pepper), rice, *pinakbet* (vegetables stewed in fish sauce), and fruit. Common beverages are soft drinks, tea, and water.

Marienda: 3:00 to 6:00 P.M. *Marienda* is an afternoon snack that originated with the Spanish who occupied the Philippines.

Cakes, sweet fritters, and tarts are served with tea.

Dinner (*hapunan*): 7:00 to 8:00 P.M. (some families, especially those of Spanish ancestry, don't dine until 9:00 or 10:00 P.M.). Dinner often includes a seafood main dish accompanied by rice, a vegetable, fruit, and dessert. Soft drinks, water, and beer are often served.

WHERE TO EAT

- Most restaurants are open from 10:00 A.M. to 2:00 P.M. for lunch and from 5:30 P.M. to midnight for dinner.
- Women dining alone might get unasked-for attention (Filipino women seldom eat alone). To avoid harassment you might want to stick to hotel restaurants or more expensive outside restaurants.
- Most menus are in English. Don't look for them to be posted; it isn't the custom.
- Cafeteria-style restaurants are inexpensive and numerous. Just choose from the dishes on display and pay by the dish.
- For an economical meal try a small restaurant that offers a set menu.

Set menus are often advertised on signs outside.

- If you want a quick snack — or a long respite from the street — pop into a coffee shop, where you can get sandwiches, sweets, and non-alcoholic drinks. You may sit for a long time without being asked to move on.

- Try the street vendors for fresh barbecued chicken (*lechon manok*), marinated chicken stew (*adobo*), and rice-noodle soup (*sotanghon*). Make sure the stand has quick turnover, so you'll get fresh food, and that the vendors look healthy.

FOODS TO TRY

- Filipino cuisine mirrors the land's mix of Malay, Spanish, Chinese, and Indonesian cultures. Today American-style fast foods are making headway. Seafoods are important in Filipino dishes.

- Most foods are rather bland, with few spices. They're usually cooked or served with garlic, lemon, vinegar, fish sauce, or shrimp paste.

Specialties. Try the national favorite, *adobo,* a dish made of braised pork or chicken stewed in vinegar with bay leaves, garlic, salt, and peppercorns. Other favorites are *kari kari* (oxtail or beef cooked with tripe in a spicy peanut sauce, then served with vegetables), *afritada* (beef in tomato paste and olive oil, served with vegetables and olives), and *lechon* (barbecued pig stuffed with tamarind leaves, served with a liver-and-vinegar dipping sauce).

- *Bagoong* is a popular condiment used to flavor vegetable dishes. It's a fermented mixture of fresh anchovies and salt and is often called the poor man's caviar.

- Local appetizers to try are *lumpia* (heart-of-palm salad with bits of shrimp and pork, rolled in a wafer and served with garlic) and *ukoy* (bean sprouts and bean curd mixed with tiny crayfish, seasoned with leek and shallots, covered with batter, and stir-fried).

- Soups are popular. Try *sinigang* (a sour broth made of fish, shrimp, or meat seasoned with fruits and flowers), *tinola* (chicken boiled with vegetables and seasoned with peppercorn and ginger), *batchoy* (a soup of pig's heart, liver, kidney, and blood), and *sinuam* (made from clams or

PHILIPPINES

261

mussels sautéed with garlic and onions).

- For dessert try the many cakes made from plain or glutinous rice (*biningka* or *puto*), or yams or tubers in coconut milk (*halea sa ube* or *kalamay*).

- Fruit is often served as a dessert. For a change of pace, try jackfruit, mangosteen, tamarind, *rambutan,* and *durian* (a fruit so smelly that airlines ask passengers not to bring it on board).

- If someone offers you *balut,* watch out. It's a hardboiled duck egg containing a partially developed embryo that you suck out through a hole in the shell. It might be crunchy.

Beverages. Don't drink unboiled water outside the city of Manila. As an alternative get soft drinks or beer with the caps on (sometimes water is added to dilute the beverage).

- Usually only men are served alcoholic beverages. Women drink soft drinks, orange juice, or *calamansi,* a drink made from a local citrus fruit.

- Filipinos enjoy a good pre-dinner aperitif and have developed a number of local versions. In

the north try *basi,* a sugar-cane wine. Elsewhere look for *tuba* (a beer made from fermented coconut-flower sap), *lambanog* (distilled *tuba*), and *layaw* (an alcoholic corn beverage).

TABLE MANNERS

- When you're eating in front of other people, whether in public or in a home, offer them some.

- Many Filipinos hiss to get a waiter's attention, but it's not polite. Instead, catch the waiter's eye by raising your hand with the fingers together.

Utensils. Most Filipinos eat with forks and spoons. Hold the spoon in your right hand and the fork in your left, and use the fork to push food onto the spoon.

- To signify that you've finished eating, place your fork and spoon on your plate.

- In rural areas people often eat with their right hands.

Dining with others. Having a drink before dinner is common in a restaurant, but not in a home.

- When dinner is announced look hesitant about heading

for the table (take your cue from the Filipinos). Wait until the host shows you where to sit. The guest of honor sits at the head of the table.

- It's polite to decline the first offer of seating, food, drinks, cigarettes, or anything else. You may accept the second offer. Similarly, you should always offer something at least twice.

- Guests are given their first serving by the host (or by a servant if the family has one). After that, if the serving dishes are in the middle of the table, serve yourself.

- Leave a bit of food on both your plate and the serving plates so that your hosts will know they provided enough food.

- Many middle-class and wealthy people have cooks who prepare meals in their homes, so don't compliment the woman of the house on the food. Instead, compliment her on her lovely home and the presentation of the dinner.

- Many formal dinner parties conclude with dancing after the dinner.

- At a weekend dinner party, take your leave around midnight. On a weekday night leave by 10:00 P.M.

- The person who suggests a lunch or dinner pays the entire bill. Going "Dutch" is considered bad form.

Banquets. At formal or business banquets, the seating is arranged, so wait to be directed to your seat. Guests of honor often sit at a head table.

- At some point during a banquet (usually near the beginning), the guests of honor are introduced.

- After dinner guests are often asked to sing. It's rude to decline.

ACCOMMODATIONS

Hotels. Hotel rooms are in demand from March through May and their prices reflect it. From December through February and June through November, inquire about seasonal discounts. (In July and August hotels give discounts of up to 50%.)

- Keep your valuables in a

hotel lockbox, not in your room. If you're not staying in an international-class hotel, get a receipt stating exactly what you put in the safe.

- Fires can be a problem, so look for exits when you check in. If possible get a room on the ground floor.

- In Manila look for inexpensive guesthouses around the Ermita tourist area. Most of them have fans instead of air-conditioning.

- The electric current is 220-volt, 60-cycle AC. Most hotels also have 110-volt outlets.

Rest rooms. Public toilets tend to be very dirty. They rarely have toilet tissue, so carry some with you. The men's room is a *lalake,* and the women's room is a *babae.*

TRANSPORTATION

PUBLIC TRANSPORTATION

- As a rule Filipinos don't queue for buses or taxis. You'll just have to scramble like everybody else.

Buses. Buses are fairly easy to take. Just board, tell the conductor your destination (the fare is based on distance), and hand over the money. Take small change; conductors don't change large bills.

In Manila air-conditioned blue buses called "Love Buses" ply set routes for a flat rate.

- Most Filipino men don't give up their bus seats to a woman unless she's elderly, pregnant, or carrying a baby. Always give your seat to an elderly person.

Taxis. You can hail taxis on the street or find them in front of hotels. Most taxis have meters; just make sure the flag drops before you start out. If there is no meter or it's broken, bargain the fare before the taxi moves an inch. Most rides around Manila should be about 30 or 40 *pesos*. Take small change — drivers don't carry much.

• Many taxis have meters rigged to run fast. If the meter display is digital and the driver honks his horn a lot, check to see whether the fare increases every time he honks.

• At the airport avoid the taxi touts who promise you a better deal "just around the corner." They'll have your bags locked in the trunk before you even agree on a fare. Stick to the licensed taxis in front of the airport, and act as though you've been to Manila before and know where you're going. A regular taxi into Manila should be about 40 *pesos*.

Trains. Trains run only on the islands of Luzon and Panay and are extremely slow. If you want to try them, they have three classes: first (reclining seats and air-conditioning), second, and third. Keep your ticket with you until you disembark.

Other transportation. "Jeepneys" are multicolored converted jeeps with benches in the back that seat about twelve passengers. Their routes and fares are hard to figure out, but jeepneys are inexpensive and you can find them anywhere. Hail one on the street, hop in the back, ask the driver the fare to your destination, and pay. When you want to get out, either pound on the roof or shout *"para"* (stop).

• To travel between the many islands, try the passenger ferries. Most offer three classes: First (air conditioned), second (not air-conditioned), and third (you sleep on the deck). The fares include meals. Book and buy your ticket several days before you travel.

DRIVING

• Self-drive rental cars are available, but driving is hazardous and congested. Hiring a car and driver is much easier.

• If you do drive yourself, the rental company will require an International Driver's License.

• Driving is on the right, as in North America.

• Drivers often ignore traffic regulations and signs.

At an intersection with a stop sign, don't assume that other cars will stop.

- If you have an accident while driving, get a police officer, take photos of the scene before you move the car, and get license plate numbers, names, and addresses. In rural areas bystanders have been known to attack drivers whose cars injured pedestrians.

BUSINESS

BUSINESS HOURS

Business offices: 8:00 or 8:30 A.M. to 5:00 P.M. Monday through Friday, with a one- or two-hour lunch break. Some offices are open until noon on Saturday.

Banks: 9:00 A.M. to 4:00 P.M., Monday through Friday.

Government offices: Same as business offices.

BUSINESS CUSTOMS

- The best time of year for business visits is from October to May, when there aren't as many holidays as during the summer. If you're meeting with Chinese business people, note that they close their businesses for a week around the Chinese New Year (January or February).

- Many Filipino businesses don't have telexes, so start requesting meetings by cable a month before your trip, or by letter two months in advance.

- A letter of introduction from a bank or a mutual friend greatly increases your chances of getting a reply to your request for a meeting (otherwise, the Filipinos might be suspicious of your intent).

- Filipinos prefer face-to-face talks and might not even bother to answer written communications, so don't rely on memos and letters to communicate your ideas.

- Negotiations and deals take more time than they do in the West — in the Philippines everything goes at a slower pace —

so don't expect to pop into the country and conclude a business agreement in a few days.

- When you're dealing with the cumbersome bureaucracy, you sometimes need *lagay* (small bribes) to get things up to speed — even though this form of "persuasion" is illegal. If you're pleading with a bureaucrat to find the forms you need and the desk drawer slides open, you're expected to drop something into it.

- Women might find it difficult to establish good business relationships with Filipino businessmen and gain their counterparts' respect.

Business etiquette. Exchange business cards when you're introduced. English is the language of commerce, so you don't need to have your cards (or your sales literature) translated.

- When you address business people, use their titles (Attorney Cruz).

- Smooth interpersonal relationships are the key to business relationships. Even if you have bad news, communicate it courteously and gently. In fact, to save face on all sides, it's best to have emissaries deliver negative messages.

- If you must criticize someone, do it only in private and very tactfully. If the person is an employee, follow your criticism with questions about the person's family, to show concern and convey a sense of belonging.

- Filipinos dislike saying no because they don't like to let anyone down, so get your negotiating agreements in writing as you proceed (your counterpart might have said yes without really meaning it). Don't try to back your counterparts into a corner, however. They won't react well to pushiness.

If you're dealing with a family-run business, remember the importance of family interests and social acceptance. They outweigh profit and material considerations.

Appointments and meetings. The best times of day to suggest for appointments are 10:00 A.M. and 3:00 P.M. Many companies have a noon to 2:00 P.M. lunch break, and many people take a siesta at that time.

- Your counterparts might be late for meetings. Not

only is the concept of time less rigid than in the West, but traffic in the cities can be very heavy. Foreigners, however, are expected to be on time.

- The first meeting might be taken up with small talk and conversation. Filipino business people want to get to know you before you really talk business. A relationship outside of any business context is important to a successful business relationship.

- When you meet with a group, pay particular attention and show special respect to the senior members. Never interrupt an older person who is talking. Age is respected, and you'll lose face among your counterparts for any perceived slight of an older person.

Business gifts and entertainment. Bring gifts for your first meeting with business people. Good choices are crafts indigenous to your region, imported liquor (Chivas Regal, Johnny Walker Black Label), pen sets, or calendars with your company logo.

- Before you leave the country — especially if you've reached an agreement — invite your counterparts and their spouses to dinner. A good choice is a fine restaurant in an international hotel.

- If you invite someone to dinner, remember to ask them at least three times. (It's polite to decline at least once or twice.)

- Arrange business lunches and dinners in person, or personally over the phone. Have your secretary make only the confirmation.

- If you're invited to a lunch, don't bring your spouse. Lunches tend to be for business discussion.

- If you attend a business dinner, don't be surprised if you're asked to sing. Filipinos enjoy singing, especially at dinners and parties, and will accept you more quickly if you participate.

- A Western businesswoman should not attempt to pay for a Filipino businessman's dinner, even if she invited him. If she pays it will embarrass him and harm the relationship.

TELEPHONES AND MAIL

Telephones. The red public phones are scarce outside the business district and when you do find one, it's often out of order. If you can't find a phone, ask to use one in a shop or restaurant.

- To make a local call lift the receiver, deposit 75 *centavos,* and dial. There is no time limit on local calls. If you call from a hotel, expect to pay an extra 5 *pesos.*

- Make long-distance and international calls from the Long Distance Telephone Company office or your hotel room. Before you use the hotel phone, check on the surcharges — they can be as high as 20%, and you must pay even if you don't make a connection. Most hotels don't have direct dialing, so overseas calls take fifteen minutes to an hour to put through.

Mail. Mail delivery is un-reliable. Don't send valu-ables through the mail — pilfering is a problem.

- Mailboxes are gray. You'll find them on the street and at commercial centers.

- Post offices are open Monday through Friday from 8:00 A.M. to 5:00 P.M. and Saturdays and holidays from 8:00 A.M. to noon.

LEGAL MATTERS

Customs and immigration. Visas are not required for stays of less than 21 days, but are required for stays of 21 to 59 days. You might be asked for proof of onward ticketing.

- You can't bring in porno-graphic materials, sedi-tious writings, gambling equipment, or gold or sil-ver that doesn't show its actual quality.

- It's illegal to export more than 500 *pesos* in local currency.

Other restrictions. The minimum legal drinking age

(although rarely enforced) is 21.

- Filipinos frown on hitch-hiking (although they'll usually stop to pick up foreigners).

SAFETY

Crime. Avoid walking alone after dark — robberies can happen. Women traveling alone should be especially careful and take taxis at night.

- Pickpockets can be a problem. Their favorite haunts are crowded buses. Keep your wallet in your front pants pocket or use a money belt, and keep your handbag clutched tightly.

- To prevent theft put your valuables in hotel lock-boxes rather than leaving them in your room, and make sure that each taxi driver puts all your bags in the trunk and closes it before you get in.

- Filipinos are usually peaceful, but young men (many of whom are armed) can become quite violent if provoked. If a drunk ha-rasses you, look away and move on. Staring just invites a quarrel.

Health. The water in Manila is usually considered safe to drink, but stick to boiled or treated water. Drink soft drinks only if they're opened in your presence.

- If you eat food from street vendors, be careful to eat only fresh, well-cooked foods. Don't eat dairy products outside of hotels — even if they're pasteurized, they might not be safe.

- Medical services in Manila are quite reliable. All hospitals have 24-hour emergency centers. Medical supplies are readily available.

- Because of the climate, mosquitos are a problem. Carry mosquito coils with you to rural areas.

SHOPPING AND ENTERTAINMENT

Shopping. Shop hours are 10:00 A.M. to 9:00 P.M. Monday through Saturday. Many shops close for a two-hour lunch break, and many are open on Sunday afternoons and evenings.

• Bargaining is expected in markets and most shops. Even if the price is marked, ask what the store "discount" is. Start bargaining by offering half the quoted price, and always bargain with a smile.

• Store clerks usually follow you closely. They do this to help, not to keep you from shoplifting.

• Bargains to look for are *barong* shirts, custom-made shoes, hand-woven cloth, guitars, fine embroideries, and rattan furniture and baskets.

• Reproductions of Chinese-style porcelains are common, even in the most reputable, expensive shops. Only the stamp of the National Museum guarantees that a piece has been authenticated. Rare, unique antiques cannot be taken out of the country.

Entertainment. The Ermita strip in Manila features many of the capital's wildest, earthiest nightspots. Most of them are hot, loud, and crowded. A beer usually costs US$ 1.50, and hostess drinks are double that price.

Dancers perform above the bars, and *mamasans* are there to introduce them to the patrons.

• Most bars, especially those around Manila's Del Pilar Street, have "hospitality girls" who will chat and drink watered-down drinks with patrons for a fee. An hour of conversation can easily cost 50 *pesos*. Western women are welcome in most bars. (The Unescorted Ladies Not Allowed signs usually refer to local professionals.)

HOLIDAYS

Holidays: New Year's Day (January 1), Holy Thursday (three days before Easter), Good Friday (April), Bataan Day (April 9), Labor Day (May 1), Independence Day (June 12), Philippine-American Friendship Day (July 4), Thanksgiving Day (September 21), All-Saints Day (November 1), National Heroes Day (November 30), Christmas Day (December 25), Rizal Day (December 30).

- New Year's Day is the most eagerly-awaited festival next to Christmas. Families gather on New Year's Eve for an all-night vigil, with fireworks lasting until midnight. The fireworks are followed by the *media noche,* or midnight repast, and an early morning mass.

- During Holy Week (the week before Easter), everything closes down, and people refrain from eating meat or attending entertainments. Most people stay home and worship every day.

- Rizal Day commemorates the death of Dr. José P. Rizal, a national hero. Rizal was a novelist and physician whose writing fomented the revolt against Spain.

KEY PHRASES

English	Tagalog	Pronunciation
Good morning	Magandang umaga	Mahg'ndahng oo-mahga
Good afternoon	Magandang hapon	Mahg'ndahng hah-pon
Good evening	Magandang gabi	Mahg'ndahng ga-bee
Good night	"	"
Goodbye	Paalam na po	Pa'ahlm na paw
Please	Paki	Pa-kee
Thank you	Salamat sa iyo	Sa-lahmat sa-yo
Excuse me	Ipagpaumanhin	Eepahk-pawman-hin
Don't mention it	Walang anuman	Wahlahng ahnoo-mahn
Yes	Oo	Aw aw
No	Hindi	Hindi
I understand	Naintindihan ko	Na-in-tindi-hahn
I don't understand	Hindi ko naintindi-han	Hindi kaw na-in-tindi-hahn
How much?	Magkano?	M'k-kahnaw?
Does anyone here speak English?	Mayroon ba ritong naka pagsasalita ng Ingles?	Meh-rawn ba rreet'ng nukkah-puk-sahsah-lee-ta' n'ng Ingl-glehss?
Sir, Madam	Po*	Po
Mr.	Ginoong	Ghee-noong
Mrs.	Ginang	Ghee-nhang
Miss	Binibining	Be-nee-bee-neeng

(*To be polite people insert *po* after the first word or phrase of a sentence.)

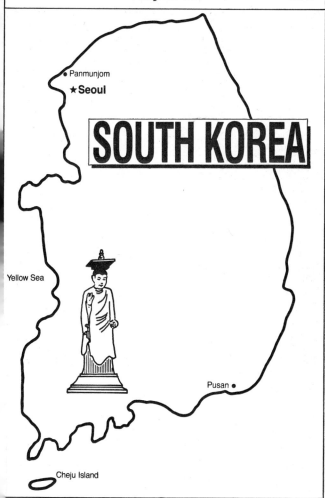

Situated between the two giants of China and Japan, the peninsula-bound Koreans have been overrun repeatedly by their powerful neighbors.

Korea's most bitter memory is of Japan's 1910-1945 occupation, and efforts to erase Korean language and culture. Ironically Japan's own culture was heavily influenced during the 4th century by Korea's Paek-che Kingdom, which transmitted to Japan Chinese writing, the works of Confucius, Buddhism, and art forms.

Today North Korea, the Democratic People's Republic of Korea, is off-limits to tourists and most other Westerners. But visitors are welcome in South Korea, the Republic of Korea, which has chic international hotels, plush restaurants, and a lively night life — at least in Seoul, the capital and the home of one out of every four Koreans. The Korean countryside is beautiful in the spring and fall and great for trekking — there are few fences. The stone temple complexes have a solid appearance unlike any others in Asia.

Don't leave Korea without experiencing a traditional Korean inn, or *yogwan,* which features floor mats for sleeping and heated floors for winter comfort.

MEETING PEOPLE

- The Koreans are not off-shoots of their neighbors. They and their language, culture, and foods are quite distinctive, and they will remind you of this in no uncertain terms.

GREETINGS

- When you greet someone for the first time that day, no matter what the time of day, say *"Annyong-hashimnikka."* It means "hello."

- Korean men greet other men by bowing slightly and shaking hands with either the right hand or both hands. Korean women rarely shake hands. Young children bow and nod their heads unless they are invited to shake hands, which is a great honor. Bow slightly when you greet either men or women.

- The senior person offers a handshake first, but the junior person bows first.

- Men should not initiate a handshake with a Korean woman; they should wait for her to offer her hand. Western women should initiate handshakes with Korean men.

- Pay complete attention to the person you're greeting, maintaining eye contact.

- When you meet a person older than yourself, be the first to offer greetings.

Names and titles. Both in speech and in writing, the family name is given first, followed by the two-part given name (a few people have a one-part given name). The first part of the given name is shared by all family members of the same generation. The second part of the given name is the individual's name. Thus, Pak Hyong Sim and Pak Hyong Su might be sister and brother. Distinguishing male from female names is very difficult.

- Never call Koreans by their given names — it's impolite and will make people wince visibly.

- Koreans often avoid using even family names by using titles, positions, or honorifics such as *sonsaengnim* (teacher or Mr.). When titles are used with a name, they follow after the name. If you aren't certain of a person's position, you may say "Mr. Kim" or "Kim *Sonsaengnim,*" but try to avoid using names whenever possible.

- Most Korean women keep their maiden names after they marry, so Mrs. Pak might be married to Mr. Yi.

- The suffix *-ssi* added to a family name can mean Mr., Mrs., or Miss. Don't be surprised if you're addressed as "George-ssi" by Koreans who think your first name is your family name.

Correspondence. The correct salutation is, "To my respected (title) (full name)." Don't separate the family name from the given name. You would address a Korean man named Pak Hyong Su, for example, as follows: "To my respected Mr. Pak Hyong Su."

- The closing paragraph of a letter usually includes good wishes for the recipient's health and business success. Always mention that you expect a reply; in general Koreans don't like to write letters.

CONVERSATION

- Good conversation subjects: Korea's cultural heritage (especially 11th-century Celadon pottery) and scenic beauty, sports such as baseball, the Olympics, your host's company, and your host's children.

- Subjects to avoid: Domestic politics, Communism, Japan, trade friction, and your male host's wife.

- Koreans might ask you rather personal questions, such as how much you earn, where you're going, or why you don't have children. Don't be offended; they're just trying to show interest or determine your position in the social order. They don't always expect an honest answer.

- When you address a mixed group of Koreans, address them as "Gentlemen and Ladies." Men come first in Korea.

PHRASES TO KNOW

- Korean is a distinct language, unintelligible to Korea's Chinese and Japanese neighbors. It is spoken by the 45 million people on the Korean peninsula and by about a half million Korean-Japanese people in Japan.

- The Korean alphabet (*Han'gul*) is phonetic and easy to learn in just a few hours. Most newspapers and books use a mixture of *Han'gul* and Chinese characters.

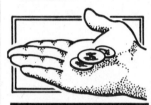

CURRENCY

- The Korean unit of currency is the *won*. One U.S. dollar is worth about 743 *won* (August 1987 rates). Coins are available in 1, 5, 10, 50, and 100, and 500 *won*. Notes are available in 500, 1,000, 5,000, and 10,000 *won*.

- Exchange rates at banks are better than those at hotels.

- Korea has an illegal black market for U.S. dollars that pays about 7% above the bank rate. When you walk through the open markets, people might approach you to buy your dollars.

- When you leave Korea reconvert all your leftover Korean *won.* Banks in Japan and some other countries will not exchange *won,* even if you have your currency exchange receipts.

- International credit cards are widely accepted at tourist hotels, department stores, and expensive restaurants. In shops where you bargain, however, you'll have to pay a surcharge of about 5% to use a credit card.

- Traveler's checks are often abbreviated to "T.C.," or *ti-sshi.* You might find them hard to change outside of Seoul, even at banks.

ETIQUETTE

GENERAL MANNERS

- Koreans don't like to say no. They sometimes indicate a negative answer by tipping their heads back and inhaling audibly through their teeth.

- "Yes" does not always mean the person agrees with you. It can also

mean, "I hear and understand you."

- Rather than admitting that they don't know the answer to your question, Koreans sometimes give the answer they think you want to hear. They believe that it's more important to preserve your good feelings than to give you accurate but unpleasant information.

- You might see Koreans laugh in situations where a laugh or smile would be inappropriate in the West. Koreans often laugh to cover their feelings when they're embarrassed, hurt, or shocked. It does not mean they're taking the situation lightly.

- When a potential loss of face is involved, appearing proper is far more important than being proper. Avoid embarrassing a Korean at all costs — even to the extent of being untruthful, if the truth would cause a loss of face.

- Maintaining harmony (*kibun*) is of the utmost importance. Don't upset people's feelings by publicly criticizing or disagreeing with them. Koreans avoid open criticism, abruptness, and public disagreement because they believe that no one has the right to upset someone's feelings or tarnish their self-esteem.

- Extreme modesty in talking about your status, family, or accomplishments is a social tradition. Don't be surprised if a man makes disparaging remarks about his wife and children.

- Being polite includes politely rejecting compliments and being reluctant to accept high honors. If someone compliments you politely deny the compliment. Don't say "thank you"; it's impolite.

- Older people warrant special respect. Stand when they enter a room, ask them how old they are (they're proud of their age), and don't smoke in front of them. Remove your dark glasses (or even your regular glasses) when you talk to elders.

- Men take priority in Korea. Thus, women help men with their coats and let men go through doors first.

- Men and women socialize separately at social events and dinners, whether at home or in a restaurant. They often go to separate rooms.

- Koreans prefer sons to daughters. A couple might be touchy if you congratulate them on the birth of a daughter — especially if she's the latest in a succession of daughters.

- Women visitors to South Korea shouldn't misinterpret stares or attempts at conversation; they usually result from simple curiosity. In rural areas foreigners with blonde or red hair might find themselves the center of attention and might even have their hair touched out of curiosity (especially by elderly people).

- A queue is a fragile thing in Korea and usually disintegrates into chaos when a bus or subway train arrives. If you hesitate even slightly in a taxi queue or ticket line, people might either jump in front of you or reach around you to put their money down. Be as aggressive as everybody else or you won't get anywhere.

- Pushing and jostling are the norm in streets, subways, and department stores. Don't take it personally; everyone gets pushed.

- On sidewalks and stairs, keep to the left.

- If you're talking to someone in a hallway and someone else wants to pass, move backwards and let the third person go between you rather than behind you.

- When you go through a doorway, don't expect the people in front of you to hold the door open for you. Women shouldn't expect men to let them go first.

- Party invitations are usually given on very short notice — typically by telephone, often on the same day as the party. If written invitations are sent, RSVP requests are often ignored.

- Eating in the street is considered crude.

- Koreans eat lots of garlic but don't like to hear disparaging remarks about their food or breath. To Koreans meat-eating Westerners smell bad (the odor results from bucolic acid).

- Blowing your nose in front of other people is very rude. If you use paper tissues, throw them away. Never return them to your pocket or purse.

BODY LANGUAGE

- Koreans of the same sex often hold hands in public. However, don't put your arm around someone's shoulders or pat someone on the back unless you're very good friends.

- Be particularly careful not to touch older people or people of the opposite sex.

- When you're talking to people, keep your hands in full view, not in your pockets or behind your back. Use both hands when you give or receive any object, putting your left hand under your right forearm.

- In meetings and other formal occasions, if you want to cross your legs put one knee over the other and point your soles and toes downward. In very formal situations don't cross your legs at all. Never put your feet on a desk or chair.

- To beckon someone hold your arm out, palm down, and move your fingers up and down. The Western beckoning gesture of moving the fingers with the palm facing up is very rude in Korea.

- Korean women cover their mouths when they laugh. Men should never do this.

- Cover your mouth when you yawn or use a toothpick.

DRESS

- Dress well for all occasions. It shows respect for those you are with.

MEN For business wear a dark suit and tie with a white shirt. For informal occasions wear conservative pants and a shirt (avoid yellow or pink). For formal occasions wear a gray or navy suit and a white shirt with a tie.

WOMEN Korea is a conservative Confucian country, so women are expected to dress modestly. Don't wear revealing clothing, shorts, or sleeveless blouses. Also avoid wearing tight skirts, since in homes and restaurants you often sit on the floor.

- For business wear a suit or conservative dress. For informal occasions wear a conservative dress or pantsuit. For formal events wear a cocktail dress.

NATIVE DRESS On holidays you'll see Korean women wearing the traditional *hanbok,* a long skirt (*chima*) tied at the chest with a waist-length jacket (*chogori*) worn over the top. The sleeves of the *chogori* are curved.

TEMPLES

- You may wear shoes around temple grounds, but remove them when you enter a building.

- Many temples charge an entrance fee.

- Photography is permitted in temples unless signs specifically prohibit it.

PRIVATE HOMES

- Business associates and acquaintances seldom invite visitors to their homes, but friends often invite visitors home for dinner to try their Korean specialties. Homes are small, and all the rooms are used for sleeping, so don't expect your Korean friends to invite you to spend the night.

- Never drop in for a visit unannounced. Most Koreans prefer to meet at a favorite coffee shop.

- Tourists can arrange to visit a Korean home by contacting the Private Home Stay Advisor in the

Tourist Information Center behind the Seoul City Hall.

- Most houses have both a central courtyard, with a gateway that opens inward, and a high wall that blocks off any view from the street. Most homes also have sliding doors and windows covered with fragile paper.

- Before you enter the house, remove your shoes. Leave them at the front door with the toes pointed away from the house. Before you actually step in, wait to be invited in two or three times.

- If you're invited to a home for a meal or party, bring a small gift. Good choices are nicely wrapped foods such as fruit or cooking oils, which you can find at large department stores. Use both hands to present the gift when you arrive.

- During your visit don't expect the host to show you around the house — it's considered private. Don't wander around on your own or peek into the kitchen.

- The bathroom door stays closed all the time. To find out if the room is occupied, either knock or cough to announce your presence.

- When you leave the host will see you to the door or even outside before saying goodbye.

PERSONAL GIFTS

- When you present or receive a gift, always use both hands. Gifts are never opened in the presence of the person who gave them. If you give someone money as a present, enclose it in an envelope.

- Liquor is a good gift for Korean men, but never give liquor to a woman unless you make it clear that it's meant for her husband.

- Koreans feel obliged to reciprocate gifts in kind, and many can't afford escalated gift wars, so don't give expensive gifts.

- Accepting a gift incurs an obligation. If you wish to avoid a major obligation, return an expensive gift to the person who gave it to you, saying something like, "This is too much." Be diplomatic so the other person doesn't lose face.

TIPPING

- Tipping is not a traditional Korean custom, so when in doubt don't tip.

- Hotels: Most hotels add a 10% service charge to your bill, so tipping is unnecessary. Most hotels prohibit tipping their bellhops.

- Restaurants: Restaurant bills usually include a 10% tip, so any additional small tip is at your discretion. If the bill doesn't include a service charge, tip 10%. Tipping is unnecessary in small, family-run eateries.

- Taxis: You don't need to tip unless the driver helped with your luggage or provided an extra service. It's customary, however, to leave any change under 100 *won.*

- Porters: Tip 150 to 250 *won* per piece of luggage.

- Barbers and beauticians: Tip 10% to 15%.

- Chambermaids and cloakroom attendants: Tip 500 to 700 *won.*

FOODS

MEALS

Breakfast (*choban* or *achim*): 7:30 to 9:00 A.M. A typical breakfast is rice, fish soup, fish, *kimchi* (pickled vegetables), and coffee (*kopi*). All tourist hotels serve Western breakfasts.

Lunch (*jomsim*): Noon to 2:00 P.M. Rice, *kimchi,* soup, and fish are the usual fare. Office workers eat a quick meal of noodles.

Dinner (*chonyok*): 6:00 to 8:00 P.M. This is the main meal of the day and features soup, seafood, rice, and *kimchi,* often with several side dishes such as bean sprouts, spinach, and bean paste. All the dishes arrive at the same time and can be eaten in any order.

WHERE TO EAT

- Many Korean restaurants are on the second floors (or higher) of office buildings.

- *Hanjonshik* restaurants are expensive (between 15,000 and 28,000 *won* per person) but serve full-course Korean meals, sometimes buffet style. Many of these restaurants are in tourist hotels and feature performances of Korean classical music and dance.

- *Taejung shiksa* restaurants are cheaper; most people favor them for lunch. Typical meals are noodles, dumplings, beef-rib soup, garnished rice (*pibimpap*), and fermented soybean paste casseroles (*toin jangtijigye*). You can usually find these eateries in shopping centers.

- Try *kalbi* and *pulgogi-jip* restaurants for the famous Korean barbecued or charcoal-grilled beef ribs, pork, or marinated beef. *Naengmyuon* (buckwheat noodles) or *paekban* (rice and side dishes) will be served with the meat dish. Most of these restaurants are in the Yong-dong area south of Seoul's Han River.

- For a quick meal head for department store basements, which have a variety of inexpensive snack bars.

- Look for the covered *pojang macha* food carts set up at noon and at night around train stations, nightclub districts, and markets. They cook and serve battered vegetables, sweet pancakes, fish, dumplings, and rice cakes.

- Vegetarians can enjoy traditionally cooked mountain vegetables at the *Sanchon* restaurants in the Insa-dong and Namyong-dong districts of Seoul.

- *Makkolli* or wine houses (*suljip*) are the common man's drinking places. They're less expensive than the beer halls, which also feature floor shows. Order a *pindaedok* (vegetable pancake) to go with your *makkolli*.

- You'll find tearooms (*tabang*s) on almost every street in Korea, often in basements off the sidewalks. They serve hot and cold teas, light beverages, and coffee. Barley tea is free with every order. Very few *tabang*s serve food. Feel free to sit at the table as long as you wish.

- Coffee in a teahouse costs about half what it does in a hotel coffee shop. It's also available from street vending machines for about 150 *won*.

- Menus are usually signs (in Korean) posted on the wall; individual menus are seldom available.

- Few restaurants have no-smoking sections.

FOODS TO TRY

- Korean food tends to be very hot and spicy, demonstrating use of hot pepper and garlic.

- Glutinous (sticky) rice is the foundation for all meals except noodle dishes. Besides *kimchi,* soup, and rice, dinners include three, five, or seven side dishes such as bean sprouts, spinach, or kelp.

- All the dishes of the main meal are served at once, not in courses. Soup is eaten with (not before) the other foods. Salads and desserts are uncommon.

- Koreans don't drink alcohol without accompanying it with a meal or snack. Cocktails are not served before a meal.

Specialties. Try these Korean specialties: *pulgogi* (barbecued beef), *kalbi* (marinated, barbecued short ribs), *kimchi* (pickled vegetables), *mandu* (stuffed dump-

lings), *pibimpap* (rice topped with vegetables and egg), and *pam* (roasted chestnuts).

- *Pulgogi* is a Korean delicacy made from barbecued beef slices seasoned with garlic and spices and cooked over a grill. The beef is wrapped in a piece of lettuce with more garlic and bean paste.

- *Kimchi* is served with every meal. It can be made from cabbage (*paechu*), radishes (*daikon*), or other vegetables depending on the season. The vegetables are mixed with chili pepper, garlic, spring onions, and ginger, and left in a cool place to ferment.

- Try *shinsollo,* a mixture of beef, pine nuts, and vegetables cooked in a brass bowl heated by a tube in the center. Charcoal is burned under the tube, slowly cooking the bowl's contents at the table.

- Other dishes to try are *mulmandu* (dumplings filled with meat and vegetables), *champong* (noodles with vegetables or meat), *udong* (noodle soup with vegetables and meat), and *takgogi* (fried chicken).

- Dessert is rarely served

with meals; when it is, it usually consists of fresh fruit. Coffee shops serve desserts such as *sujongwa* (dried persimmons and pine nuts in ginger tea) and rice cakes filled with sweet red bean paste or a mixture of cinnamon, honey, and sesame seeds.

Beverages. Don't drink the water outside of the major hotels or use ice unless you know it was made from boiled water.

- *Boricha,* a weak beverage made from burned barley or rice, accompanies most meals.

- Coffee often has milk and sugar added automatically. If you don't want either one, make that clear before you're served.

- *Makkolli* is a potent, milky white Korean liquor with a long history. It's made from rice and barley and is best consumed in *makkolli* houses while listening to traditional Korean music. It's considered a low-class drink.

- *Soju* is "white lightning" watered down to 20% or 35% alcohol. It's usually served with such dishes as hot fish soup and barbecued pork. *Soju* tends to creep up on you and leave you with a very bad hangover.

TABLE MANNERS

- At lunch hour you might get seated with a stranger. You don't need to start a conversation.

- To get a waiter's attention, say *"yobo-seyo"* (hello).

- At traditional meals in homes or some restaurants, you'll sit on the floor at a low table. Seat yourself on the cushion and cross your legs. When this position becomes unbearable, bend your legs to the side but don't stick them straight out under the table.

- Some restaurants require payment before the meal.

Utensils. Chopsticks and large spoons are the utensils used. The chopsticks might be of either the thick, blunt Chinese type or the thin, metal Korean type (these are unique to Korea). To use the chopsticks hold the upper stick between your thumb and first two fingers while you keep the lower stick stationary with your ring finger. For maximum leverage hold the sticks one-third of the way down.

- Eat rice and *kimchi* with either the chopsticks or the spoon. Use the spoon for the soup; when you're done put the spoon either in your soup bowl or over your rice bowl, not down on the table.

- While you're eating rest your chopsticks either on top of a dish or bowl or on the chopstick rest. Never leave chopsticks or the spoon sticking into the rice — that's how offerings are made to ancestors. You can leave the spoon in the soup or on a plate, but not with the concave side down.

- Take the top off the rice bowl and put it on the floor under your place at the low table.

- When you eat don't raise the rice bowl or any other dishes to your mouth.

- When you pick up any food, don't use your hands. Use toothpicks to pick up pieces of fruit.

- Koreans often serve food from the communal dishes with their used soup spoons.

- When you finish eating lay your chopsticks neatly on the table.

- When you're served tea or coffee, the spoon will be on your side of the cup. After you use the spoon, put it on the side of the cup away from you.

- Napkins aren't used, but you'll often be given a hot or cold damp towel before the meal to wash your hands and face.

- When you use a toothpick cover your mouth with your hand.

Dining with others. In a home elders will be served first and children last, a reflection of the Korean respect for age.

- Talking a lot during dinner is impolite. Don't be surprised if the conversation lags during dinner and picks up again afterwards.

- To be polite pour soy sauce into your neighbor's small sauce dish; your neighbor will do the same for you. Do the same with tea and alcoholic drinks.

- Drinking partners trade and fill each other's cups. Refusing someone's cup is rude.

- People never pour their own drinks. Diners pour each other's drinks, watch the glasses, and pour refills when their neighbor's glass is dry. Younger people pour for older or more senior drinkers. Women pour for men but never for other women.

- When you pour a drink for someone else, hold the bottle with one hand and support your forearm with your free hand. Always lift your glass when someone pours for you.

- If you don't want a refill, leave some of the drink in your glass.

- Koreans forgive drunkenness easily.

- Pass food with your right hand, and with your left hand supporting your right forearm.

- When you offer a toast, say *"kon-bae,"* (dry cup).

- Show appreciation for the meal by slurping the soup and smacking your lips. A belch after the meal compliments the host.

- No matter how you feel, don't joke about the food or show any hint of revulsion at dishes such as chicken feet, soup made with whole fish, or small, dry whole fish eaten as a snack.

- Completely cleaning your plate is bad form. It implies that you're still hungry because your host didn't provide enough food.

- Hosts urge guests to eat more but respect a firm refusal. If you want another serving, politely refuse your host's first two offers and accept the third. If you're hosting the dinner, make sure you offer three times.

- If you dine in a home, let the hostess know you appreciated her work. Don't eat all the food; the children will appreciate the leftovers.

- The person who suggested the meal should pay for everyone, but it's polite to argue good-naturedly over the privilege of paying. Younger people might be expected to treat their elders.

- After a meal Koreans like to entertain by having each person sing a song. If you're asked to sing, don't decline — it spoils the mood and leaves a bad impression. Sing any traditional Western song in English.

- At a dinner party leave soon after the entertainment finishes. It's not customary to linger long after a meal.

Banquets. At a banquet the host doesn't put food on the guests' plates; however, women attendants might do this.

- Dishes are served not all at once, but rather in a

sequence of up to twelve courses preceded by appetizers. Soup is usually served just before the main course. Make sure you at least taste every dish.

- The first course is *kujolpan,* a large platter of meat-and-vegetable hors d´oeuvres and thin pancakes. Select some of the meat-and-vegetable tidbits and roll them up in a pancake.

ACCOMMODATIONS

Hotels. Most Western-style hotels are first rate. They'll include a service charge in the bill, so you don't need to tip.

- If you're visiting during the peak travel seasons (April-May and September-October), make reservations well ahead of time.

- Many tourist hotels have a few Korean-style rooms modifed for use by foreign visitors.

- The bottom floors of many of Seoul's tourist hotels lead into underground shopping arcades that turn into a vast labyrinth interconnecting different parts of the city. Mark your trail; it's easy to get lost.

- Many hotels (as well as some other buildings) have no fourth floor. The Korean word for "four" sounds the same as the word for "death."

- Some smaller hotels might ask for your passport when you register, or might even keep it overnight. Don't worry; they'll return it to you.

- For an adventure try the inexpensive Korean-style inns called *yogwan*s. These traditional inns have *ondol* (charcoal-heated floors — leave your windows cracked open to avoid asphyxiation) and cushions rather than chairs. Your maid will roll out a mattress (*yo*) at bedtime and give you hard pillows made from grain husks.

- Remove your shoes before you enter the rooms of a *yogwan* and use the slippers provided for walking in the rooms and on the veranda.

- *Yogwan*s don't have dining rooms or restaurants. If the rate includes a meal, the owner will either prepare it for you or have the food delivered from a restaurant, and serve you in your room.

- *Yogwan* rooms don't have locking doors (it would be an insult to the other guests). Leave your valuables with the manager.

Rest rooms. Department stores, hotels, and parks have public rest rooms. Those in department stores and hotels are Western-style; those in public parks and other places are of the squatting type.

- *Yogwan*s have communal rest rooms and washing areas. The washing area is usually in the center of the compound, surrounded by the *yogwan* building. Koreans usually wash their face, hands, and feet before they retire. While you're in the rest room, wear the slippers that you'll find just inside the door, and leave your other slippers or shoes outside the door to indicate your presence. Don't wear the rest room slippers anywhere else.

TRANSPORTATION

- Heavy morning fog around Seoul sometimes forces planes to divert to Pusan, so try to book flights into Seoul that arrive after 10:00 A.M.

- Try to avoid traveling in Seoul during the rush hours from 8:00 to 10:00 A.M. and 6:00 to 7:30 P.M.

- To find your destination, especially in Seoul, you might need the help of police officers or taxi drivers. Seoul has 426 small districts, or *dong*. Some streets have no names. House numbers don't follow a sequential order down the street, as they do in the West; instead, they follow the order in which the houses within each district were built.

- Korean place names are romanized according to several different systems, so you might see town names written several different ways (for example, Chamsil, Chamshil, and Jamshil are all the same place).

PUBLIC TRANSPORTATION

- On trains, buses, and subways the passengers sitting down usually hold packages for those who are standing. Offer your seat to anyone who looks over sixty years old.

- Smoking is not permitted on buses or subways.

Buses. Buses are recommended for inter-city travel; they're inexpensive and easy to find. In rural areas just stand along any remote, rough dirt road and a bus will come along in a few minutes. Try to find a seat near the front — traveling over unpaved roads, these buses offer one of the world's roughest rides.

- Most buses between major towns are air-conditioned and you must catch them at a bus station. *Kosok* buses are speedy highway-express buses that require reserved tickets. *Chikhaeng* buses are first-class, direct-route buses a bit slower than the *kosok*s.

- For local buses save money by buying tokens at shops and kiosks near marked bus stops. Most places that sell tokens have a Bus Tokens sign in English. You can also pay the female conductor after you board — just hold out a handful of change and she'll take the correct amount (about 120 *won* regardless of distance). Buses run from 5:00 A.M. to 11:30 P.M. every day.

- Some buses don't allow passengers to stand. These buses are more expensive (350 *won*) than the regular city buses, which are often packed like sardine cans.

Taxis. You can catch a taxi either in front of a hotel or at a yellow taxi stand. At a stand move quickly when your turn comes, or someone will jump in front of you. To catch a taxi on the street, shout your destination as one pulls near you; if the driver doesn't want to go there, it'll just zip by.

- Taxis come in two basic kinds, both with meters. Regular taxis are very small and are often green or yellow. "Call" taxis are beige, larger, and more expensive. You can get a call taxi by dialing 414-0151.

- If a call taxi pulls up to a taxi stand when it's your turn, or you're led to one at the airport, and you'd prefer a cheaper regular taxi, just extend your hand palm outward with the fingers outstretched and rotate your hand. This is a polite gesture that means "No, thank you."

- Taxi trunks are very small, so your luggage will usually join you in the back seat.

- Some drivers try to get two or three people going in the same direction to share a taxi, with each rider paying the full fare. This practice, called *hapsung,* used to be common but is now illegal.

- Look for taxi drivers wearing yellow shirts and jackets adorned with awards. They've been recognized for their safe driving records.

- Trips between midnight and 4:00 A.M. cost 20% more than the usual fare. This surcharge should appear on the meter.

- You can use taxis for long-distance travel, but negotiate the fare before you get in.

- Some taxis, called *koax* taxis, are for American military personnel and have signs in English. If you look like a member of the military, you can

sometimes catch one near a military base. You must pay for them in U.S. dollars.

Trains. For inter-city travel trains are a safe alternative to express buses. The five classes of trains, in order of increasing speed, are *Pidulgiho* (has frequent stops), *Potong kuphaeng* (has berths and runs at night), *Tukkup* (limited express with reserved seats), *Mugunghwaho* (air-conditioned), and *Saemaul ho* (air-conditioned express with dining car). Purchase your tickets in advance. Round-trip tickets are not available.

- On express trains waitresses pass through the cars selling sweets, drinks, snacks, and box lunches (*toshirak*) containing rice, eggs, fish, and pickled vegetables.

Subways. Seoul's rapidly expanding subway system is both quick and inexpensive. The subways operate from 5:00 A.M. to 12:30 A.M. every day, and the different subway lines are color-coded.

- You can buy your ticket at either a machine or a ticket window. A trip within downtown Seoul costs 170 *won.* After you buy your ticket, insert it into the turnstile at the station entrance and retrieve it from the other end. Keep the ticket with you; you'll need to insert it into another turnstile at your destination.

DRIVING

- Korean drivers are extremely reckless. Driving is very dangerous and foolhardy for a foreign visitor to attempt. If you have an International Driver's License, car rental is possible (but complex).

- Driving is on the right, as in North America.

- Traffic accidents are common. Police automatically arrest the principals until they determine who was at fault.

- When you get on a toll superhighway, stop at the entrance gate to get a ticket. To get the correct ticket, you must know what exit you plan to use.

BUSINESS

BUSINESS HOURS

Business offices: 9:00 A.M. to 5:00 or 6:00 P.M. Monday through Friday, with an hour off for lunch around noon. Many offices open on Saturday from 9:00 A.M. to 1:00 P.M.

Banks: 9:00 A.M. to 4:30 P.M. Monday through Friday, and 9:00 A.M. to 1:00 P.M. Saturday. During the winter (December through February), opening and closing times are moved back thirty minutes.

Government offices: Same as business offices.

BUSINESS CUSTOMS

- The best months to travel to Korea on business are February through June, September, November, and early December. Avoid holiday-filled October, as well as July through mid-August, when many Koreans take their vacations. The second half of December is a poor time to visit because of the Christmas holiday.

- Korean business people are slow to accept someone they don't know, so have a mutually respected third party introduce or refer you. Without a referral your request for an appointment probably won't even be answered.

- Businesswomen are rare in Korea.

- Before you begin negotiations or meetings, find out who from the Korean side will be present. Sending a high-level corporate officer to meet with Korean middle-managers will embarrass both sides.

- In negotiations Koreans are more direct than the Japanese but place just as much importance on trust and a comfortable relationship. Negotiations will take a long time and might require more than one trip.

- Be well prepared for negotiations. Admitting that you don't know the answer to a question might cause the Koreans to lose faith in you and feel embarrassed for having asked you the question.

- Korean negotiators usually start off with an extreme position, expecting to back down. You should do the same and leave room for compromise.

- In negotiations emotional considerations are often more important than Western-style logic.

- Korean business people sometimes use appeals to sentiment during negotiations, reminding you that Korea is a poor country that deserves special concessions. Be sympathetic but firm. Build some negotiating room into your proposal before you start so you can grant concessions without jeopardizing your position.

- If you plan to conduct long-term business in Korea, plan on making frequent trips there. Personal contact is essential.

Business etiquette. Bring business cards; they're very important in introductions. Your hotel can help you get some printed with one side in Korean. Never hand a Japanese-language card to a Korean.

- After you receive your counterpart's name card, place it on the table in front of you. Address your counterpart occasionally during the meeting.

- If you know a person's title, use it in address — for example, Deputy Manager Lee. Over half of all Koreans have the family names Kim, Lee, or Pak; using titles helps to differentiate individuals.

- Korean business people are proud of their nation's cultural history and will appreciate your showing some knowledge of Korean culture. Be very careful not to confuse Japanese and Korean culture. Koreans are very sensitive about any hint of Japanese influence because of the 1905-1945 occupation.

- Boasting about your company's achievements is bad manners. Instead, include this information in the written materials you leave with your Korean counterparts.

- Until the Koreans begin to let down their reserve, be formal and polite. Don't be too familiar with your counterparts, especially those of higher or lower rank.

- Koreans don't like to give or receive a flat no, so they might say yes (even if they don't mean it) just to avoid upsetting you. Phrase your questions so they don't require a yes-or-no answer ("When can you provide it?" is a better question than, "Can you provide it by Wednesday?").

- Koreans, including business people, express frustration and anger much more freely than do their Asian neighbors, so be prepared for histrionics. Threats to cut off discussions are often made indiscriminately; don't take them literally and don't respond in kind.

- When you're speaking with people, maintain eye contact with them.

- Contracts might be signed with a personal seal (*tojang*) made of wood or stone, with the person's name carved on the end. The *tojang* is used with crimson ink.

- Don't sign a contract with a red pen.

Appointments and meetings. Before you visit a company or government office, you must secure an appointment. The Koreans will want to research your company before you arrive.

- The best times to schedule appointments are around 10:00 or 11:00

A.M. and 2:00 or 3:00 P.M. You might also suggest a business dinner. Business breakfasts are rare.

- Koreans expect Westerners to be on time for meetings and are usually punctual themselves. Meetings often last past normal business hours.

- The meeting will probably take place in a small reception room at the Korean company's office. You'll sit opposite your Korean counterparts at a low table. Sit where they indicate. As an honor they'll probably seat you opposite the door.

- Before the meeting begins you'll be offered tea, or perhaps coffee or soda. A "tea girl" will serve yellow-green tea (the white things floating in it are pine nuts, not lemon seeds), kneeling as she hands it to you. Accept it with both hands and drink it without comment.

- Meetings sometimes take place in coffee shops, especially those in the lobbies of international hotels. The coffee shop at your hotel is a good place to suggest if you want to meet on neutral ground.

- The first meeting is to get acquainted, so don't launch right into your business proposal. Start at the periphery and gradually zero in on the business.

- To ensure that what you said during a meeting was understood, exchange notes with your Korean counterparts after the meeting and send a typewritten version later.

- Observe the greeting and exit bows at a meeting. If the Koreans bow longer and deeper at the end of the meeting than at the beginning, they felt the meeting went well. A perfunctory departing bow might mean trouble.

Business gifts and entertainment. Bring gifts to present at your first meeting. It's best to present your gift after your host has given one to you. Good gift choices are crafts, foods, or other items from your region: pens, whiskey, Scotch, or fruit packages. If you don't want to carry gifts to Korea, department stores sell packaged foods designed to be given as gifts.

- Business entertaining takes place at restaurants and bars; don't expect to be invited to a home. Spouses are not included.

- Koreans like to take business guests to dinner at a restaurant. It gives them an opportunity to judge their guests' character and determine whether they want to keep working with them. At dinner avoid talking business unless the Koreans bring the subject up.

- After dinner your hosts might invite you to go drinking with them. Refusing is impolite. They'll probably take you to a nightclub or bar where hostesses will sit between you and pour drinks, ask questions, and feed you snacks. Their job is to help (along with the alcohol) to break down your reserve and permit an informal relationship to develop between businessmen.

- Members of the group will pour drinks for each other. Some will probably begin to sing to the group using the microphone provided. If you're asked to sing it's very impolite to refuse. Singing something in English is acceptable.

- Your hosts might also take you to one of Seoul's very expensive *kisaeng* houses, where talented, charming women (*kisaeng*) entertain guests with talking and music while they eat. Don't expect more than flirtation and singing from a *kisaeng*. You need local references to get a reservation at a *kisaeng* house.

- If you invite Korean businessmen to dinner or drinking, don't invite their wives — it's improper. Don't bring your spouse or anyone else not involved in the business relationship.

TELEPHONES AND MAIL

Telephones. Public telephone booths are usually orange; you'll see them on many sidewalks in the cities. Other public phones are in train stations, subways, hotels, and restaurants. Most people can't afford phones in their homes (they cost between 450,000 and 750,000 *won*).

- To make a local call, use the red or green public phones in stores and restaurants. Insert two 10-*won* coins and dial. The connection will automatically cut off after three minutes unless you insert more coins

- You can make direct long-distance calls at yellow public pay phones in post offices and major hotels. These phones take only 10-*won* and 100-*won* coins, so have your money ready. If you hear beeps during your call, insert more money quickly or you'll be cut off. Extra coins will be returned.

- To take advantage of a 20% lower tariff, make international calls between 11:00 P.M. and 7:00 A.M.

- To make an overseas call, dial 1035 or 1037; to send a cable, dial 115.

- When you answer the phone say *"yobo-seyo"* (hello).

Mail. Main post offices are open from 9:00 A.M. to 6:00 P.M. weekdays.

- You can buy stamps at hotels, shops, and post offices.

- Mail carriers deliver letters door to door, but you must pick up parcels at the post office.

- Large post offices offer a parcel-packing service for a small fee.

LEGAL MATTERS

Customs and immigration. Visas are required for entry into Korea. Transit visas are valid for 15 days, and tourist visas are valid for 60 days. Both types permit multiple entries for five years.

- When you enter Korea don't try to bring in any narcotics, firearms, pornographic materials, or Marxist literature. It's also illegal to bring in Korean currency.

- Each time you exchange currency, keep the receipt. You'll need the receipts to change any leftover *won* when you depart.

- Selling cameras, stereos, and similar items without paying the large duty on them is illegal. If they were noted on your entry papers, you must have them when you leave or you'll have to pay import duty.

Other restrictions. Don't take photos from airplanes, at airports, harbors, or underground shopping areas, near military bases, or from anywhere you can see the entire city of Seoul. South Korea is sensitive about security risks because of the military threat posed by North Korea.

SAFETY

- Nationwide air-raid drills are held at 2:00 P.M. on the fifteenth day of each month. When you hear the sirens, head for a nearby building to wait out the fifteen-minute drill. Nighttime drills are sometimes held at 9:00 P.M. All traffic stops during the drills.

Crime. Physical assault is very rare in Korea, but beware of pickpockets on crowded buses and subways. Keep your wallet in your front pocket or your purse tightly clutched in your arms. Walking alone at night is fairly safe.

- Women traveling alone are quite safe in Korea and are unlikely to be harassed.

- If you need help look for one of the many police boxes on major streets. They're marked by a lighted yellow sign on the building.

- A large black market exists for U.S. dollars, cameras, and similar items. Don't be surprised if someone approaches you, but don't sell anything.

Health. Water is safe to drink in the major hotels, but avoid it elsewhere unless it's been boiled.

- Many rivers, lakes, and harbors are heavily polluted with sewage and industrial waste. Don't swim in them.

- Before you eat fruit peel it or wash it thoroughly. Wash vegetables as well — human waste is sometimes used as a fertilizer.

SHOPPING AND ENTERTAINMENT

Shopping. Most shops, eateries, and service establishments are open every day from 9:00 A.M. to 10:00 P.M., including on weekends and public holidays. The larger department stores close earlier, usually about 7:00 or 8:00 P.M., and close on one weekday. Department stores are unbearably crowded on Saturday and Sunday.

- Bargaining is the rule, except in department stores and shops clearly marked as "one price" stores. Department store jewelry counters do negotiate prices.

- Haggling should always be good-natured. Start by offering one-half to two-thirds of the price the merchant is asking. If your offer is accepted, you're obligated to buy.

- If you don't plan to buy anything, avoid being a shop's first customer of the day. Shop owners believe that if the first customer doesn't buy anything, the whole day will be bad.

Entertainment. For a taste of the local social life, go to a neighborhood beer hall (*pee-ah hol*) featuring stage shows and Korean beer. There are three types of beer halls. Some have live entertainment but no dancing. Their beer and snacks (*anju*) are moderately priced; you're expected to order snacks,

but you needn't tip the waitress. Others have semi-private booths and hostesses for whom you buy expensive drinks. Still others are inexpensive places with bottled or draft beer and canned music.

- Discos (nightclubs) are popular. Most of them are in hotels. The international tourist hotels have plush discos where locals and hotel guests mingle; expect the tab for four people to be about 70,000 to 100,000 *won.* Most (but not all) of the women sitting in hotel discos are actually there to conduct business and will try to negotiate a "deal" while they're on the dance floor.

- Most of the discos south of the Han River in Seoul serve no liquor and are crowded with teenagers.

- Nightclubs in the Itaewon area of Seoul cater to the American military and can be quite rowdy.

- At movie theaters don't be surprised to find chicken feet and dried squid served as snacks.

HOLIDAYS

Holidays: New Year (January 1-3), Independence Movement Day (March 1), Labor Day (March 10), Arbor Day (April 5), Children's Day (May 5), Memorial Day (June 6), Constitution Day (July 17), Liberation Day (August 15), Armed Forces Day (October 1), National Foundation Day (October 24), Han'gul Day (October 9), United Nations Day (October 24), and Christmas Day (December 25). Holidays with variable dates include Buddha's Birthday (May) and the Moon Festival or Ch'usok (September or October).

• Han'gul Day celebrates the anniversary of *Han' gul,* Korea's written language, invented by King Sejong in the 15th century.

• Buddha's Birthday, or the Feast of the Lanterns, is one of Korea's most colorful celebrations. This festival takes place on the eighth day of the fourth lunar month and features parades of gaily dressed people carrying lanterns. Look for rituals at temples throughout Korea.

• The Moon Festival (Ch'usok) is the Korean Thanksgiving and takes place the day of the full moon in late September or early October. People visit family tombs and make offerings of food. Bus and train seats are scarce, and many shops close.

KEY PHRASES

English	Korean	Pronunciation
English	*Korean*	*Pronunciation*
Good morning	Annyong hasimnika	Ahn-yohng hah-shim-nee-kah
Good afternoon	"	"
Good evening	"	"
Goodbye (leaving)	Annyonghi kasip-siyo	Ahn-yohng-he kae-sip-si-yo
(staying)	Annyonghi kesip-siyo	Ahn-yohng-he kae-sip-si-yo
Please	Chom	Chum
Thank you	Kamsa hamnida	Kahm-sah hahm-nee-dah
Excuse me	Silre hamnida	Sheel-ray hahm-nee-dah
You're welcome	Ch'onmaneyo	Chon-mahn-ay-yo
Yes	Ye	Yeh
No	Anio	Ah-nee-yo
I understand	Amnida	Ahm-nee-dah
I don't understand	Morumnida	Mawroom-nee-dah
How much?	Olma yimnikka?	Oylmah yim-nee-kah?
Do you speak English?	Yong-o halsu is-sumnika?	Yhong-oh hall-su ee-some-nee-kah?
Sir, Mr.	Sonsaang-nim	Song-saeng-nim
Mrs.	Puin (after name)	Poo-een
Miss	Yang (after name)	Yahng

PRONUNCIATION

Vowels a, e, i, o, and u are pronounced as ah, eh, ee, aw, oo but spread the lips as in a smile for a, e and i. The consonants b, d, g, and j are lightly sounded, especially at the beginning of a word. Consonants can change their sounds in different contexts.

ae = "a" as in "sank"
aa = "a" as in "hat"
ng = as in "singer"
s = "sh" if before an "i"

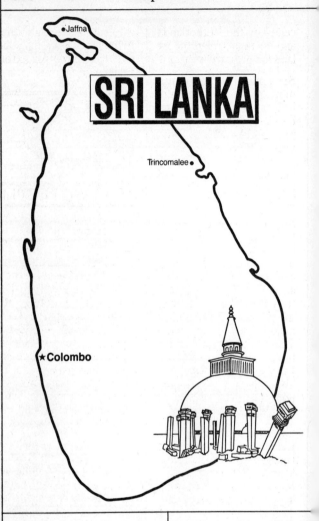

In case you wondered where "Ceylon" had gone, it's still the island at the southern tip of India, but its name was changed to

Sri Lanka in 1972 — not t‹ confuse tourists, but t‹ leave the colonial past (in cluding the British-mad‹ name) behind. Britain, pr‹

ceded by the Netherlands and Portugal, ruled the island for over 150 years.

Sri Lanka is becoming more popular with tourists, and luxury hotels and beach resorts are springing up in many choice spots. It's harder now to escape to unspoiled beaches and coastal villages and enjoy their unhurried pace.

Seventy percent of Sri Lanka's people are Sinhalese, most of them Buddhist, who came to the island from India centuries ago. They have a reputation as an easy-going, friendly people. The other major ethnic group are the Tamils, Hindus the British brought from India to work European plantations. The Tamils make up 20% of the population, concentrated in the east and north.

Since the early 1980s Sri Lanka has been torn by conflict between the Sinhalese and Tamils who want to create an independent Tamil state in the north. Terrorism has escalated, and some tourists have stayed away even though the conflict is strictly Sri Lankan against Sri Lankan.

If you decide that you like Sri Lanka, you can stay. The government welcomes Western residents who can prove (as author Arthur C. Clarke did) that they have a regular external income.

MEETING PEOPLE

GREETINGS

- Forms of greeting vary among different ethnic groups and castes. The traditional greeting, still widely practiced, is to place your palms together under your chin and bow slightly (as in India's *namaste* gesture). Foreigners are not expected to initiate this gesture but should return one if it's offered.

- A Western handshake with a common English greeting is also quite acceptable. Westerners may shake hands with Sri Lankans of either sex.

- The Sinhalese greeting *"aaibowan"* has multiple meanings: Hello, good day, and even goodbye. For informal situations the greeting *"kohomede?"* (How are you?) is often used.

- When Western men greet Sri Lankan women, they should not hug or kiss them. Sri Lankans of the same sex often embrace if they haven't seen each other for a while.

- When greeting someone don't smoke; it's impolite. If Sri Lankans are smoking when you approach them, they'll try to conceal or extinguish their cigarettes.

- At a party you'll be introduced to all the guests. Shake hands with everyone.

Names and titles. In Sinhala *mahattaya* and *nona* (or *nona mahattaya*) are used more often than their English counterparts, sir and madam. If you refer to someone as Mr., Mrs., or Miss, put the Sinhalese title after the name (you may abbreviate *mahattaya* to *mahata* in this case).

- In Sinhala the given name comes first, followed by the surname. Quite a few Sri Lankans are descendants of Dutch and Portuguese settlers and have European surnames.

- Tamil has no words for Mr., Mrs., or Miss. Instead, *Aiyaa* (father) and *Ammaa* (mother) are often used in place of sir or madam. To indicate respect to an older person or superior, include the participle *ngal* at the end of a sentence or after a key word.

- If you meet Sri Lankans who are medical doctors or have degrees, address them as "Doctor."

Correspondence. Business and formal letters to foreigners are usually written in English, with English salutations ("Dear Mr. Kremer,").

CONVERSATION

- English is widely spoken, especially in tourist areas. Sri Lankans are very interested in foreigners and will often strike up a friendly conversation. Speak slowly and show interest in what your conversation partners are saying.

- Good conversation subjects: Hobbies, families, hometowns, and schools. Ask for recommendations on sights to see.

- Subjects to avoid: Strife between the Sinhalese and the Tamils, relations with India, the caste system, religion, and sex. Until recently caste was a major factor in what people were permitted to do for a living, so don't ask people about their parents' occupations.

PHRASES TO KNOW

- Sinhala is the language of the Sinhalese majority (74% of the population). Tamil is the language of the three million Tamils concentrated in northern Sri Lanka. English is widely understood. All three are official languages.

- A good phrase book is *Sri Lanka Phrasebook* by Margit Meinhold (Lonely Planet, Victoria, Australia, 1987, $2.95).

CURRENCY

- The unit of currency is the Sri Lankan *rupee,* abbreviated "Rp" (singular) or "Rs" (plural), which is divided into 100 cents. One U.S. dollar is worth about 26 *rupee*s (August 1987 rates). Coins are issued in denominations of 1, 2, 5, 10, 25, and 50 cents and 1, 2, and 5 *rupee*s. Notes come in Rs 2, 5, 10, 20, 50, 100, 500, and 1,000.

- To change money you'll need the exchange control card that's attached to your passport when you enter the country. Every time you exchange money, make sure it's recorded on the form or that you keep the receipt. You'll need the form to reconvert money when you leave.

- Banks offer better exchange rates than those at hotels or other authorized money changers. Rates vary from bank to bank, however, so shop around.

- Traveler's checks usually bring a higher exchange rate than does cash.

- When you exchange currency or get change, don't accept torn or soiled notes. Some merchants won't accept them. Because of a small change shortage, large-denomination bills might also be hard to change or use for small purchases. If you do get soiled or large notes, change them at banks.

- International credit cards are accepted in hotels and tourist shops. Some shops try to add an additional charge to use them; if that happens report the incident to the card company.

- A black market for hard currency does exist. Changing money with black market operators can be dangerous — many of them are experts at sleight-of-hand rip-offs.

- Touts or tour guides might claim to have a "friend" who can change currencies. Don't fall for it. You'd probably have to pay an extra charge on top of the exchange rate, to cover the tout's commission.

ETIQUETTE

GENERAL MANNERS

- The caste system is still evident in Sri Lanka, especially among the Tamils of the Jaffna area. People of some "inferior" castes (fishermen, barbers, and similar professions) are not supposed to sit at the same table as members of higher castes. If someone looks reluctant to sit where they're invited, don't press the issue.

- Sri Lankans usually smile instead of saying "thank you." The Sinhalese phrase that comes closest to "thank you" is *"bohoma stutiy,"* but to use it seems a bit unusual.

- Men and women segregate at dinners and parties. Visitors should go along with this custom. Men should not talk to a Sri Lankan woman very long; her husband might resent it.

- Many professional beggars congregate near tourist hotels and temples. The government asks tourists not to give money to them because it only encourages more to take up the practice. Other Sri Lankans won't consider you rude if you decline to give beggars money.

- Before you photograph people, ask permission — some people object. If you do photograph people, they might ask you for money. Don't give them more than three *rupees*.

- If you see people with their teeth and lips stained dark red, or find what looks like dried blood on the sidewalk, don't be alarmed. Chewing betel, an areca nut wrapped in betel leaf, is a popular activity that causes red-stained mouths and much expectorating.

BODY LANGUAGE

- The left hand is considered unclean, since Sri Lankans use it for cleaning themselves after they use the toilet. Don't eat or hand something to another person with your left hand.

- Smiling in Sri Lanka can be flirtatious, so don't smile as much as you would in the West. Local women usually smile only to family members.

- Wiggling your head from side to side, much like the Western gesture for "no," means "yes" in Sri Lanka. Nodding your head up and down, the Western gesture for "yes," means "no."

- To refuse something politely say, *"E-pa"* (No thanks) and wave your hand.

DRESS

- Sri Lanka is hot and humid, and dress is usually casual. Sri Lankans dress conservatively but are more tolerant than Indians are of foreigners' dress styles.

MEN For all but the most formal occasions, wear a light shirt and trousers. For formal events wear a lightweight dark suit. Jackets and ties are rarely worn for business meetings or any other occasion.

WOMEN Wear a light blouse with a skirt or pants for most occasions. For formal events wear a cocktail dress or pantsuit. Leave your nylon stockings at home; it's much too hot for them. Don't wear shorts anywhere but the beach, and don't wear low-cut dresses, sleeveless blouses, or other revealing clothing.

- Check with your hotel to see what's acceptable beach attire. Bikinis are acceptable on most beaches. Toplessness is illegal but is evident on some resort beaches.

TEMPLES AND MOSQUES

- When you visit a temple or mosque, wear conservative clothing that covers your arms and legs.

- Before you enter a temple or any other holy place — even if it's abandoned or in ruins — remove your shoes and hat. Stockinged feet are sometimes permitted. If you're temple-hopping wear slip-on shoes or sandals. They're cooler, and you can slip them on and off easily.

- To be polite don't wear or carry any leather articles into a temple, even those where leather is not strictly prohibited.

- Posing for photographs in front of religious paintings or monuments is very impolite. Most Sri Lankans are devout Buddhists or Hindus. Show respect for all religious objects.

- Sitting or standing on one of the large Buddha statues is one of the worst things you can do. Not only is it a sacrilege, it's also illegal. Treat any Buddha image, no matter what size, with the utmost respect.

- To greet a Buddhist monk, raise both hands in prayer fashion to just below your mouth. Don't try to touch him, shake hands, or photograph him. To hand anything to a monk, offer it with both hands.

- Buddhist monks must refrain from touching money, so don't try to

hand money to them. Instead, place your donation in the box at the temple entrance.

- Monks of Sri Lanka's three Buddhist sects (*nikaya*s) dress differently. Those of the Ramanya sect wear their robes over both shoulders and carry palm-leaf shades. Amarapura monks also cover both shoulders but carry umbrellas. Monks of the Siyam sect cover only one shoulder.

PRIVATE HOMES

- Sri Lankans are very friendly and often invite new acquaintances home to meet their families. (Some locals take advantage of this reputation for friendliness, inviting foreigners to their homes and then using the opportunity to make sales.)

- Dropping by friends' houses unannounced is acceptable, especially if they (like most Sri Lankans) don't have a phone. It's polite, however, to limit your visit to between 4:00 and 7:00 P.M.

- If you're invited to dinner in a home, bring a gift (it's not expected but it will be appreciated).

- If the family has a phone and you use it to make calls, offer to reimburse them. They pay a charge for each call.

- Hindu homes often have a prayer room with statues or pictures of Hindu deities. Never wear shoes in this room, even if the family wears shoes elsewhere in the house.

- If you stay in a private home, keep some clothes on all the time, even in your bedroom. Laundry boys and maids often pop into rooms without warning.

- If you stay with a family that has servants, discreetly hand each one 20-50 *rupees* (depending on how long you stayed) when you leave.

- If you go out while you're staying with a family, let them know where you'll be. Most families will either invite you to use their car (if they have one) or offer to escort you. Decline their first and second offers, but if they offer a third time, feel free to accept.

PERSONAL GIFTS

- Good choices are European chocolates, cosmetics, radios, fruit packages, and crafts from your home region. If you know that someone drinks liquor, a bottle of imported whiskey would be treasured. For teenagers bring books or T-shirts with college logos. Avoid giving meats or cheeses.

TIPPING

- Restaurants and hotels: A 10% service charge is usually added to your bill, but give something extra to waiters (10% of the bill if no service charge has been added), room maids (Rs 20-25 per week), and bellhops (Rs 9-10 per errand).

- Taxis: Give the driver 10% of the fare.

- Porters: Tip Rs 3-4 per bag.

- Tour guides: Tip Rs 20-40.

- Barbers and beauticians: Tip 10% of the fee.

- Gas station attendants: Some people tip Rs 3-4, but for normal service it's not expected.

FOODS

MEALS

Breakfast (*ude kaama*): 7:00 to 8:00 A.M. Sri Lankans eat large breakfasts that usually include fruit, eggs, bread, curry, fish, and hoppers (rice-flour pancakes). Rice balls and rice cooked in milk are also common. Westerners might like to ask for egg hoppers (*bittara appa*).

Lunch (*dawal kaama*): Noon to 2:00 P.M. The main meal of the day. Typical fare is a fish or meat curry, rice, hoppers, and a dessert such as pudding or fruit.

Dinner (*raa kaama*): 7:00 to 10:00 P.M. (People in Colombo tend to eat later than other Sri Lankans.) Similar to lunch.

WHERE TO EAT

• Sri Lankans rarely dine out unless they're away from home, so restaurant choices are limited — especially if you're looking for first-class restaurants that serve native cuisine.

• Women eating alone in restaurants will not be harassed by men (unlike in India).

• To sample authentic native cooking, try to either wrangle an invitation to a home or stay in a guesthouse that features home cooking.

• Many restaurants automatically serve foreigners mild curry because they think they won't like the hot dishes Sri Lankans prefer. If you like your curry hot, ask for red curry. White curry is mild.

• Restaurants post their menus either in the window or on the wall. The menus are seldom in English, but you can usually find an English-speaking person to help you.

• At a restaurant ask for "short eats," a plate of assorted spring rolls, meatballs, vegetable patties, and other goodies placed on the table. The bill is calculated by counting the number of snacks left on the plate, so you pay only for the ones you eat.

• Eating food from street

stalls is a bit risky. Watch to see how the food is prepared and how the dishes are washed, and evaluate the health of the food server.

- You'll find bars only in tourist hotels. Even these bars close during the monthly Full Moon festivals.

FOODS TO TRY

- Most Sri Lankan dishes are closely related to those of India. They're highly spiced — sometimes to the extreme. Curry and rice is a typical dish; it includes a wide variety of small servings of curried vegetables and meat that are eaten with the rice. Seafood plays a more important role in Sri Lanka than in India. Most areas of Sri Lanka have fresh fish and prawns.

- Rice is the staple of the diet and the basic food for all meals.

- Strict Buddhists don't eat flesh of any kind; some Buddhists eat fish or eggs.

- Hindus don't eat beef or pork, and Muslims don't eat pork. If you're invited to a Tamil home for dinner, it will probably be completely vegetarian.

- Most curries contain fish or other meats. If you want a vegetarian curry, ask for *venjene*.

- When you eat hot curries, use the dishes of grated coconut on the table to cool your mouth. Drinking cold water will only intensify your discomfort.

- After a meal fruits such as papaya, pineapple, or bananas are served for dessert. The meal concludes with a cup of hot Ceylon tea.

Specialties. Sri Lankans prefer round-grain rice, served either plain or yellow (cooked in coconut milk and spices). It often has a musty taste. *Biriyani* rice, popular with Muslims, is cooked in stock and served with hard-boiled eggs and chopped meat or fish.

- A combination salad (*sambol*) of dried fish, grated coconut, pickles, onions, and lemon juice is often served as a first course or with curried dishes.

- Try *lamprai,* a curried snack made from rice boiled in meat stock, mixed with dry curry, and baked wrapped in a banana leaf.

- Try hoppers (*appa*), the

crisp, cup-shaped pancakes made from fermented rice-flour batter and coconut. They're often eaten for breakfast, frequently with an egg cooked inside. String hoppers (*indiappa*) are like rice vermicelli; they're eaten with vegetable or fish curries.

- In the northern Jaffna region, try *kool,* a boiled, fried, and sun-dried vegetable mixture.

- The *durian,* a smelly, spiny fruit, is the Sri Lankans' favorite fruit. Break it open and then scoop out and eat the smelly yellow-green contents.

- If you are given an unopened mango, stand it on end and slice it into vertical sections by running a knife down each side of the flat stone in the center. Leave the fruit in the skin and cut the sections with crisscrossed incisions. When you turn the skin inside out, the fruit will pop up.

- For dessert try *wattallapam,* a baked caramel custard of Malaysian origin, or (a bit riskier) one of the many curds made from buffalo milk. *Pan pol* (coconut and honey cake), *kiri buth* (a rice, coconut, and honey mixture), and *jaggery* (hardened palm-tree sap) are unique to the island and worth a try.

Beverages. Don't drink water or eat ice unless you know the water's been boiled. This is hard to verify (some people take offense when you ask them), so to be safe ask for bottled soft drinks or boiled tea.

- Sri Lanka's tea is famous, but it's served quite strong in local restaurants.

- Local brands of soft drinks are numerous; the most popular is Elephant House. International brands are available but more expensive. The legal maximum price for a soft drink is printed on the label or can; don't pay any more than that.

- Another safe, thirst-quenching alternative is *thambili,* the milk of the king coconut drunk straight from the shell with a straw.

- The most popular local alcoholic drinks are *toddy* and *arrack.* Toddy is a cider-like drink made from fermented coconut flowers or palmyrah sap; *arrack* is distilled toddy.

TABLE MANNERS

- If a restaurant is crowded and has no empty tables, you may join strangers at theirs. Sri Lankans usually welcome foreigners to their tables and will often start a conversation with them.

Utensils. Most people eat with the fingers of their right hands. Follow your host's lead in using bread (*roti*) or rice balls to scoop up the curries and vegetables. Never use your left hand for eating or for passing or receiving dishes.

- Communal dishes are usually placed in the center of the table, not passed around. Serve yourself but be careful not to let the serving spoon touch your plate. Curries are messy and you'll probably spill some, but don't worry about it.

- If you're given food on a large plantain leaf, don't eat the leaf. It's the dish.

Dining with others. If you're invited to dinner, eat a snack before you go. (Drinking and chatting before the meal often lasts a couple of hours.) Women should drink nothing stronger than wine. Muslim hosts serve soft drinks.

- Your hosts will seat you. The place of honor is next to them.

- Orthodox Buddhists might not eat fish or meat curries, so don't offer them any.

- Add servings of the curries and *sambol* to your plate of rice. Don't take large portions. You'll be urged to take more servings; taking two or three is polite.

- The greatest compliment you can offer is to ask for more. When you've had enough, politely refuse more helpings and put your hands over your plate to prevent refilling.

- To express thanks and compliments for a meal, smile and say *"bohoma rahay,"* the Sinhalese equivalent of "That was enjoyable."

- The person who suggested the meal pays the whole tab.

ACCOMMODATIONS

Hotels. During the off season (May to October), ask for a discount before you register. Discounts are common at this time of year.

- Firmly but politely decline the "services" of the hotel touts who harass tourists leaving the airport or getting off buses. These touts will steer you to a hotel that gives them a high commission for bringing you in. Some touts will even go the length of traveling on buses and trains, befriending travelers and leading them to "a friend's place" at their destination.

- For inexpensive accommodations look for guesthouses near city centers. They're basically bed-and-breakfasts with private baths, home-cooked meals, and fans instead of air-conditioning. Find out what's included in the quoted rate. Some places charge extra for everything,

even tea and fans.

- Hotels and, most recently, guesthouses tack on a 10% service charge. Ask about the service charges before you register. Guesthouses usually don't provide much service, so they shouldn't have a large service charge.

- Ask whether there's a telephone service charge. Local calls cost at least one *rupee,* but many hotels absorb the cost.

- Some snack shops are known as "hotels." Don't expect to rent a room in one.

- Theft can be a problem, so don't leave valuables in your hotel room. Carry them with you if a lockbox is not available.

- Most medium-class and inexpensive hotels don't serve alcohol.

- Air-conditioning is available in first- and second-class hotels; other hotels and resorts provide only ceiling fans.

- Hot running water is often available only in first-class hotels. If it's not available ask for heated water for your bath.

- Electricity is 230-240 volt, 50-cycle AC. Don't

be surprised if the lights go off occasionally. Outages are frequent, so a flashlight might come in handy.

• Mosquitoes can be a nuisance; they also spread malaria. Many hotels provide mosquito netting, but bring your own repellent or netting as a safeguard.

Rest rooms. Sri Lanka has few public toilets. Hotels will let you use their facilities, or you can head for a train or bus station or a restaurant. Carry toilet tissue with you; it's not always supplied.

TRANSPORTATION

PUBLIC TRANSPORTATION

Buses. The red government buses are extremely crowded and uncomfortable. Don't even attempt to take your luggage. Board by the front door and hand your money to the conductor (you don't need exact change). The fare is based on distance, so tell the conductor your destination. Be sure to keep your ticket until you get off. City buses operate from 5:00 A.M. to midnight.

• Pickpockets can be a problem on crowded buses, so keep your purse in your arms or your wallet in your front pocket.

• Straying hands are also sometimes a problem for women on buses. Finding a place to sit down is the best prevention.

• The first two seats on buses are reserved for Buddhist monks, so don't sit in them. Women should never sit next to a monk; monks are not permitted to have any contact with women.

• The minibuses found throughout the island are faster and less crowded than the regular buses, and only slightly more expensive. Look for them at the railway station in Colombo. Route maps and timetables don't seem to exist. Pay the conductor as you board. To ensure that you aren't overcharged, check the price before you board and make sure you get a ticket. The fare is based on the distance traveled. If you want to travel long-distance, be sure to arrive at the station early in the day.

Taxis. Taxis are easy to find on the streets of large cities; they have yellow tops and white license plates with red numbers. (Colombo taxis are yellow and black.) In most areas a puzzled look on a tourist's face will attract taxis immediately.

• Most taxis outside of Colombo don't have meters. In a metered taxi make sure the meter flag drops before you set out. If the meter doesn't work, settle on the fare before the car moves. Many meters seem to run fast, so you might be better off negotiating the fare anyway, especially for a long trip.

• Taxi service from the airport to Colombo follows a set rate. Pay for the trip at the counter in the airport; the attendant will call your taxi.

Trains. Train travel is very slow. For comfortable travel choose first-class, air-conditioned cars with sleeping berths and observation cars. Second- and third-class cars have wooden benches and open windows. Reserve your tickets in advance at the railway station.

Other transportation.

You can rent bicycles at beach hotels or through a travel agent. Many rental bikes are in poor condition, so check the brakes and lights before you pay. And don't accept the quoted price — bargain.

• Three-wheeled scooters called "autoshaws" can be hailed on the street in Colombo and Galle, and should cost about half the taxi fare. Most have meters (many of which spin faster than they should).

DRIVING

• It's cheaper to rent a chauffeur-driven car than a self-drive car. That's because driving is so hazardous that rental companies want only trained professionals to drive their investments. Drivers speak English and can act as guides.

• You can arrange to rent a car, with or without a driver, through travel agencies or the international car-rental firms in Colombo. An air-conditioned car costs about 25 cents a mile plus US$ 2 a day for your driver's expenses.

• To rent a car you must be between 25 and 65 years old, and you must have a passport and a temporary Sri Lanka driving license (available from the Automobile Association).

- Before you hire a car and driver for overnight trips, negotiate the driver's overnight and meal rates (they should total about Rs 30 per night). Many hotels and guesthouses provide drivers' quarters at no extra charge.

- Driving is on the left, as in Britain. Crowds of pedestrians, animals, motorbikes, bicycles, and cars make driving hazardous. Few observe traffic regulations.

- If your car is involved in an accident, don't move it until the police have come and filled out the report required for insurance claims. As a foreigner you'll probably be found at fault.

- In Colombo park at car parks. You pay the attendant for the first hour when you leave your car and pay the rest when you return. Outside Colombo parking isn't a problem.

- You can rent motorcycles if you have a national driver's license. You must pay the rental charges in advance and

put down both a refundable 20% deposit and a smal "collision damage waiver" fee. You might also have to surrender your passport or airline ticket as security. Insist that a helmet be provided with the bike.

BUSINESS

BUSINESS HOURS

Business offices: 8:30 A.M. to 4:30 or 5:00 P.M. Monday through Friday. Some businesses close for lunch, and many close earlier than their posted closing times. Some also open on Saturday morning.

Banks: 9:00 A.M. to 1:00 P.M. on either Monday or Friday, and 9:00 A.M. to 1:30 P.M. on other weekdays.

Government offices: Same as business offices.

BUSINESS CUSTOMS

- The best time for business visits is from October to April (so you can avoid the southwest monsoon season). Avoid trips around Christmas and New Year's and during April, the time of the Sinhalese and Tamil New Year's. Many businesses close around these holidays, and travelers clog public transport.

- Arrange appointments by telex or letter well before you arrive. Many businesses do not have a telex, and international mail can be quite slow.

- Sri Lankan business people want to get to know you before they commit themselves to a business arrangement. Be patient. Don't expect to introduce yourself, negotiate a deal, and complete a contract during a single visit.

- Businesswomen will find themselves taken more seriously in Sri Lanka than in India or Pakistan.

- Before your Sinhalese counterparts make important decisions, they might consult an astrologer.

Business etiquette. Name cards are usually exchanged when you're introduced. English is widely spoken in business circles, so there's no need for a translation on one side. (In fact, it could do more harm

than good — you wouldn't want to hand a Sinhalese-language card to a Tamil.)

Appointments and meetings. Many businesses close for lunch, so don't request appointments between 11:30 A.M. and 2:00 P.M.

- Some first meetings take place over lunch at a restaurant.

- If your counterparts are late, don't act upset. Sri Lankans expect Westerners to be punctual, but are not always punctual themselves.

- At the beginning of a meeting, you'll be offered tea. Don't refuse it, and be sure to comment on its quality.

Business gifts and entertainment. Your Sri Lankan business associates might invite you home for dinner. If you're invited out for dinner, reciprocate in kind. Sri Lankan business people greatly appreciate dinner invitations to Western restaurants in the international hotels.

TELEPHONES AND MAIL

Telephones. You'll find public pay phones in hotel lobbies, restaurants, and post offices and, occasionally, in phone booths on the street. Deposit one *rupee* and dial. When you hear a warning buzz after three minutes, deposit another *rupee* immediately or you'll be disconnected. Power outages are common, and making a connection might take up to a half hour.

- Long-distance direct dialing is available from most tourist hotels. If it's not available at your hotel, book the call with the operator and be prepared to wait up to an hour for an international call to go through.

- You can also make long-distance calls from post offices or the Central Overseas Telephone Exchange, which has English-language telephone books. Be prepared to wait a long time for your connection, especially if you're calling from outside Colombo. At post offices you might have to pay in advance.

- To send domestic telegrams by phone, dial 133. Fast or slow rates are available.

- Both telephone and postal services are available in privately operated post offices, which display red signs with white lettering. The phone service is often more efficient at these establishments, but you'll pay a slightly higher rate.

Mail. Mailboxes are painted red and look like British letter boxes. In rural areas mailboxes might not be emptied for days, so post your letters at hotels or post offices.

- If you want to mail a parcel, take it to the post office counter.

- At the post office make sure the clerk cancels the stamps on your letter or parcel so they can't be peeled off and resold.

- Both the Colombo general post office and the Tourist Information Center offer general delivery services.

LEGAL MATTERS

Customs and immigration. U.S. and Canadian citizens can stay up to thirty days without a visa if they obtain an entry permit when they arrive. These permits can be extended for two more one-month periods. A fee is usually charged for extensions, payable in stamps obtained near the immigration office. Don't buy stamps from the hawkers outside the building.

- When you arrive be sure to declare all your currency. A currency exchange form, which you'll need to change money, will be placed in your passport. When you leave the country, you'll need to have all your exchange transactions recorded on the form (or receipts from them) to change *rupees* back into your own currency.

- It's illegal to bring Indian or Pakistani *rupees* into Sri Lanka.

- To enter the country you might need an international certificate of vaccination against cholera. You might also need smallpox and yellow fever immunizations if you've recently been in an infected area.

- When you leave customs will check your baggage.

- Tourists may take up to six pounds of tea out of the country duty free. You'll have to pay duty on extra tea unless you buy it in the duty-free airport departure lounge.

- Antiques over fifty years old cannot be exported.

- You may take gems out of the country only if you purchased them with money declared on the foreign exchange form. You'll have to show customs the receipts for the gems as well as those for the money exchanges.

Other restrictions. Photography is sometimes prohibited inside temples, museums, and caves (see whether there are any signs). You might need a special permit to photograph archeological sites; you can obtain one from the Commissioner of Archeology in Colombo or from museums at the sites.

- Smoking is prohibited in cinemas, buses, and theaters.

- It's illegal to exchange currencies through unlicensed dealers. Don't let touts steer you into a "friend's" shop to change money (even if it's an authorized shop).

SAFETY

Crime. Theft is a problem in tourist areas. Don't leave your valuables on the beach while you're swimming. Keep them in hotel lockboxes rather than in your room.

- On buses and in street markets, beware of pickpockets.

Health. Except in tourist hotels, water is usually unsafe (it carries organisms that can give you amoebic dysentery). Don't use ice or drink water unless it's been boiled or treated. Fruit juices might not be safe either. The water from the king coconut (*zambili*) is safe.

- Avoid ice cream and other dairy products. They're often the sources of visitors' stomach disorders.

- Medical and surgical care is free to locals. Some services are also free to tourists.

- Malaria is a problem in some parts of the country. Get anti-malaria medications from your doctor before you leave home.

- Bring anti-mosquito preparations, sunscreens and sunburn lotions, and medications. Good brands are hard to find locally, and imported drugs are very expensive.

- Most other health-care products are available, although expensive. Sanitary napkins and tampons are available.

SHOPPING AND ENTERTAINMENT

Shopping. Shop hours are 9:00 A.M. to 5:00 or 6:00 P.M. Monday through Friday, and until noon on Saturday. In tourist areas shops stay open until 8:00 or 9:00 P.M.

- Shops and markets have two price levels, one for locals and a much higher one for tourists.

- Bargaining is the norm. Ask the price, then offer half that amount. Always bargain good-naturedly.

- Gems, shoes, batik clothing, and handicrafts are good bargains if you negotiate the prices.

- Gems such as moonstones, garnets, quartz, and star rubies are usually good buys, but avoid buying in the streets, where authenticity is questionable. Check the prices in several hotel shops and at the government gem shops, where the gems are guaranteed.

- Many nations prohibit the import of ivory and tortoise-shell products like those sold in Sri Lankan shops.

Entertainment. Like shops, many attractions such as zoos and museums have two entrance fees, one for local residents and a higher one for visitors. In many cases the government sanctions or requires this discriminatory policy.

HOLIDAYS

Many of Sri Lanka's holidays are based on the lunar calendar, so their dates vary from year to year. Muslim holidays move forward ten days every year; the Muslim calendar is ten days shorter than ours.

Official holidays: Hadji Festival Day (December/January), Thai Pongal Day (January 14), Independence Day (February 4), Maha Sivarathri Day (February/March), Tamil and Sinhalese New Year (April 13-24), Good Friday (March/April), May Day (May 1), Wesak Poya Day (May), National Heroes Day (May 22), Deepavali and Ramadan (October/November/December), and Christmas Day (December 25).

- June 30 and December 31 are bank holidays.

- Full Moon holidays, which occur every month, are religious holidays during which people are expected to behave conservatively. All places of entertainment (except those in tourist hotels) are closed, and no liquor is sold.

- Thai Pongal honors the Hindu sun deity with special observances held in homes. Madu Pongal, which follows Thai Pongal, is more noticeable to the visitor. A day or two after Thai Pongal, Hindus wash their domestic animals and pets, mark the animals' foreheads with auspicious smears of red, and adorn them with garlands of marigolds.

- Sinhalese and Tamil New Year is a secular festival celebrated most intensely in rural areas. People stop all activities (including eating and drinking) when the new year begins. At an hour specified by an almanac, they light fires in their kitchens, put on new clothes, and begin activities. They make token gestures of starting work by touching the tools of their trade. An anointing ceremony is the climax of the observance. Family members have a spot of oil rubbed on their heads, and then sit in a chair and trample a white cloth beneath their feet. Soon after the new year begins, merchants and other

people exchange money with someone nearby to ensure prosperity throughout the coming year.

- Wesak and the day after it are the two holiest days in the Buddhist calendar. Temple bells begin the festival by calling pilgrims dressed in white to temples around the island, where they spend the day reading religious books. Colombo is filled with huge paintings of Buddha hung on bamboo frames and lit with colorful lights. Coconut-oil lamps line streets, driveways, and temples.

- During the Hindu Festival of Lights (Deepavali) in late October or early November, people put on new clothes and refurbish their homes. Lamps are burned to welcome Lakshmi, the Hindu goddess of prosperity.

KEY PHRASES

SINHALA

English	Sinhala	Pronunciation
Good morning	Aaibowan	Ahyoo-bo-wahn
Good afternoon	"	"
Good evening	"	"
Good night	"	"
Goodbye	Aaibowan gehillia ennam	Ahyoo-bo-wahn geh-hil-la ehn-nam
Please	Karunakara	Kahrroo-nahka-rra
Thank you	Istutiy	Issttoo-tee
You're welcome	Matak karanna epa	Mahttak ka-ranna eh-pah
Excuse me	Samawanna kana-gatui	Sa-mah-wanna kahna-gah-tooee
Yes	Owu	Oh-oo
No	Naa	Naah
I understand	Mata terenawa	Mahta tehrreh-na-wah
I don't understand	Mata terenne naa	Mahta tehrreh-neh naah
Do you understand?	Terenawa da?	Tehrreh-na-wah da?
How much?	Kiiyada?	Keeya-da?
Does anyone here speak English?	Kavuruth Ingrisi ka takaranavada?	Kau-voo-root een-gree-see kah-tah-kah-rah-nah-vah-dah?
Sir	Mahattaya (follows surname)	Mah-ta-yaa
Mr.	Mahata (follows surname)	Mah-ha-ta
Madam, Mrs., Miss	Nona (follows surname)	Noh-na

KEY PHRASES

TAMIL

English	Tamil	Pronunciation
Good morning	Gud marning	Good mawning
Good afternoon	Gud aftarnun	Good ahftarr-noon
Good evening	Gud iivning	Good eevning
Good night	Gud nait	Good night
Goodbye	Poyitu varen	Poyit-oowa-rehn
Please	Dayavu seydu	Dahya-voo sehdoo
Thank you	Nandri	Nahndri
Excuse me	Manniyangal	Mannee-yangga
Don't mention it	Adu paravaayilla	Ahduh prra-vahyil-la
Yes	Aamaa	Ahmah
No	Illai	Illa
I understand	Puriyudu	Poorriyu-duh
I don't understand	Puriyillai	Poorri-yilla
How much?	Yevlavu?	Yevva-la-vuh?
Does anyone here speak English?	Inge yaarukaavadu Inglish pesa teriyuma?	Inga yahra-kahva-duh Ingglish peh-sa terri-yoo-mah?
Sir	Aiyaa	Eye-yaa
Madam	Ammaa	Ah-maa
Mr., Mrs., Miss	Not used	—

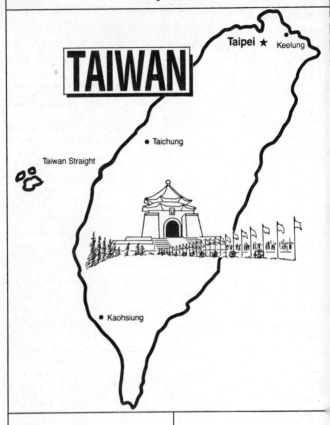

Chinese settlers first came to Taiwan in the 13th century, soon after China made the island a protectorate. Successive waves of immigration continued up to 1949, when three million Nationalist Chinese fled the mainland after the Communist takeover, moving the government of the Republic of China to Taiwan province. Today, the Nationalists still proclaim theirs to be the only legitimate government of all China. Although small, this island of 18 million people continues to outproduce in many ways the one billion inhabitants of the mainland.

This "other China" prides

itself on its preservation of traditional Chinese values and culture. Taiwan has over 2,000 Taoist and 2,500 Buddhist temples, and the people follow Confucian philosophy regardless of their religious affiliation. You can sample the best of China's art history in Taipei's National Museum, which houses artifacts that the Nationalists brought from mainland museums.

Dates in Taiwan are based on the number of years since the 1911 founding of the Republic of China — thus, July 12, 1988, is written as 77/7/12.

MEETING PEOPLE

- The Taiwan Chinese are very friendly to Western visitors, especially Americans. Although learning a bit of Mandarin Chinese will greatly enhance the pleasure of your stay, many young people speak good English and are extraordinarily helpful to foreigners. You won't be hassled by touts, and you can look forward to being treated by the people of Taiwan as a friend and equal.

GREETINGS

- Nodding your head is appropriate when you meet someone for the first time, but friends and acquaintances usually use a handshake. Westerners are expected to offer a handshake. You may bow slightly to show special respect, but don't exaggerate it.

- Elderly people are highly respected in Chinese society, so always acknowledge and speak to them first. When you're introduced to elderly people, spend a few minutes talking with them, and compliment them on their health. To show special respect when you greet them, put your right hand over your left fist and raise both hands to your heart.

- Introductions are preferred. Try to avoid introducing yourself; instead, have a third person introduce you. Always wait to be introduced at parties and business meetings — the host will introduce you to everyone there. At a banquet, however, introduce yourself to the other people at your table.

- When you greet young people, ask them about their schoolwork. Education is important in Chinese society.

- Asking someone whether they've eaten is a common greeting. If someone greets you this way, say yes to be polite.

- When you greet an elder, take off your glasses.

Names and titles. Chinese names consist of a one-syllable family name followed by a generation name (cousins on the father's side have the same middle name) and an individual given name. If a man is named Chiang Ching Guo, Chiang is his family name, Ching is his generation name, and Guo is his given name.

- When you address people, always use their titles and family names, not their generation or given names. Address Chiang Ching Guo, for example, as Mr. Chiang or, in Chinese, *Chiang Shinshung* (*Shinsung* means "Mr."). Never refer to people by their given names unless asked to do so — even if you're talking about a third person.

- On business cards the English side usually shows the person's name Western-style, with the family name last. A hyphen is usually inserted between the generation and individual names.

- Many Chinese who deal with foreigners adopt an unofficial English name (for example, Patrick) that they ask foreigners to use.

- Many Chinese women retain their maiden names after marriage and call themselves Madam (abbreviated "Mdm.") to make it clear that they're married. If you don't know a woman's maiden name, use Mrs. and her husband's family name until you find out.

Correspondence. In the salutation use only the person's family name (Dear Miss Chiang), not the generation or given name.

- If you address an envelope in Chinese, remember that all the information is listed in the reverse order from that used in Western-style addresses. The country comes first followed by the province, the county, the city and street, and finally the recipient's name.

CONVERSATION

- Good conversation subjects: Chinese food, calligraphy, and art; what you like about Taiwan; and families. Ask about the health of a person's family, and ask children about their schools.

- Subjects to avoid: Domestic politics, trade friction, and mainland China. The Taiwan-based government of the Republic of China considers itself the only rightful government of all China and does not recognize the People's Republic of China on the mainland. If you must talk about the mainland, refer to it as "mainland China." The name of Beijing, the mainland capital, means "Northern Capital," so while you're in Taiwan refer to Beijing as "Beiping" (Northern Peace) or Peking.

- If people ask you personal questions such as "How much money do you make?" or "Why don't you have children?" don't consider it an invasion of privacy. If you don't want to answer truthfully, give a joking reply.

College-aged "English-pirates" will probably approach you to practice their English. Be courteous and encourage their efforts.

PHRASES TO KNOW

- The Mandarin dialect of Chinese is the Republic of China's official language, taught in all the schools. The island's people came from various areas of mainland China, however, and speak many different dialects in their homes.

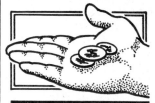

CURRENCY

- Taiwan's unit of currency is the New Taiwan dollar (abbreviated "NT$"), commonly called *kuai* in conversation. One U.S. dollar is worth about 31.8 New Taiwan dollars (August 1987 rates). Coins are available in NT$ 0.5, 1, 5, and 10, and notes are available in NT$ 10, 50, 100, 500, and 1,000.

- Save all currency exchange receipts for reconverting your money when you leave the country.

- Banks usually offer better exchange rates than those at hotels.

- Traveler's checks can be cashed only at the Bank of Taiwan and its branches.

ETIQUETTE

GENERAL MANNERS

- Most Chinese don't appreciate Western straightforwardness. Don't be too open or brusque, especially if you're criticizing someone.

- The Chinese also dislike noisy, untactful, or boisterous behavior. They believe that Westerners are too loud and forceful in conversation.

- Age is greatly respected. Treat the elderly with special deference, and don't smoke or wear sunglasses in their presence.

- If someone compliments you, politely refuse it. Saying "thank you" in response is considered immodest. The Chinese appreciate receiving compliments (even though they'll deny them) on their English ability or other talents.

- Queues break down easily. When that happens you must push and shove with everyone else. People trying to board buses sometimes bump aside even elderly or crippled people.

- Chinese usually make initial invitations to social events by phone, then confirm them by mail.

- Eating or drinking in the street is considered crude.

BODY LANGUAGE

- Young friends of the same sex often hold hands, but putting your arm around another person's shoulders is considered inappropriate.

- The Chinese believe that children's heads are very sensitive and too precious to risk damage by touching. Don't touch anyone — especially a child — on the head.

- Women may cross their legs when they sit down, but men should keep their feet flat on the floor.

- The Chinese consider the feet dirty and unsuitable for touching either objects or people. Don't use them to move anything, even a chair.

- Shaking your hand from side to side with the palm forward means "no." Tilting your hand from side to side while holding it horizontal means that something is "so-so," or "sometimes good, sometimes bad."

- For pointing use your open hand rather than your index finger. Never beckon anyone with one finger, Western-style. Instead, extend your arm, palm down, and wave your fingers up and down.

- Winking, even in jest, is impolite.

DRESS

- Dress modestly. Low-cut dresses or other revealing clothing will mark you as a "loose" person.

MEN For business or formal occasions, wear a conservative suit and tie. For informal dinners in the summer, you may forgo the tie. Men often remove their jackets during a meeting; follow your Chinese counterparts' lead. Shorts are acceptable casual attire for young men.

WOMEN Wear a conservative pantsuit or blouse and skirt for business, and a long dress for formal occasions. Young women may wear shorts for casual occasions. You may also wear a bikini at the beach or pool (although few Chinese women do).

NATIVE DRESS Only a few Chinese women, primarily waitresses and hostesses, still wear the traditional dress (*cheongsam*) with the slit up the side. The Chinese find it amusing when Western women wear them.

- The Chinese consider red the color of good luck and often wear it on holidays and for weddings. They also believe gold to be an auspicious color and often combine it with red.

- If you attend a funeral, wear black clothing — not red. The family of the deceased will wear white sackcloth.

- If you attend a wedding, don't wear black.

TEMPLES

- You may wear shoes around a temple courtyard, but remove them before you enter any of the covered buildings.

- When you pass through the temple gate or any of the inner doorways, be sure to step over, not on, the raised threshold.

- When you're in a Buddhist temple, don't take photographs without permission.

PRIVATE HOMES

- People in Taiwan don't usually drop in on acquaintances. Always phone ahead or make arrangements in advance. Many Chinese women work and are not home during the day.

- Before you enter a home, remove your shoes. You'll find slippers provided at the doorway.

- When you greet the family, always greet and talk to the eldest members first. Be sure to defer to them — age is venerated in Chinese society.

- After you're seated, your hosts will serve you tea, candy, fruit, juice, or a soft drink. Even if you don't like the drink they serve you, take at least a few sips before you put it down, to be polite.

- Dinner conversation in a home often centers on the meal — how it was prepared, what the ingredients were, and where they were obtained. If you can, eat whatever you're offered.

- During the meal the hostess might spend most of her time in the kitchen preparing the series of courses. It's Chinese custom, so don't ask her to join you.

- You're not expected to help clean up after the meal, although it's not improper to ask.

- Your hosts will appreciate sincere compliments but will deny them politely out of modesty.

- Complimenting your hosts on a particular object in the house might make them feel obliged to give it to you.

- When you leave, bow to your hosts.

- Your host will usually escort you a considerable distance from the home. To be polite, give a token show of resistance and express your thanks for the special hospitality.

PERSONAL GIFTS

- When you visit a family, particularly around the New Year, bring a small gift such as fruit — preferably, something you can give in pairs. Other good gifts are top-quality teas from special tea shops, imported coffee, cosmetics (especially top Japanese brands), chocolates, and crafts from your home region.

- When you give or receive a gift (or any other object), use both hands. The recipient will politely refuse the gift, but you're expected to persist. Don't expect the recipient to open a gift in your presence.

- When you choose gifts, keep in mind that Chinese custom requires people to reciprocate gifts in kind. Don't give an expensive gift to someone of limited means. If someone gives you a gift or a dinner, reciprocate with one of about equal value.

- If you're in Taiwan during the Chinese New Year, give the children of friends a *hong bao* (red bag) of money. Use new money, available from banks, and place an even number or a pair of banknotes in a red envelope.

- If you're invited to a Chinese wedding, bring a gift of money wrapped in a small red envelope with your name on it. A functionary will probably open the envelope and count the contents in front of everyone, entering the amount on a register.

TIPPING

- Both the government and the hotel industry discourage tipping, so don't over-tip service people.

- Hotels: Hotels usually include a 10% service charge in the bill, so tipping is not necessary. A small tip to the bellhop won't be refused. If the maid or concierge performs a special service, you may tip NT$ 10-15.

- Restaurants: Leave 10% if the service charge isn't included in the check.

- Taxis: Drivers don't expect a tip unless they help with your luggage. It's customary, however, to let them keep the small change.

- Porters: Tip NT$ 10 per piece of luggage.

- Barbers and beauticians: Tip 10%.

FOODS

MEALS

Breakfast (*zaocan*): 7:00 to 8:00 A.M. A typical breakfast is fried bread (*yu-tiao*) dipped in warm soy milk. Rice *congee* (gruel) is also quite popular, as is a selection of rice, bean curd, a salty egg, peanuts, and pickled vegetables. Tea is the usual beverage.

Lunch (*wucan*): Noon to 2:00 P.M. Workers often eat a quick noodle or ramen dish and use the rest of their lunch break for a nap. Steamed or fried rice with vegetables or meat is also typical fare.

Dinner (*wancan*): 6:00 to 8:00 P.M. The largest meal of the day, dinner usually consists of steamed rice with three or four dishes of meat, fish, and vegetables, and soup.

WHERE TO EAT

- For a traditional, inexpensive breakfast, look for food stands or small, open-front shops that serve warm soy milk and *yu-tiao,* an oily fried bread that is dipped into the soy milk.

- For inexpensive meals try the small food shops near the open markets or train stations. You'll usually find menus posted on the walls, but they're seldom in English, so make sure you know the name of your favorite dish to tell the waitress. During the hot summer, stick to the cleaner cafes that have doors.

- In hotel restaurants ask for the set or guest meal (*ke fan*), which usually includes a soup, one or two dishes, and all the rice you can eat — all at a very reasonable price.

- You'll see many inexpensive cafeteria-style eateries with trays of various meats and vegetables to choose from. Every item is on display (for flies as well), so just point to whatever looks good. The rice and soup are often free.

- You'll find night markets in every town. Food stalls line the street, and people walk back and forth between them dodging cars and sampling a wide variety o foods. You can taste seafood, dog meat, dried squid, and deep-fried tofu (bean curd), among other delicacies. Don't eat at a stall where the cook looks dirty or the dishes are sitting in cold, grungy water. Deep-fried or well-cooked foods are safest.

FOODS TO TRY

- You'll find all of China's regional cuisines in Taiwan, prepared by chefs who fled the mainland. It's a great place to try Shanghai, Mandarin, Cantonese, Hunan, and Sichuan cuisines, along with the local Taiwanese dishes.

- Rice or noodles form the foundation for every meal. You'll usually get rice with any meal, sometimes served free with a main dish. Other typical foods are soup, seafood, pork, chicken, vegetables, and fruit. Most foods, including vegetables, are fried.

- The Chinese like to eat in groups, sharing a meal of several courses, with each course brought to the table in turn. The meal usually includes appetizers, a fish or meat dish, a vegetable dish, sweet curds or fruit, and

soups. Soup and fish are served at any time during the meal.

Specialties. At restaurants specializing in Taiwanese cuisine, you'll get dishes that are less salty and less highly seasoned than those typical of the other regional cuisines. Typical Taiwanese selections are glutinous rice dumplings, prawns, fried fish with bean oil, and assorted firepot.

- Chinese cuisine features many unique soups. Try cabbage-and-bean-curd soup, scrambled-egg soup, lily-flower-and-shredded-pork soup, shark's fin soup, bird's nest soup, and corn soup.

- Other dishes to try are *schwei jiao* (steamed dumplings), *jiaozi* (fried dumplings), *bao-ze* (steamed buns filled with meat or vegetables), fried rice noodles with shredded pork, spring rolls, curried rice, and *mifen* (rice noodles with meat and vegetables).

- Taiwan grows many fruits, among them watermelon (*syi gwa*), persimmon (*shir dze*), papaya (*moo gwa*), mango (*mang gwo*), banana (*shiang jiao*), and tangerine (*jyu-dze*).

- Two dishes about which

you should be fore-warned are "fragrant meat" (dog meat) and "Fight between Tiger and Dragon" (a mixture of cobra and civet cat).

Beverages. Drink tap water only in the international hotels. Don't drink water anywhere else unless you know it's been boiled.

• Although you can order beverages such as beer and soft drinks with any meal, the Chinese usually use clear soup to wash the food down.

• Every meal includes tea, unsweetened and without milk. It's usually free with the meal. Taiwan produces many different varieties; the most popular are green, oolong, and jasmine.

• The Chinese make a cool beverage from fruit, sweet milk, and ice mixed in a blender. To order it just add *ze* (juice) to the end of a fruit name and it will be prepared from fresh fruit on the spot. Look for shops with signs saying "500 cc." Be careful, though — the ice is rarely made from boiled water.

• Taiwan Beer, the only domestic beer, is very good and has won many international awards.

Maotai (fermented sorghum liquor) and *shiuhing* (rice wine) are also popular.

TABLE MANNERS

• If an eatery is crowded, you may seat yourself at a table with strangers. Before you sit down, however, look at them and dip your head slightly to ask their permission.

Utensils. The Chinese use chopsticks for every meal, with a porcelain spoon provided for soup. The Chinese believe that food tastes better eaten with chopsticks and will appreciate your effort to use them. All food except fish is cut into bite-sized pieces, so chopsticks suffice for eating everything except soup.

• Chinese chopsticks are longer and rounder than their Japanese counterparts. To use them, hold one in the crook between your thumb and index finger, resting it on your little finger. Put the second between the tips of your thumb and index finger. Use your middle finger to support the side of the second chopstick, so you can manipulate it while keeping the first one firmly in place. Hold the sticks at the same height, about two-thirds of the way up.

- When you're not using the chopsticks, set them on the small wooden or porcelain rest. Never set them down parallel on a rice bowl — it's thought to bring bad luck or death to someone at the table.

- Many people hold their bowls near their mouths and use their chopsticks to shovel in the food. Eating this way is all right in casual situations, but it's considered unrefined in more formal settings.

- Don't rummage through the serving dishes with your chopsticks to get the best morsels. It's very impolite.

- When you take food from a serving plate, don't put it straight into your mouth. Transfer it to your own plate first.

- When you're finished eating, lay your chopsticks neatly on the table.

- Instead of a napkin, you might be given a damp cloth to clean your hands before and during a meal. Keep it on the table, not in your lap. Since few restaurants provide napkins, it's wise to carry a handkerchief.

- If you use a toothpick,

cover your mouth with your free hand.

Dining with others. You'll probably be invited to a meal at a restaurant rather than at your host's home. If you are invited to a home, consider it an honor.

- If you're the guest of honor at a round table, you'll be seated facing the door. Wait to be shown to your seat.

- Cocktails are not served before a dinner or banquet, but tea is often poured before the guests are seated.

- The host usually selects the foods served to the guests and gives them their first servings. After that, guests help themselves.

- If you're the guest of honor, be the first to sample any dish brought to the table. If you don't everyone will sit there waiting for you while it gets cold.

- Serving dishes are placed in the center of the table, often on a lazy Susan, so everyone can reach them.

- Put bones, shells, or other rejects either on the table or on the plate provided, but not in your rice bowl or on your own plate. The Chinese often spit bones onto the table or floor, considering it unsanitary to remove them from their mouths with their fingers.

- You should finish all the rice in your bowl; feel free to ask for a refill. Leave a little food on each serving dish and on your plate, however, or the host will feel obliged to have more food prepared.

- Soup will usually be served toward the end of a meal.

- Slurping hot soup and belching (not too raucously) after the meal are acceptable behavior. The belch is even considered a compliment.

- Warm rice wine is often served in small cups. Drink it only when making or receiving toasts. Hold the cup with two hands, one under it and the other around it. For a toast, you need only take a sip unless your host says *"Gan bei"* (Dry cup), in which case you should drink it in one gulp.

- If someone toasts another person's health, stand up, take your glass in both hands, and say a few kind words yourself.

- At a restaurant your Chinese host will expect to foot the bill. A guest may also offer to pay, but should not insist. Polite disagreements over the bill are part of the eating ritual.

- If you dine at someone's home, don't stay long after the meal.

- In either a home or a restaurant, don't let the meal last over two hours. The Chinese like to talk during the meal, but don't like to chat at the table after the meal is finished. Once you leave the table, it's time to go home.

- After the meal the honored guest should be the first to leave. The other guests will sit and wait for this signal.

- Hosts usually accompany their guests to their cars or taxis.

Banquets. If you're invited to a formal banquet, it's very important to arrive at the restaurant precisely on time.

- If you're the guest of honor at a formal banquet, you'll sit to the left of the host. As another privilege, you might be given the head of any chicken served with the meal. Chicken brains are a delicacy.

- When everyone is seated, the host will offer the guests a welcoming toast. If you don't drink alcohol, toast with a soft drink or water. Don't drink wine without toasting.

- The host might also make a speech and a toast to mutual cooperation. Have some complimentary remarks prepared so you can respond.

- Cold dishes are served first at a banquet. If sanitation is lacking, avoid them.

- Soup will be served throughout a formal banquet.

- Although some business might be discussed, Chinese banquets are not business meetings. The favorite conversation topic is the food.

- Additional servings of rice, noodles, or tea brought to the table might signal that the banquet is over.

- If you host a banquet, arrange to pay the bill before the meal begins. Otherwise, your guests will all squabble over picking up the tab.

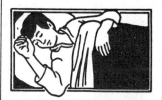

ACCOMMODATIONS

Hotels. If you plan to be in Taiwan during October, make reservations in July or August. Many overseas Chinese visit the island for the Double Tenth (October 10) celebrations, a time when they receive discounts from hotels and many other businesses.

- If you need a room for a few days, look for a guesthouse. You should be able to get a discount. Also look for cheap hotels near train stations.

- Also check with the China Youth Corps office in Taipei for the locations of their hostels throughout Taiwan. These hostels offer a choice of dormitory-style or private rooms, but they're very crowded from July through September and during January and February, when Chinese schoolchildren are on holiday.

- In smaller, inexpensive hotels and guesthouses, don't expect the staff to speak or understand much English. They might pretend to understand it, however, to save face. Be prepared for your requests to meet with good intentions but no results.

- Unless you're in an international hotel, don't drink the tap water. If you find a carafe of cold water in your room, use that for drinking or brushing your teeth. Many hotels provide bottled water in a small refrigerator placed in each room.

- Before you go anywhere, pick up the hotel's card with the address on it, so you can show it to taxi drivers when you're ready to return.

- Whenever you go out, make sure you leave your room key with the front desk.

Rest rooms. Western-style toilets are increasingly common in Taiwan, but you might run into some of the squat-type. Carry your own toilet paper; it's rarely supplied.

- If you visit a public bath, soap yourself and rinse off before you get into the hot bath. Many people use the bath water, and soap will ruin it.

TRANSPORTATION

- Try not to travel during the rush hours from 7:30 to 9:30 A.M. and 5:00 to 7:00 P.M. Buses are so packed you'll be lucky to get either on or off.

- Only Bangkok's traffic is more chaotic. Taiwan's drivers, from bus, taxi, and truck drivers to motorcyclists, totally disregard both safety and traffic regulations. No matter whether you're in a car or on foot, never assume that a vehicle is going to stop for you — even if you're at a crosswalk, wearing bright orange clothes, and carrying a baby. Police rarely bother to collar traffic violators until they actually hurt somebody.

- For traveling around Taiwan buy maps showing town and street names in English transliteration as well as in Chinese. That way you can find your way around even if signs are written in Chinese, and you can pronounce the names correctly when you ask for directions.

PUBLIC TRANSPORTATION

• When you buy tickets for travel within Taiwan, try to have your destination and desired departure time (with an alternative) written on a piece of paper to show the ticket seller. Ticket sellers are always hidden behind thick plexiglass that's difficult to even see through, much less speak through. If you try shouting the ticket seller might ignore you out of embarrassment at not being able to understand you. Just slip your request through the tiny hole in the window and hope they aren't sold out.

Buses. There are two kinds of buses, air-conditioned (costs NT$ 8) and regular (NT$ 6). You may either buy bus tokens at the kiosks near bus stops or pay the conductor on the bus. All buses run on numbered routes and have their route numbers displayed in Arabic numerals. Bookstores sell maps showing the routes. City buses in Taipei operate from 6:00 A.M. to 11:30 P.M.

• For inter-city travel first try the trains, but if they're booked up you can usually catch a bus. Bus stations are usually near train stations. Intercity buses depart every five or ten minutes, so don't get in line for a bus until the sign says it's ready for boarding. Seats aren't numbered, so take any one. Either write down your destination or show people your ticket — they'll help you find the right bus and get off at the right station.

Taxis. Taxis are inexpensive and easy to find; puzzled-looking foreigners seem to attract them. Catch one in front of a hotel, at a taxi stand, or by hailing it in the street. Most drivers don't speak much English, so have your destination written in Chinese.

• Taxis are metered. Make sure the meter flag drops when you start out. Some meters still display old rates, and the driver might produce a fare adjustment card with the higher rates at the end of your trip. If you don't think the card is official, get the taxi's number and report it to the tourist bureau.

Trains. Taiwan's excellent trains are ideal for inter-city travel. Only the express class is more expensive than the highway buses, and it's well worth the extra money. In order of decreasing speed and luxury, the classes are *Chu Kuang* (air-conditioned, first-class express), *Tzu Chiang* (electrified, air-conditioned express), *Chu Hsin* (air-conditioned limited express), and Express (not air-conditioned).

- The Taipei train station is downtown, near the tourist hotels. Trains are heavily used, so reserve your seats several days before your trip. You can buy round-trip tickets, but you must wait until you reach your destination to reserve your seats for the return trip.

- Once you have your ticket, look on the back to find your carriage and seat numbers, and sometimes the platform number. Most station employees don't speak English but will point you in the right direction if you show them your ticket. Many of the destination signs are in English as well as in Chinese.

- On the train stewardesses will serve complimentary tea and bring carts of box lunches that

you can buy at mealtimes.

- Overnight trains between Taipei and Kaohsiung have sleeper berths that include free tea, Chinese magazines, and wet towels.

DRIVING

- Both chauffeured and self-drive cars are available for rent. Driving in Taiwan is frightening because drivers are so reckless, so you might want to let someone else drive for you. Most roads are in very good repair, but all the signs (except on the north-south freeway) are only in Chinese. Accurate road maps are hard to find.

- Driving is on the right side of the road, as in North America.

- Have your destination written in Chinese on a piece of paper so you can show it to people when you ask them how to find the right roads.

- Keep your tank about half full. Gas stations in rural areas are scarce and close early.

BUSINESS

BUSINESS HOURS

Business offices: 8:30 A.M. to noon and 1:00 to 5:00 P.M. Monday through Friday, and 8:30 A.M. to noon Saturday.

Banks: 8:30 A.M. to 3:30 P.M. Monday through Friday, and 8:30 A.M. to noon Saturday.

Government offices: 8:30 A.M. to 12:30 P.M. and 1:30 to 5:30 P.M. Monday through Friday, and 8:30 A.M. to noon Saturday.

- A six-day, 48-hour work week is common. The government now discourages the traditional break from noon to 2:00 P.M.

BUSINESS CUSTOMS

- The best time to visit Taiwan on business is April through September, when there aren't too many holidays. Taiwanese business people usually vacation from January to March. Don't come near the Chinese New Year (January or February), when many businesses and shops close for a week.

- You might need either a letter of introduction or a personal introduction from a mutual friend or a bank to get an appointment — or even a reply — from business people you want to meet.

- When you visit Taiwan don't expect to return home with a contract or completed negotiations. Before they make a decision, Chinese business people will want to get to know you, evaluate your integrity, talk about your proposal, research it, talk some more, and then think about it for a long time. Be patient and plan on multiple trips.

- When you select a negotiation team, choose people with knowledge of overall company operations. Whether they're corporate officers is less important.

- The Chinese are very patient and often try to wear down foreign negotiators or frustrate them into making concessions. Don't disclose your deadline, and if your counterpart asks the date of your return flight, say that you have an open ticket.

- Taiwan is a major source of counterfeit products, so companies wishing to do business there should protect themselves by applying for patents or registering their trademarks in Taiwan.

Business etiquette. Catalogs, promotional literature, and instructions in English are acceptable.

- When someone gives you a business card, take a moment to look at it and remember the name and title. Don't put it away without looking at it, and don't put it in a wallet that goes in your back pocket.

- Instead of boasting about your company's successes, let your written material speak for you. It's polite to downplay your achievements and possessions — even when you talk about your family. If your host refers to his house as a hovel and his son as an idiot, don't agree with him. Just respond by complimenting him and being modest yourself.

- "Yes" can mean either "yes" or merely "I understand what you said." "Maybe" usually means "no." Flatly disagreeing

with someone is impolite, so say "maybe" instead.

- Western-style frankness is not appreciated. Be subtle when you speak, and become attuned to the nuances of what your counterpart says. If you can't interpret these nuances, bring along someone who can.

- In business negotiations it's inadvisable to admit frankly that you don't know the answer to a question. It might cause both you and your counterpart to lose face.

- If someone asks you a difficult question, don't sigh. It could be interpreted as a refusal to answer.

- Before you open an office in Taiwan, have the layout and arrangements approved by a geomancer or *fengshui* (wind and water) man. Doors, windows, and opening dates must all follow the laws of geomancy; the Chinese will blame any hint of poor business on failure to consult a geomancer. Your business neighbors will refer you to a reputable *fengshui* man.

Appointments and meetings. The best times for appointments are

11:00 A.M. and 4:00 P.M. Business entertaining often lasts late into the night, so executives don't like early morning appointments. Many business people eat quickly at noon (unless they have a business lunch) and nap until 1:30 or 2:00, so they might be groggy for 2:00 P.M. meetings.

- If your counterpart doesn't arrive on time for a meeting — or doesn't arrive at all — don't get upset. Westerners are expected to be punctual, but many Chinese dislike absolute punctuality. If people don't show up at all, it probably means they didn't want to come but had no way to tell you that.

- At follow-up meetings inquire about the health of your counterpart's family.

Business gifts and entertainment. To be successful in Taiwan, you must develop a friendly relationship separate from any business context. This will require after-hours entertaining and going to sporting events and dinners. Thoughtful gifts also help to establish a feeling of friendship.

- Bring a small gift for a person you are meeting for the first time, or for your host at a dinner. Good business gifts are pen sets, Johnny Walker Red Label Scotch (purchased duty-free on the airplane before you arrive), ginseng (if you are coming from Korea), and folk crafts from your region. Taiwan has high taxes on foreign luxury goods, so most imported items are appreciated.

- Always present or receive a gift with both hands, to show respect. The recipient never opens a gift in the presence of the person who gave it. (Opening it might cause embarrassment if the gift is not very expensive or appropriate.)

- Business entertaining takes place at good Chinese restaurants. Don't be fooled by outward appearances; some of the best restaurants look anything but fancy. Invitations to a business dinner at someone's home are rare.

- Don't discuss business while you're eating unless your Chinese host brings up the subject.

- Entertaining continues long into the night. You might be invited to a bar after dinner; it's impolite to say no. Businessmen may be taken to a bar or nightclub with flirtatious hostesses.

- After someone treats you to a dinner, reciprocate with an equivalent one. If you invite your male counterpart to dinner, you may invite his wife as well; she might or might not come.

TELEPHONES AND MAIL

Telephones. You can find public pay phones on the street and in shop entrances, hotels, restaurants, and coffee shops. Deposit a NT$ 1 coin for local calls or a NT$ 5 coin for long-distance. You have three minutes to talk before you're automatically disconnected; to continue the conversation you'll have to redial.

- The Chinese answer the phone with a loud *"wai!"* (pronounced "why"), which means "hello" and is used only for answering phones.

- To make overseas calls go to a government telecommunications office or

call from your hotel. The telecommunications offices accept some foreign telephone charge cards.

Mail. The postal service is very efficient. Most post offices are open from 8:30 A.M. to 5:00 P.M. Monday through Saturday. The red mailboxes are for air mail and special delivery, and the green mailboxes are for local letters only.

- When you mail a local letter, write the address on the envelope in reverse order from the way it's done in the West. (Start with the town name and end with the person's name.)

- The larger post offices offer packing and mailing service for overseas parcels.

LEGAL MATTERS

Customs and immigration. Visas are required for all visits to Taiwan; you must obtain one before you arrive. Transit visas are good for visits of under two weeks. Tourist visas are valid for six months and for multiple entries.

- You must declare all your currency when you arrive and when you leave. It's illegal to bring in or take out more than NT$ 8,000 in Taiwanese currency.

- When you come to Taiwan, don't try to bring in any products made in mainland China.

Other restrictions. Taiwan prohibits photography at the airport, near military bases, and on most beaches because of the perceived threat of mainland Chinese espionage.

- Literature from mainland China and Communist reading material of any kind are illegal in Taiwan.

SAFETY

Crime. Taiwan has a low crime rate, and foreigners are rarely bothered. Women can feel free to walk alone at night. The only threats are pickpockets on buses, so keep your purse or wallet in a safe place.

Health. Don't drink water outside of the international hotels unless you know it's been boiled. Hot tea made with boiled water is usually a safe alternative.

- Dairy products are not always pasteurized, so avoid ice cream and milk. Buying foods from street vendors is risky — sanitation is often inadequate — so stick with fried and well-cooked foods.

SHOPPING AND ENTERTAINMENT

Shopping. Most shops open at 9:00 A.M., and many stay open past 10:00 P.M. (Many merchants live behind or above their shops.) Department stores are open from 10:00 A.M. to 9:30 P.M. everyday.

- Bargaining is common in shops where items are not marked with the price. Look at several objects in a shop and then very casually ask the price of the item you're interested in. When the merchant quotes you a price, offer half and begin to haggle good-humoredly. If the merchant doesn't meet your offer halfway, start to walk out and your offer might be accepted. If it is accepted, you're obligated to buy.

- Bargains are easier to find in the couple of weeks before the Chinese New Year, when shopkeepers need cash to pay off old debts. Food, however, is more expensive.

- The night markets in each city are good places to haggle and find bargains. If you don't speak Chinese, you might need to carry a pen and paper so you can make written offers and counteroffers.

Entertainment. On holidays and festival days, as well as on full-moon nights, look for plays being performed on the grounds of Buddhist temples. The performances often feature Taiwanese operas and puppet plays during February and March, and Peking operas during April.

HOLIDAYS

Holidays: Founding of Republic of China (January 1 and 2), Chinese New Year (January or February — dates depend on the lunar calendar), Youth Day (March 29), Tomb Sweeping Day and Death of Chiang Kai-shek (April 5), Dragon Boat Festival (June), Mid-Autumn Festival (September/October), Birthday of Confucius (September 28), Double Tenth National Day (October 10), Taiwan Retrocession Day (October 25), Chiang Kai-shek's Birthday (October 31), Dr. Sun Yat-Sen's Birthday (November 12), Constitution Day (December 25).

- The Dragon Boat Festival, also known as Poet's Day, commemorates the drowning of poet-statesman Chu Yuen in 299 B.C. Boat races are held on the Tamsui River in Taipei.

- During the Mid-Autumn Festival, Taiwanese gather outside to watch the full moon and eat moon cakes (rice cakes filled with sweet bean paste).

- Confucius's Birthday, also celebrated as Teacher's Day, honors the philosopher who was also known as the Great Teacher. Confucian temples throughout Taiwan hold impressive ceremonies featuring ancient music and dance.

- The Double Tenth National Day celebrates the founding of the Republic of China by Dr. Sun Yat-Sen in 1912. Overseas Chinese visit Taipei for the spectacular celebrations, and hotel rooms are scarce. Lion dancers, bands, and floats parade past the Presidential building in Taipei.

KEY PHRASES

English	Mandarin	Pronunciation
Hello	Nin hao ma	Neen how ma
Good morning	Tsao an	Zaow ahn
Good afternoon	Nin hao	Neen how
Good evening	"	"
Good night	Wan an	Wahn AHN
Goodbye	Zaijian	Dzigh jyen
Please	Ching	Chying
Thank you	Xie xie	SYEH syeh
You're welcome	Bu xie	Boo syeh
Excuse me	Duibuqi	Du-way-boo-chi
Don't mention it	Mei shenme	MAY SH'ma
Yes	Shi	SHER
No	Bu shi	BOO SHER
I understand	Wo dong	WAW dawng
I don't understand	Wo budong	Waw BOOdawng
How much?	To shao chien?	DWAWshao CH-YEN?
Does anyone here speak English?	Shei hui shuo ying wen?	Sjay hu-way shwo ying win?
Sir, Mr.	Xian sheng	SYENSH'NG
Madam, Mrs.	Tai tai	TIGH tigh
Miss	Xiaojie	SYOWjyeh

There seems to be a natural affinity between Thais and Americans. Americans will find themselves welcome in Thailand.

Thailand has more neighboring countries than any other Asian nation and has fought frequently over the past seven centuries with the Burmans, Lao, and Khmers. Thailand (a word meaning "land of the free") was also the only Southeast Asian nation able to resist European colonization. Nevertheless, the Thais are an incredibly laid-back people, devoted to their country, their royal family, and Buddhism.

Bangkok's traffic is surely the most chaotic in Asia. It is therefore all the more remarkable that the calm Thais are able to maintain their composure in the heat and congestion of Thailand's capital city. You won't see taxi drivers shouting and gesticulating at drivers who cut in front of them — after all, everyone does it!

If you think that the residents of Bangkok are gentle and impeccably polite, wait until you visit the countryside. The people are invariably open and friendly to foreigners, and visitors can strike up friendships easily.

MEETING PEOPLE

GREETINGS

- When introduced or greeting someone, women should say, *"sawatdee-kah"*, and men should say, *"sawatdee-krap."* Thais accompany this verbal greeting with the *wai* (pronounced "why"), a gesture of respect made by placing the palms together, elbows down, with a slight bow of the head.

- Foreigners, or *farangs* (not a derogatory term) seldom initiate the *wai* gesture, but it would be very impolite not to return one. Unless you receive a *wai,* shake hands with men and smile politely to women.

- In the *wai,* the height to which the hands are raised varies with respective age and social status. Equals or strangers unaware of their relative social status bring their fingertips to about throat level and hold their hands close to their bodies. Inferiors greeting superiors always initiate the *wai* and bow their heads until their fingertips are just above the nose, but not above eye level. Superiors returning the *wai* gesture to inferiors keep their hands at throat level but incline their heads only slightly.

• Thais also use the *wai* when they say goodbye, thank someone, or excuse themselves in embarrassing situations. And don't be surprised to see them using the gesture toward sacred places and Buddha images, even when riding in a bus or driving a car.

• If your hands are full when you receive a *wai,* just bring them together and as close as possible to the proper position.

• When you greet children, servants (even if they're elderly), street vendors, or laborers, don't use the *wai* gesture. It would embarrass them and make you look ridiculous.

• People might greet you with, "Where are you going?" rather than "Hello." It's the direct translation of the common Thai greeting and does not require an elaborate explanation of your destination. "Just down the street" is a polite reply.

• Introductions are not part of Thai convention, so feel free to introduce yourself or ask for someone's name. Introductions are more common in formal situations. The inferior is always addressed first; thus, if you're introducing your spouse to an important Thai, mention your spouse's name first.

Names and titles. Thais address each other by their first names, reserving their last names for very formal occasions and correspondence. In formal situations you may use Mr., Mrs., or Miss before the person's last name.

• Introducing yourself by your first name will make it easier for the Thais they'll probably call you (Mr. Bob or Mrs. Mary anyway). Foreigners are often addressed by their first names; it does not imply familiarity.

• Most Thai family names are quite long (they're some of the longest in the world) and difficult even for Thais to pronounce. If two people share the same last name, they're almost certainly related. In the 1920s each Thai family was required to choose a unique family name.

- On a name card, the person's given name comes before the family name, as in the West.

- A person's given name is preceded by the all-purpose title *Khun,* which is used for both men and women, married or single, unless they have a higher title such as Doctor. A man named Montri Chareonlarp, for example, is *Khun Montri* (Mr. Montri).

- Married women are also addressed by their first names, so the wife of Khun Montri is not Mrs. Montri. If you don't know people's names, address them simply as *Khun.*

- Nicknames are common in Thailand. Thai friends might ask you to call them by their nicknames — usually disparaging names like "rat," "pig," or "fatty." Still, preface the nickname with the respectful *Khun* (for example, *Khun Moo,* which means Mr. or Ms. Piggy).

Correspondence. In a letter use "Dear *Khun* (first name):" as the salutation.

- Note that Thais often mention a mutual acquaintance in the last paragraph and convey their regards to the person.

CONVERSATION

- Good conversation subjects: Thai food, the weather, and favorable impressions of the country. Thais often ask visitors what they think of Thailand. They'll appreciate polite answers, but few people will be offended if you complain about the traffic, the pollution, or the hot weather, since these are also favorite complaints of their own. All Thais appreciate compliments.

- Subjects to avoid: Politics, corruption, the royal family. Let the Thais take the lead if they want to discuss these topics. Thais also dislike discussing personal problems, even with friends.

- Thais have great respect for their royal family and resent any slight directed at them or the institution. (The musical *The King and I* was banned in Thailand for this very reason.) Also refrain from any criticism of the Buddhist religion.

- Joking is best kept to obvious lies ("The weather is too cold for me"). Much Western humor is taken seriously and thus misunderstood. Subtle sarcasm is not appreciated.

- Personal questions such as "How much do you earn?" or "How old are you?" show friendly interest and are not impolite in Thai society. Thais use such questions to determine relative social standing so they can observe rules of correct social conduct. If you prefer not to answer truthfully, give a vague answer and smile.

- Personal questions such as "Have you had a bath today?" or "Where are you going?" are meant to either show concern or function as a greeting. A serious answer is not expected.

PHRASES TO KNOW

- The national language of Thailand is Thai, the most widely spoken member of a language family that also includes Lao. Thai is a five-tonal language that uses inflection to make each sylla-

ble's meaning clear. The inflections make Thai hard to learn, but visitors can make themselves understood by breaking the words into well-defined syllables.

CURRENCY

- Thailand's unit of currency is the *baht,* which is divided into 100 *satang.* One U.S. dollar is worth about 26 *baht* (August 1987 rates). Coins are available in 25 and 50 *satang* and 1 and 5 *baht.* Notes come in denominations of 10, 20, 100, and 500 *baht.*

- No black market for Thai *baht* exists. Importing or exporting more than 500 *baht* is prohibited.

- Bangkok has the best exchange rates. Hard currency and traveler's checks are changed readily at hotels, banks, and money changers. For the best rates use traveler's checks and cash them in banks or at authorized money changers.

- If you're in a bind, many

merchants, taxi drivers, and restaurants will accept U.S. dollars.

ETIQUETTE

GENERAL MANNERS

- Talking in a loud voice is impolite (especially for women).

- Displays of anger are regarded as extremely boorish. Any show of temper will embarrass the Thais and end any hope of cooperation.

- Public criticism is equated with violence, whether or not the criticism is fair. If you deliver any criticism (even well-meaning criticism) before a third party, you'll end the relationship. Criticism must be extraordinarily subtle even in private.

- If you make a mistake or offend someone, smile, apologize by saying *"khau thode"* (excuse me), and make the *wai* gesture (see Greetings). Thais smile or laugh when they're embarrassed; don't misinter-

pret their behavior as indifference.

- If you see any image of the king, whether it's a photograph in a building or a picture on paper money, show great respect. Whenever the national anthem (written by the king) is played, stop your activities and stand.

- Before you take photographs of a Buddhist statue or any person (especially a monk), ask permission.

- At a social gathering a man shouldn't spend too much time talking with a married Thai woman. Her husband might be offended.

- Thais often refer to babies in a disparaging manner to avoid drawing the attention of negative spirits to them. Don't engage in this custom of compliment-insults yourself, since many Thais do not practice it, but don't be alarmed if someone compliments you on your "ugly" baby.

- When you go through a doorway, step over the threshold rather than on it. According to tradition, a spirit resides in the threshold.

- Throwing an object either toward or over

someone is impolite.

- Smoking is acceptable almost anywhere.

BODY LANGUAGE

- Touching anyone's head or hair is a grave insult. The head is considered the most important part of the body. Thai men are especially averse to having a woman — or even a woman's clothing — touch their heads.

- The feet are regarded as the lowest part of the body. Never point them at anyone or use them to move anything such as a door or chair — soccer balls excepted. (Westerners' frequent use of their feet for tasks they could perform with their hands has led Thais to refer to feet as "foreigner hands.")

- Public displays of affection between men and women are inappropriate. A woman can lose face if a man touches her in public.

- Friends of the same sex often hold hands. This gesture does not have the connotations that it does in the West. If a Thai of the same sex takes your hand while you're walking, either smile and go along with it, or explain that you're unused to this practice and gently withdraw your hand. A hand on the knee is a similar gesture of friendship.

- A smile is used to show amusement, apologize, thank someone, greet someone, defuse a tense situation, or show embarrassment. Expressing thanks with a smile is usually more appropriate than a verbal thanks.

- If other people are sitting on the floor, don't sit on a chair. Never sit with your head higher than that of an older or more senior person.

- Sitting with your legs crossed in the presence of elderly people or monks is impolite. If you're sitting on the floor, tuck your feet under your body, out of sight.

- When you pass between or in front of people, lower your head and upper body a little.

- If you want to point out someone, you may use your chin but don't point with your hand (especially with one finger).

- To beckon someone extend your arm palm down and flutter your fingers up and down. Don't snap your fingers, clap, hiss, or yell.

- Waving your hands about while you're talking will give the impression that you're angry.

- The left hand is considered unclean. Don't use it to pass any object.

- If someone is sitting in a chair, don't put your arm over the back.

- When you're talking with someone, don't have your hands in your pockets. It's impolite.

DRESS

- Thailand's heat and humidity make cotton and other natural fabrics the most practical. Nylon and other synthetics will prove very uncomfortable. The hottest season is during March and April, the rainy season is May through October, and the coolest months are November through February.

MEN For most business occasions wear pants and shirts (white or colored) with or without a tie. For most evening functions you may wear a dark business suit. You may also wear the traditional collarless Thai silk shirt, even to very formal functions. A white jacket, black pants, and black tie are also appropriate for very formal functions.

WOMEN For most functions wear conservative dresses or skirts and blouses (not sleeveless). Shorts are not accepted street attire in some areas. Hats and gloves are rarely worn and are not required in churches. It's too hot to wear nylons.

- Since you must remove your shoes when you enter temples and homes, wear slip-ons. Don't wear your best — because they might be stolen when you leave them outside a temple, and Bangkok streets are often wet. Rubber thongs, however, are inappropriate.

- If you go to a wedding, don't wear white, a color reserved for the bride. Also avoid wearing purple and black, since purple is worn by widows in mourning, and black signifies sorrow and is worn only to funerals. (Don't wear black to a party or social affair.)

- If attending a funeral, women should wear a black dress with sleeves. Men should wear a dark suit, white shirt, and black necktie, and a black armband on the jacket sleeve.

TEMPLES AND MOSQUES

- If you visit a shrine, temple, or mosque, dress conservatively and remove your shoes before entering.

- When you enter a Buddhist temple (*wat*), remove your shoes and hat and step over, not on, the threshold. Talk as little as possible and only in a low voice. Some of the royal *wat* in Bangkok refuse entry to men in short-sleeved shirts and women wearing pants. Leave your umbrella outside.

- Desecrating a Buddha image can result in severe punishment. Don't touch — and never, ever climb onto — an image of Buddha either inside a temple or outside. Treat all such images, regardless of size, with respect. Don't carry a Buddha image in your pants pocket; contact with the lower body defiles it.

- In a Buddhist temple observe the following customs:

Don't sit with your back against a wall and your legs stretched out in front of you.

You may talk with a monk, but don't shake his hand.

Monks are forbidden to have any contact with women. Women should never touch a monk, hand anything to him, or sit next to or at a higher level than him.

- When you visit mosques in southern Thailand, remove your shoes before you enter and dress conservatively. Men should wear long pants and a shirt with a collar. Women should wear slacks or a long skirt, a long-sleeved blouse buttoned to the neck, and a headscarf.

PRIVATE HOMES

- Thais often drop in on each other unannounced, but usually only when visiting close friends or delivering a small gift to a superior.

- Before you enter most Thai homes, remove your shoes even if the host, to be polite, invites you to keep them on. Check to see whether there's a pile of shoes around the doorway or other family members are going shoeless inside. You'll often be provided with slippers.

- When you enter the home, don't step on the doorsill. According to tradition a spirit dwells in the threshold.

- You need not bring a gift when you visit a home, but it's perfectly acceptable to give the host fruit, flowers (not carnations or marigolds), or cakes. Have the gifts wrapped, if possible.

- If your host sits on the floor, do the same so that you're not seated higher. Don't cross your legs — keep them tucked under you and pointed away from everyone else — and don't expose the soles of your feet to anyone.

- Never step over any part of someone lying on the floor, no matter how much of a hurry you are in. Either go around them or excuse yourself so they'll move.

- Show genuine interest in your host family but, if you are in a traditional rural home, don't rave about the family's "beautiful baby." Some Thais believe that such praise attracts negative spirits to the baby.

- When passing a gift or other object to someone, use your right hand and, to be very polite, cup your left hand under your right forearm. Remember not to use your left hand for eating or for handing objects to anyone.

- After a meal offer to help in the kitchen only if you can see that there are no servants. You should leave no later than 10:00 P.M.

- If you admire items of decor, don't compliment your hosts on them to excess or they might feel obliged to give them to you.

- If you stay in a Thai home, keep in mind that Thais are very modest, and wear a full-length robe to and from the bath. The toilet is usually separate from the washroom and bath.

PERSONAL GIFTS

- Good choices for presents are gift packs of cooking oils, sweets, or other foods available in department stores. Teenagers appreciate T-shirts from overseas colleges.

- Offer gifts with your right hand, and with your left

hand supporting your right arm. If you receive a gift, you should *wai* (see Greetings).

- When you give a gift to a Thai, it won't be opened in your presence. If Thais present you with a gift, just thank them; don't open it then unless they invite you to do so.

TIPPING

- Hotels: Hotels normally add a 10-15% service charge to the bill; tipping service people is not expected.

- Restaurants: Most tourist restaurants add a 10% service charge to the bill, so tipping is not essential, but as a rule leave the loose change from the bill. Don't leave one *baht;* it's an insult. In inexpensive restaurants that don't add a service charge, leave the change.

- Taxis: Most taxi and *samlor* fares are bargained, so don't leave a tip. It isn't expected.

- Porters: Luggage porters have a fixed charge per bag of two *baht* at the airport and one *baht* at railway stations. Tip hotel porters five to ten *baht*.

- Hairdressers and barbers: Tip about 10%.

FOODS

MEALS

Breakfast (*'ah-hahn-chau*): 7:00 to 10:30 A.M. The usual fare is *kao-tom-moo* (mild rice soup with pork) and *pa-tong-go* (fried bread) with tea or coffee.

Lunch (*'ah-hahn glahng-wan*): 11:00 A.M. to 2:00 P.M. This is often a quick meal of noodles or a curry with side dishes.

Dinner (*'ah-hahn-yen*): 5:00 P.M. to midnight. (Most Thais like to eat early, usually about 6:00 P.M., and many restaurants close at 8:00 P.M.) The first course is usually a clear soup with shrimp balls, fruits, and other tidbits added. Desserts are usually coconut confections followed by fruits and beer.

WHERE TO EAT

- Bangkok has a wide variety of international restaurants. Most of them require proper dress (except that men don't need jackets because of the heat).

- Many tourist hotels feature Thai-food buffets, often with performances of classical dance. These hotels usually prepare Thai dishes with the foreign stomach in mind and go easy on the chili and garlic.

- The Patpong Road area of Bangkok, although wild by night, has reasonable international lunches during the day.

- Noodle shops, crowded during lunch, often have selections on display in glass cases. Just point to the thick or thin noodles, onions, bean sprouts, or other ingredients and say what kind of meat you'd like: *kai* (chicken), *moo* (pork), *goong* (shrimp), or *neua* (beef). Thai men gather at noodle shops and gossip long into the night.

- Street vendors and night markets are everywhere. They rarely have menus, so either memorize the Thai names for your favorite foods or just point. To avoid overcharging know the price of what you order. Notice how much the previ-

ous customer paid and let the vendor know you noticed. Take a good look at the sanitary situation before you order.

FOODS TO TRY

- Thai food features lots of tiny but very hot chilies. Most dishes are fiery, not just spicy, and are seasoned with basil, garlic, coriander, and cardamom. Every Thai meal includes rice (*kao*), often accompanied by curries and seafoods. Many dishes are cooked in coconut milk.

Specialties. Sample these foods throughout Thailand: *pla too* (fried and salted mackerel), *tom yam* (a spicy soup made with prawns, chicken, or fish), *mee krop* (sweet and crispy noodles with shrimp and banana-flower stamens), *poo-cha* (a deep-fried mixture of crab, vegetables, and herbs), and *phak bung phat* (morning-glory vine fried in garlic and bean sauce).

- If you're a vegetarian try *pad Thai,* a delicious dish made by mixing raw vegetables over fried noodles and sprinkling on ground peanuts, salt, and sugar. On any other dish say, *"Mai sai neua"* to request that the meat be left out.

- For dessert try *kluay-buat-chii* (banana in coconut milk) and *sang-kha-yaa* (Thai custard).

- Depending on your mood, you might want to either seek out or avoid elephant's penis soup or eggs in horse's urine.

Beverages. Better restaurants serve bottled water. Most restaurants serve a weak tea to show that the water has been boiled. You might prefer an alternative, such as soft drinks and beer, to be on the safe side.

- Thais are fond of adding salt to their orange juice (*nam som*) and lime juice (*nam manao*) because of the tropical heat. To get drinks without salt say, *"mai sai klua"* (don't add salt).

- For *Mehkong,* the local rice whiskey, go to local food stores. It's cheap but difficult to find in tourist places. You can also get well-known brands of imported liquor, but beware of fakes.

- Beer and cocktail prices at bars tend to increase after the night staff comes on duty at 6:30 P.M. Most bars in the Patpong Road area are hostess bars that offer expensive drinks and are not frequented by local Thais.

- Locally made beers are Amarit, Singha, and Kloster. Amarit is the most potent, but Kloster is favored by upwardly mobile Thais.

- Sweet, black iced coffee called *oleang* is a favorite beverage.

- Asking for a "Pepsi-Cola" will confuse most Thais, since Pepsi-Cola is called *"pepsii"* and Coca-Cola is known as *"kholaa."*

TABLE MANNERS

- People might stare at you, especially if you're dining alone. Don't get offended. Foreigners are considered interesting under any circumstances, and dining alone is a bit unusual in Thailand.

- If a restaurant is crowded, expect to either be seated or seat yourself at a table with other diners.

- To attract a waiter's attention, use an unobtrusive waving gesture, palm down. *"Nong,"* which means "brother" or "sister," is a polite word to catch their attention.

Don't embarrass your Thai companions by being assertive with waiters (clapping your hands, snapping your fingers, or raising your voice).

- When a waiter or waitress makes the *wai* gesture, simply smile. Returning the gesture would be interpreted as sarcasm.

Utensils. Thais eat most meals with a fork and spoon rather than with chopsticks, which are used only in Chinese restaurants. Hold the spoon in your right hand and the fork in your left, and push the food onto the spoon with the fork. Food is served in small pieces, so knives usually aren't necessary. Use the side of the spoon to cut anything too large.

- Except at restaurants you'll seldom find napkins or place mats at the dinner table. Table salt is also uncommon; fish sauce is used instead for its salty taste.

- Some food, especially in the Lao-influenced northeast, is eaten with the fingers of the right hand. Either roll the sticky rice into a small ball or flatten it between your palms, and use it to scoop food from the large communal meat and vegetable dishes. Use a damp cloth to clean your hands.

- When you use a toothpick, cover your mouth with your free hand.

Dining with others. Invitations to eat are given frequently and are not always meant seriously. The invitation is like the Western "How are you doing?" If you're really interested in sharing a meal, politely decline the first invitation and wait for the other person to repeat it. If you're not interested, say that you've just eaten. Never excuse yourself by saying you don't have time.

- In a formal situation, such as a ceremony, refusing to eat is impolite.

- Thais will be delighted if you suggest a Thai food restaurant for meetings.

- When you arrive for dinner, your hosts will offer you a drink — beer, water, or a soft drink — often without asking which you would prefer.

- Rice (served at every meal) will be heaped onto your plate, and several dishes and sauce bowls will be placed in the center of the table. Dishes are not passed from person to person.

- All the dishes are placed

on the table at the beginning of the meal; everyone is free to serve themselves and eat the foods in any order. Thais, however, usually eat one dish at a time with their rice. They don't take large portions or mix many different kinds of foods together on their plates.

- If a dish looks unappetizing, it's perfectly all right to avoid it, but don't express displeasure with it.

- The host usually serves the guests a second helping and insists that they eat as much as they desire.

- In a home the hostess sometimes waits until everyone else is finished before eating. Don't eat everything — the servants' meal is often made up of the leftovers.

- When you finish place your spoon and fork neatly on your plate, and leave a small amount of food to show that you've had enough.

- After dinner wait for the Thais to smoke before you light up, and offer your cigarettes to any other men at your table. Thai women seldom smoke.

The person who issued the invitation always pays the tab. If it's not clear who invited whom, the superior pays. Never offer to pay only your own share; it's considered cheap. If you issued the invitation, ask the maitre d' (not the waiter) to bring you the bill; otherwise, your Thai guest will receive it.

Banquets. Banquets usually feature either Chinese food at Chinese restaurants or Thai food.

- At Thai buffets eating habits are very informal. After your host invites you to start, feel free to help yourself.

ACCOMMODATIONS

Hotels. Many first- and second-class hotels in Bangkok fill up from November to February, so be sure to book well ahead of time.

- The service in tourist hotels is extraordinary.

- Many hotels extend a discount if you ask. In nontourist (first- or second-class) hotels, bargaining is the norm. Ask for 30%

to 50% off the quoted price. If possible have a Thai friend bargain for you.

- Tourist hotels add a 10% service charge and a government tax, which varies from 8% to 16% of the bill.

- When you go out leave your key at the desk. Don't give your room number to anyone outside the hotel. Always put valuables, extra money, and passports in a hotel safe-deposit box.

- The electric current is 220-volt, 50-cycle AC power. Some hotels have transformers for 110-volt appliances.

- Many hotels offer massage service. If you want a massage, ask for a "Western massage"; otherwise, they might assume that you want a "body massage," in which the masseuse disrobes and massages your oiled body with hers. Women receive the services of a masseur.

Rest rooms. Thailand has few public toilets. Ask in any hotel or restaurant for the *hong nam,* or rest room. Many places have squat toilets with a bucket of water that you pour down the toilet and refill. Carry toilet paper with

you; most rest rooms don't provide it.

TRANSPORTATION

- Try to avoid using any form of transportation during the rush hours from 7:00 to 9:00 A.M. and 4:00 to 6:30 P.M.

PUBLIC TRANSPORTATION

Buses. Buses are crowded but cheap. Fares range from 1.5 *baht* for regular buses to 5 *baht* for air-conditioned buses (for trips under 10 kilometers). Route signs are in Thai, so pick up a tourist map that shows the route numbers and look for the corresponding red numbers on the buses. When you read the bus map, remember that traffic moves on the left. Buses stop running at 11:30 P.M.

- Bus drivers work largely on commission, so they race to beat the competition to the next stop. To flag a bus simply stick out your hand. Once you get on try to get near the driver so you can signal for your stop.

- If a group travels by bus, the first one to board is usually expected to pay the fare for everyone in the group.

- Adults (but not small children) are expected to give their bus seats to elderly passengers.

- Monks customarily sit in the rear of buses to avoid contact with women. People sitting in the rear are expected to make room for them.

- In some areas outside Bangkok, especially in southern Thailand, intercity buses are occasionally robbed. On any bus keep your wallet in your front pocket or your handbag in your arms.

Taxis. Taxis are easy to catch — just hail one wherever it has room to pull over (away from intersections).

- Taxis use no meters; you must bargain the fare before you get in. Most fares in Bangkok should be around 30-50 *baht,* and there should be no extra charges. Many taxi drivers speak no English, so hold up one finger for each 10 *baht* you are offering. Add 5 or 10 *baht* during rush hours and rain.

- Hotel taxis are more expensive but provide a rate card. If you are paying a set rate, tip the driver if he helps with your luggage.

Trains. Trains are much safer than buses and usually more comfortable. Domestic express trains have first-, second-, and third-class carriages. Many slower trains have only third-class seats.

Other transportation. Riverboats speed up and down the Chao Phya River in Bangkok making regular stops. They're a great way to avoid the rush-hour street traffic (if you're going where the river goes). These express river taxis have numbers on their roofs. Fares (3-7 *baht*) are based on the number of stops, so tell the operator where you're going and get the ticket on board.

- *Samlors,* more commonly known as *tuk-tuks* after the sound they make, are motorized tricycles that cost less than taxis for short distances. They can be hazardous. Negotiate the fare before you get in.

- *Song-taos* are pickup trucks with benches in the back. They usually ply set (but somewhat flexible) routes, cost about 2 *baht,* and can be flagged down anywhere.

DRIVING

- International Driver's Licenses are recognized; however, traffic is chaotic and traffic signs are usually only in Thai, so driving is inadvisable for foreign visitors. Instead, hire a car and driver.

- Driving is on the left, but buses can legally travel in the opposite direction on one-way streets, and motorcyclists tend to go wherever they wish.

- Many of the common driving courtesies practiced in North America are not practiced in Bangkok, so be patient and calm. In general, the larger the vehicle, the greater its right-of-way.

- Few drivers are insured, and traffic accidents are common.

BUSINESS

BUSINESS HOURS

Business offices: 8:00 A.M. to 5:00 P.M. Monday through Friday. Many businesses are open Saturday morning until noon.

Banks: 8:30 A.M. to 3:30 P.M. Monday through Friday.

Government offices: 8:30 A.M. to 4:30 P.M. Monday through Friday, with a noon to 1:00 P.M. lunch break.

BUSINESS CUSTOMS

- The best time for business travel to Thailand is November through March. Don't plan trips during the Songkran Festival in April or around Christmas, when many businesses are closed. Many Thais take their vacations in April or May.

- Many small companies accept visits without appointments, but any large company prefers or insists upon prior notice. It is best to write for an appointment two months before you come to Thailand.

- Business decisions can take a long time, so give yourself twice as long to reach a goal as you would in the West. Correspondence and decisions pass through several levels in large Thai companies, a reflection of respect for superiors.

Business etiquette. Visiting cards are expected. Get cards made locally with Thai on one side. (Most hotels will help you with this when you arrive.)

- Many people in top positions have royal titles displayed in abbreviated form on their name cards. Some of the more common abbreviations are P.O.C. (grandchild of the king), M.C. (child of P.O.C.), M.R. (child of M.C.), and M.L. (wife or child of M.R. and wife of M.C.).

- If a person's title is on the name card, use it. To make matters easier for foreigners, name cards often have an English side; use the English title in place of "you," "he," or "she."

- Directness and frankness are not appreciated

and can backfire badly. Don't expect the Thais to be frank if you ask them for an opinion or a commitment.

- "Maybe" or "It's very difficult" often means "no." Thais will avoid saying no if at all possible. You should be similarly subtle in delivering a negative reply.

- When you negotiate never lose your temper. Showing anger is one of the worst things you can do and will bring the relationship to a halt.

- Thais tend to become very obstinate if they sense that a foreigner is trying to take advantage of them.

Appointments and meetings. The best times to schedule business appointments are 11:00 A.M. and 3:00 P.M. Try to avoid Mondays and Fridays; many executives like to take long weekends.

- Punctuality is appreciated, so be sure to arrive on time for appointments, but don't be surprised if the person you're meeting is late. It's not uncommon to arrive for an appointment only to find that the person you're meeting is out of the office. Any show of displeasure will result only in future noncooperation.

- If you're concerned about punctuality for an important meeting, stress that the appointment is in *nat farang* (foreigner time) rather than *nat Thai* (Thai time). Say it with a smile, of course.

- When you're scheduling appointments, ask local contacts how much travel time to allow. Allow at least an hour if you're not sure. Bangkok's traffic is often (and correctly) blamed for late arrivals.

- Dress well for appointments. Appearance is very important in Thailand, and wealth is admired.

- Hand your visiting card to the senior person first.

Business gifts and entertainment. Business people appreciate small gifts for their children Dolls in native dress, games, and picture books are good choices. Men appreciate brandy and liquors from overseas, which can be purchased duty-free on the arriving planes. Women appreciate cosmetics.

- Thais like to begin a business relationship over lunch so they can get to know you better. During the lunch talk about your counterpart's family and interests, but don't discuss business or try to negotiate.

- Thai business people like to invite visitors out to dinner about 6:00 P.M. They'll appreciate it if you suggest that you'd like Thai food.

- After dinner visiting businessmen are often taken to a bar on Patpong Road. Declining would be impolite.

TELEPHONES AND MAIL

Telephones. You'll find public phones in department stores and streetside phone booths (where traffic noise makes conversation difficult).

- To call from a public phone, insert 2 *baht* (up to 3 *baht* at public phones in hotels and clubs), dial, push the button, and speak. When you hear a beep or tape recording, insert more coins to avoid being cut off. Public phones are often unreliable.

- Two sizes of one-*baht* coins are in circulation; some telephones accept one size but not the other.

- Private phone owners are charged 3 *baht* for each local call, so offer to pay for your call. Restaurants, hotels, and clubs often charge 3 *baht* for phone calls to cover this cost.

- Domestic long-distance calls can be dialed direct on both private and public (blue) phones. It's often easier to dial direct from Bangkok to other cities than vice versa. In smaller cities make long-distance calls from the local telephone exchange.

- You can get assistance from English-speaking operators at the Tourism Authority of Thailand. Phone 2821143 or 218151.

Mail. Mailboxes are red.

- The main post office in Bangkok is near the Oriental Hotel and is open from 7:30 A.M. to 5:30 P.M. Monday through Friday, and from 9:00 A.M. to noon on Saturdays, Sundays, and holidays.

LEGAL MATTERS

Customs and immigration. In-transit passengers with confirmed onward tickets may stay for up to 15 days without a visa, but the stay cannot be extended. You can also get a 60-day tourist visa that can be extended once for up to 30 days. The "Non-Immigrant" visa, valid for up to three months, is best for business travelers. Multiple-entry visas are available.

- If you're arriving by land (by train from Malaysia), you might need a transit or tourist visa.

- When you enter Thailand you may bring in no more than 500 *baht* per person. (Since there's no black-market money exchange for *baht,* there's no reason to import them.)

- Exportation of Buddha images is prohibited.

Other restrictions. Saying or writing anything deemed offensive to the royal family can get you arrested or deported.

- Nude sunbathing is highly offensive to Thais and is strictly prohibited.

- Narcotic drugs, pornography, and firearms are banned.

SAFETY

Crime. Thailand has one of the highest crime rates in the world, but tourists are seldom bothered. In case of theft contact the Tourist Police, who are responsible for the protection of visitors, at the Tourism Authority of Thailand (TAT) headquarters. Call 2815051 between 8:00 A.M. and midnight.

- Many young Thai men carry weapons and will use them in a face-saving situation. If Thais are provoked their smiles and reserve can give way to raw violence with little warning.

- In the bar areas of Bangkok's Patpong and Sukhumvit roads, be very careful after dark and be prepared to fend off young men and taxi drivers offering you a variety of exotic delights. They usually accept friendly rejection of their offers with no problem.

- Intoxicated foreigners might become the robbery victims of incredibly realistic female impersonators.

- In some areas young men with feather dusters might "watch" your car while it's parked. To avoid damage to your car, tip them a small amount when you return.

Health. Tap water is chemically treated, but don't drink it. Drink only boiled or bottled water, hot tea, or soft drinks.

- On trips outside Bangkok, take anti-malaria tablets and mosquito spray. Cholera, smallpox, and yellow fever vaccinations are required in infected areas.

- Health services are limited in rural areas.

SHOPPING AND ENTERTAINMENT

Shopping. Shop hours are 9:00 A.M. to 7:00 P.M. Monday through Saturday for major stores. Most small shops are open from 8:30 A.M. to 10:00 P.M. seven days a week.

- You'll need to bargain for everything except daily necessities and books. Don't try to bargain, however, in department stores or designated one-price shops.

- Bargaining will work best if you approach it with a sense of humor. The merchant's first price is often two to three times the fair price.

- If a shop tries to add a surcharge for using a credit card, report the incident to the card company.

- If you buy gemstones or jewelry, buy them in government-registered stores and obtain certificates of guarantee. Obtain receipts for every major purchase.

Entertainment. The bars in Bangkok known as upstairs bars are virtually synonymous with indecency. They're found on and around Patpong Road. Drinks are reasonably priced.

- Several international hotels in Bangkok and Chiang Mai feature performances of Thai classical dance, often preceded by a Thai buffet.

HOLIDAYS

Holidays: New Year's Day (January 1), Makha Bucha Buddhist Day (full moon day of third lunar month), Chakri Day (April 7), Thai New Year or Songkran Day (April 13), Labor Day (May 1), Coronation Day (May 5), Ploughing Day (May 9), Wisaka Bucha Day (full moon day of sixth lunar month), Mid-Year Holiday (July 1), Buddhist Lent Day (full moon day of eighth lunar month), Queen's Birthday (August 12), Chulalongkorn Day (October 23), King's Birthday (December 5),

Constitution Day (December 10), New Year's Eve (December 31).

- Songkran Day is the traditional New Year celebration and includes three days of merrymaking and water-throwing. Water-throwing originated with the sprinkling of perfumed water on the hands of monks, elderly people, and Buddha statues, but has been extended to include the good-natured dousing of passersby (especially young women and foreigners) with buckets of water. Don't lose your temper. Songkran Day is celebrated everywhere in Thailand except in Bangkok, where complaints from foreign residents led to banning of the revelry.

- Ploughing Day is for government workers only.

- Wisaka Bucha Day is the holiest Buddhist day and commemorates Buddah's birth, enlightenment, and death. Buddhist temples (*wat*) are scenes of colorful celebrations open to the public.

- Mid-Year Holiday is observed only by banks.

- Chulalongkorn Day honors Thailand's most beloved king. Wreaths are laid at his statue in Bangkok's Royal Plaza.

- Loy Krathong, a festival celebrated on the full-moon night of the twelfth lunar month, is not an official holiday but it is breathtaking. People float banana-leaf boats decorated with candles and flowers on rivers, canals, and ponds. Thais believe that if the boat sails out of sight without sinking, the maker's wish will come true.

PRONUNCIATION

There are nine vowel sounds in Thai: a, e, i, o, u, are ah, eh, ee, oh, oo but short.

aw = as in "raw"	aa = "a" as in "ran"
eu = er (said with teeth tightly closed)	uh = neutral "e" as in "the"
ng = as in "singer"	dt = unvoiced d
bp = unvoiced b	gh = ai

Syllables are well-defined and should be pronounced distinctly.

KEY PHRASES

English	Thai	Pronunciation
Hello	Sa'watdee krap/ka'	Sawt-dee KRAHP-/kahk
Good morning	"	"
Good afternoon	"	"
Good evening	"	"
Good night	"	"
Goodbye (leaving)	Lah gawn krap/ka'	Lawgahn KRAHP-/kahk
Goodbye (staying)	Sa'watdee krap/ka'	Sawt-dee KRAHP/kahk
Please	Ga'ru'nah	Ga-roonah
Thank you	Kawp-kun krap/ka'	Kawpkoon KRAHP/kahk
Excuse me	Sia jai duai krap/ka'	Seea? jigh DOOEH! KRAHP/kahk
Don't mention it	Mai bpen rai krap-/ka'	MIGH!pen-righ KRAHP/kahk
Yes	Krap/Ka'	KRAHP/kahk
No	Bplahu krap/ka'	Blow KRAHPkahk
I understand	Kaujai krap/ka'	KAW!jigh KRAHP/kahk
I don't understand	Pom/Chan mai	Pom?/Chan? migh
How much?	Rahkah taurai krap/ka'?	Rahkah TOW!righ KRAHP/kahk?
Does anyone here speak English?	Krai pud angklid daibang?	Kry pudahn-kleed dy-bahng?
Sir, Mr.	Khun (see Greetings)	Khun
Madam, Mrs.	"	"
Miss	"	"

Includes Complete Packing Checklist

THE BEST EUROPEAN TRAVEL TIPS

2001 Tips for Saving Money, Time and Trouble in Europe

Save Money on Currency Exchanges, Airfare, Tours, Hotel Rates

Save Time on Transportation, Customs and Scheduling

Save Trouble with Local Customs, Laws and Weather

by John Whitman

The Best European Travel Tips

How to save money, time, and trouble in Europe

by John Whitman

The travel guides don't tell you about new baggage limits, customs regulations, hotel reservation snarls, and shifting currency values. The Best European Travel Tips does! Plus, it tells you how to get low-cost airfares, hotel rates, etc., and what the weather will be, what to pack and how to beat a no-vacancy sign.

A perfect companion to any European travel guide because it is a "how to" not a "where to" guide. If you're spending thousands of dollars on a once-in-a-lifetime trip to Europe, you owe it to yourself to take this book! $6.95

THE TRAVELERS' GUIDE TO
EUROPEAN CUSTOMS & MANNERS

HOW TO GET ALONG WITH EUROPEANS ...
How to converse, dine, tip, drive, celebrate, bargain, dress, make friends and conduct business while in Europe.

The Travelers' Guide To European Customs & Manners

How to converse, dine, tip, drive, bargain, dress, make friends and conduct business while in Europe

by Nancy L. Braganti and Elizabeth Devine

When it comes to European customs and etiquette, this book tells you what the travel agents and sightseeing guides don't. Whether your trip is for business or pleasure, this easy-to-use guide will help make it more successful. It includes sections on greetings, conversation, dress, table manners, transportation, visiting private homes, business practices and even legal matters for over 25 countries.

A must for travelers who want and need to fit in and act like a European, not a tourist. $6.95.

Mother Murphy's Law

Bombeck's wit and Murphy's wisdom on the pitfalls and perils of parenthood

by Bruce Lansky

"Parenthood is a lot easier to get into than out of." So begins a collection of Murphy style laws that details the perils and pitfalls of parenthood and provides helpful advice you won't find in any baby care manual. This hilarious book includes a sure-fire method for conception, the ideal timing between two babies and how to make love with a baby in your bed.

Like Mother Murphy, you will be able to cope with day to day family crisis much better after you find out that "everything your parents did was wrong. Now that you're a parent, everything that you do is wrong." $2.95.

In the battle of the sexes...no one ever wins.

Mother Murphy's 2nd Law

Love, sex, marriage and other disasters

Bruce Lansky

R This book contains language that may not be appropriate for the tender-in-years or the faint-of-heart.

Mother Murphy's Second Law

Advice like this you won't find in a marriage or sex manual

by Bruce Lansky

Everyone is looking for the perfect mate, perfect marriage, perfect sex life, or at least, an amicable divorce. C'mon, quit dreaming! This book is about the real thing—life. Mother Murphy knows what she's talking about. She learned about love, sex and marriage the hard way: a shotgun wedding, a nuclear divorce and a son who gave us Murphy's Law and her a permanent migraine headache.

This book will tell you about every painful situation that you've ever encountered or can expect to encounter in your search for Prince Charming (or one of his cousins). $2.95.

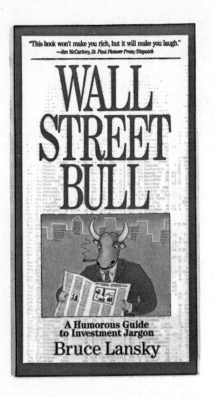

"This book won't make you rich, but it will make you laugh."
—Jim McCartney, St. Paul Pioneer Press/Dispatch

WALL STREET BULL

A Humorous Guide to Investment Jargon

Bruce Lansky

Wall Street Bull

The wittiest guide to Wall Street jargon

by Bruce Lansky

Wall Street professionals aren't really any better at investing their customer's money than a monkey with a dart and a copy of the Wall Street Journal pinned to the wall. Their big secret is the ability to sling Wall Street bull. This humorous guide to investment jargon was written for several reasons: to help customers figure out what brokers are talking about, to help professionals add sparkle to their sales rap, and to help the author recover the huge sums of money he lost In the market.

A witty lexicon of over 500 investment terms that won't make you rich, but will make you laugh. $4.95.

How to give a reference for someone who can't manage his own sock drawer.

L E X I C O N
OF
I NTENTIONALLY
A MBIGUOUS
R ECOMMENDATIONS

Robert Thornton

You'll Be Lucky To Get Him to Work For You!...

Lexicon of Intentionally Ambiguous Recommendations

How to recommend a bozo without lying

by Robert Thornton

If you have to write a recommendation for someone you wouldn't even hire to shine your shoes, what do you do? You don't want to lie, and if you tell the truth, you might get sued.

Robert Thornton's Lexicon of Intentionally Ambiguous Recommendations (LIAR) gives you hundreds of phrases such as "I can't say enough good things about him" to describe the total loser. LIAR helps you to create your own recommendations like "you'll be lucky to get him to work for you," that is, if you find him! Learn the art of mutilating punctuation marks and creating chaos with deliberate typographical errors.

An intentionally helpful guide that allows reference writers to sound positive while telling the painful truth. $6.95.

"Mary McBride is the undiscovered Bombeck."
— JOAN RIVERS

Don't Call Mommy at Work Today Unless the Sitter Runs Away

Hilarious helpful hints for working mothers.

Mary McBride
with Veronica McBride

Don't Call Mommy At Work Today Unless the Sitter Runs Away

A comic relief for working mothers

by Mary McBride

Here is a humorous guide for working mothers to keep them from giving financial reports to their baby and pablum to the boss. Mary McBride gives hilarious advice to mothers who leave their children in daycare, in school or in the bathroom as they pursue the glory of a career. Learn how to get the family to help out with housework when their idea of help is lifting their feet while you vacuum. Find out how to turn on the sex appeal after working all day, cooking dinner, washing dishes, doing laundry and emptying the cat's litter box. Discover how to dress for success with the money you saved on supermarket coupons. $4.95.

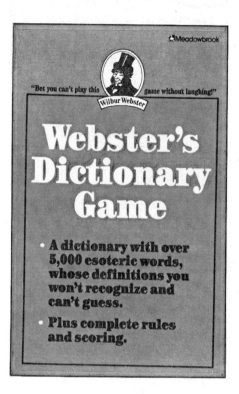

Webster's Dictionary Game

Bet you can't play this word game without laughing

by Wilbur Webster

Wilbur Webster is the black sheep of the famous dictionary family—and for good reason. As a child he discovered it was a lot more fun to make up definitions than to look them up in the dictionary. As a young man, he invented a game based on making up phony but plausible definitions to unfamiliar words. Webster compiled over 7,000 of the most esoteric, abstruse, deceptive and just plain weird words into a unique dictionary to make life easy for dictionary game players. He added the rules, scoring, and hints to maximize the fun. You'll discover it's the most hilarious and clever word game you've ever played. $5.95.

ORDER FORM

_____ 5090	Asian Customs and Manners	Chambers, K.	$7.95
_____ 5070	Best European Travel Tips,The	Whitman, J.	$6.95
_____ 4020	Don't Call Mommy at Work Today Unless the Sitter Runs Away	McBride, M.	$4.95
_____ 5080	European Customs and Manners	Braganti/Devine	$6.95
_____ 4009	Grandma Knows Best But No One Ever Listens	McBride, M.	$4.95
_____ 6040	How to Find Romance in the Personals	Price/Dana	$4.95
_____ 4050	How to Survive High School With Minimal Brain Damage	Lansky/Dorfman	$4.95
_____ 1280	Letters From a Pregnant Coward	Armor, J.	$6.95
_____ 4070	Lexicon of Intentionally Ambiguous Recommendations (LIAR)	Thornton, R.	$4.95
_____ 1149	Mother Murphy's Law	Lansky, B.	$2.95
_____ 4010	Mother Murphy's 2nd Law	Lansky, B.	$2.95
_____ 1269	Successful Single Parenting	Wayman, A.	$4.95
_____ 4040	Wall Street Bull	Lansky, B.	$4.95
_____ 6030	Webster's Dictionary Game	Webster, W.	$5.95

Please send me copies of the books checked above. I am enclosing $_____ which covers the full amount per book shown above plus $1.25 for postage and handling for the first book and $.50 for each additional book. (Add $2.00 to total for books shipped to Canada. Overseas postage and handling will be billed. MN residents add 6% sales tax.) Allow up to four weeks for delivery. Send check or money order payable to Meadowbrook, Inc. No cash or C.O.D.'s please. **Quantity discounts available upon request.**

For purchases over $10.00, you may use VISA or MasterCard

☐ MasterCard   Account #_____ Exp. date_____

☐ VISA   Signature_____

Name_____

Address_____

City_____State_____ Zip_____
s/a:03

Meadowbrook, Inc., 18318 Minnetonka Boulevard, Deephaven, MN 55391, (612) 473-5400, Toll free (800) 338-2232.